The New Sexuality

The
New
Sexuality

Edited by HERBERT A. OTTO

SCIENCE AND BEHAVIOR BOOKS, INC.
Palo Alto, California

Library of Congress Card Number 72-153849

ISBN 0-8314-0028-5

CONTENTS

CONTRIBUTORS

BEN N. ARD, JR., Ph.D., is a Professor of Counseling at San Francisco State College and was formerly a Professor of Psychology at Central Michigan University. He has written articles for the *Family Coordinator, Sexology, Rational Living,* the *Personnel and Guidance Journal,* and *Marriage Counseling Quarterly.* He edited *Counseling and Psychotherapy: Classics on Theories and Issues* (Science and Behavior Books, 1966) and the *Handbook of Marriage Counseling* (with Constance C. Ard, Science and Behavior Books, 1969).

JESSIE BERNARD, Ph.D., is a Research Scholar, Honoris Causa, at Pennsylvania State University. Dr. Bernard has written articles for *American Sociological Review, American Journal of Sociology, Social Forces, Social Problems,* and *Journal of Marriage and the Family.* Some of her books are: *American Family Behavior* (Harper, 1942), *Remarriage: A Study of Marriage* (Dryden Press, 1956), *Marriage and Family among Negroes* (Prentice-Hall, 1966), *The Sex Game* (Prentice-Hall, 1968), *Women and the Public Interest* (Aldine, 1971), and *The Future of Marriage* (Macmillan, 1971).

MARY S. CALDERONE, M.D., M.P.H., is Director of the Sex Education Council of the U.S. (SIECUS); formerly she was Medical Director (1953–64), Planned Parenthood Federation of America. Dr. Calderone has published articles in *Clinical Pediatrics, American Journal of Public Health, Journal of the International College of Surgeons, Life* Magazine, and *Playboy.* Her books include *Abortion in the United States* (Hoeber-Harper, 1958), *Release from Sexual Tensions* (Random House, 1960), *Manual of Family Planning and Contraceptive Practice* (William and Wilkins, 1964, 1970).

LEMON CLARK, M.D., is a physician in private practice. His articles have appeared in *Sexology* and *Medical Economics*. His books include *Emotional Adjustment in Marriage* (C. V. Mosley, 1937), *Sex and You* (Bobbs Merrill, 1949; paperback edition titled *The Enjoyment of Love in Marriage*, New American Library, 1969), *101 Intimate Sexual Problems Answered* (New American Library, 1968), and *101 More Intimate Sexual Problems Answered* (New American Library, 1968).

JOHN F. CUBER, Ph.D., is a Professor of Sociology at Ohio State University. His articles have been published in the *American Journal of Sociology, Journal of Marriage and the Family, American Sociological Review, Medical Aspects of Human Sexuality,* and *Sexual Behavior.* Among his books are: *Sociology: A Synopsis of Principles* (Appleton-Century-Crofts, 1947, 1951, 1955, 1959, 1963, 1968), *Problems of American Society: Values in Conflict* (Holt, Rinehart and Winston, 1948, 1951, 1956, 1964), *Social Stratification in the United States* (Appleton-Century-Crofts, 1957), and *The Significant Americans: A Study of Sexual Behavior among the Affluent* (Appleton-Century-Crofts, 1965).

ALBERT ELLIS, Ph.D., is Executive Director of the Institute for Advanced Study in Rational Psychotherapy. His articles have appeared in *Saturday Review, Playboy, American Journal of Psychiatry, American Psychologist,* and *American Sociological Review.* His books include *Reason and Emotion in Psychotherapy* (Lyle Stuart, 1962), *The Art and Science of Love* (Lyle Stuart, 1969), *Encyclopedia of Sexual Behavior* (with Albert Abarbanel; Hawthorn Books, 1961, 1967), *Sex Without Guilt* (Lyle Stuart, 1970), and *A Guide to Rational Living* (with Robert A. Harper; Prentice-Hall, 1963).

O. SPURGEON ENGLISH, M.D., Professor of Psychiatry and formerly Chairman of the Department of Psychiatry, Temple University, Philadelphia. He has written articles for *Explorations in Human Potentialities* and *Voices.* He has written: *Psychosomatic Medicine* (with Edward Weiss; W. B. Saunders, 1943, 1949), *Emotional Problems of Living* (W. W. Norton, 1945, 1962), *Introduction to Psychiatry* (W. W. Norton, 1954), and *Direct Analysis and Schizophrenia* (Grune and Stratton, 1961).

MARILYN A. FITHIAN is an instructor in Comparative Literature at California State College at Long Beach and is Associate Director of the Center for Marital and Sexual Studies. She has written *Nudist Colony* (with W. Hartman and D. Johnson; Crown Publishers, 1970) and "Desert Retreat" (with W. Hartman) in *An Analysis of Human Sexual Inadequacy* by Jan and June Robbins (New American Library, 1970).

JOEL FORT, M.D., is the founder and leader of Fort Help, the Center for Solving Special Social and Health Problems, in San Francisco. He is a lecturer at the University of California at Berkeley and San Francisco State College. Dr. Fort is also co-director of the National Sex and Drug Forums in San Francisco; he has served as a consultant on drug use and abuse for the World Health Organization. Dr. Fort has published articles in the *California Law Review, Playboy* Magazine, *Human Sexuality, American Journal of Psychiatry*, and *Saturday Review*. He has also written *The Pleasure Seekers* (Grove Press, 1970).

ELIZABETH GARFIELD is formerly President of the Phenomenology Shop (a Chicago advertising agency) and is currently doing freelance writing and photography.

S. JEFFREY GARFIELD, Ph.D., is President of Educational Resources, Inc., in Chicago, and was formerly vice-president of Psychological Affiliates. He has written articles for the *Journal of Educational Research* and *Psychotherapy: Theory, Research and Practice*.

HAROLD GREENWALD, Ph.D., Fullbright Professor at the University of Bergen, Norway, 1969–70, is a psychologist in private practice in New York City. He is Past President of the National Psychological Association for Psychoanalysis and has published articles in *Voices*, the *Psychoanalytic Review, Psychotherapy*, the *International Journal of Group Psychotherapy*, and *Playboy*. He is the author of *The Call Girl* (Ballantine Books, 1958) and *The Elegant Prostitute* (Ballantine Books, 1970), and editor of *Active Psychotherapy* (Atherton Press, 1967).

BERNARD GUNTHER for the past seven years has been a resident staff member of the Esalen Institute, Big Sur, California, and is the author of *Sense Relaxation* (Macmillan, 1968), *Love View* (Macmillan, 1969), and *What to Do Till the Messiah Comes* (Macmillan, 1970). He is the creator of the experimental feature film *Come to Your Senses* and is one of the pioneers in the use of touch, relaxation, body awareness, and nonverbal communication in the total growth process.

ELEANOR HAMILTON, Ph.D., is a Marriage Counselor and Director of the Hamilton School for Marriage & Family Life Education. Her articles have appeared in *Modern Bridge* and *Cosmopolitan*. She has written *Partners in Love* (A. S. Barnes, 1968), *Sex Before Marriage* (Hawthorn, 1969), *Your Engagement* (Bantam Books, 1970), *New Approaches to Intimacy* (Bantam Books, 1970), and *What Made Me* (Hawthorn, 1971).

ROBERT A. HARPER, Ph.D., has a private practice of psychotherapy and marriage and family counseling in Washington, D.C. His articles have been printed in the *Journal of Sex Research, American Psychologist, Journal of Marriage and the Family, Journal of Individual Psychology*, and *Eugenics Quarterly*. His books include *Marriage* (Appleton-Century-Crofts, 1949), *Psychoanalysis and Psychotherapy: 36 Systems* (Prentice-Hall, 1959), *Problems of American Society* (with J. Cuber et al.; Holt, Rinehart & Winston, 1961), *A Guide to Rational Living* (with Albert Ellis; Prentice-Hall, 1961), and *Creative Marriage* (with Albert Ellis; Lyle Stuart, 1961).

WILLIAM E. HARTMAN, Ph.D., is a Professor at California State College at Long Beach and was formerly chairman of the Sociology Department there. He is also Director of the Center for Marital and Sexual Studies in Long Beach. He has written *Nudist Colony* (with M. Fithian and D. Johnson; Crown Publishers, 1970) and "Desert Retreat" (with M. Fithian) in *An Analysis of Human Sexual Inadequacy* by Jan and June Robbins (New American Library, 1970).

PHYLLIS LYON is one of the founders of the Daughters of Bilitis, Inc. A member of the Board of Education of the Council on Religion and the Homosexual since its inception in 1964, she is currently assistant director of the National Sex and Drug Forums, a service of Glide Urban Center. Ms. Lyon has written articles (with Del Martin) for *Motive, Les Gals, The Ladder,* and various homosexual publications. She has written chapters in two books with Ms. Martin: *Sexual Latitude: For and Against,* edited by H. Hart (Hart, 1971) and *Is Gay Good? A Symposium on Homosexuality, Theology and Ethics* (Westminster Press, 1971).

DAVID R. MACE, Ph.D., is a Professor of Family Sociology at Bowman Gray School of Medicine and was formerly Executive Director of the American Association of Marriage Counselors (1960–67). Dr. Mace has traveled extensively, leading training seminars and consulting with various governments on family and marriage counseling. His books include *The Christian Response to the Sexual Revolution* (Abingdon, 1970), *Youth Considers Marriage* (Nelson, 1966), *Marriage: East and West* (with Vera Mace; Doubleday, 1959), and *Whom God Hath Joined* (Westminster, 1953).

SANDER I. MARCUS, Ph.D., is a training director at Educational Resources, Inc. He has written for the *Journal of Experimental Psychology.*

DEL MARTIN is also one of the founders of the Daughters of Bilitis, Inc. She served in 1965–66 on the Joint Committee on Homosexuality appointed by the late Bishop James A. Pike. Ms. Martin has been a member of the Board of Education of the Council on Religion and the Homosexual since its inception in 1964. Together with Phyllis Lyon, she has contributed articles to *Motive, Les Gals, The Ladder,* and other homosexual publications as well as chapters in two books: *Sexual Latitude: For and Against,* edited by H. Hart (Hart, 1971) and *Is Gay Good? A Symposium on Homosexuality, Theology and Ethics* (Westminster Press, 1971).

ETHEL M. NASH, M.A., is Clinical Associate Professor of Obstetrics and Gynecology and Senior Research Associate of the Carolina Population Center at the University of North Carolina, Chapel Hill. She has written articles for the *Journal of the American Medical Association, Medical Opinion and Review, Journal of the American College Health Association,* and *Clinical Obstetrics and Gynecology.* Her books include *With This Ring* (Association Press, 1942) and *Marriage Counseling in Medical Practice* (University of North Carolina Press, 1964).

HERBERT A. OTTO, Ph.D., is Chairman of the National Center for the Exploration of Human Potential, La Jolla, California. He has published articles in such journals as *Journal of Marriage and the Family, Mental Hygiene, Psychiatric Quarterly, Sexology, Social Casework,* and *International Journal of Social Psychology.* He is editor of *Explorations in Human Potential* (Charles C. Thomas, 1966), *Human Potentialities: The Challenge and the Promise* (Warren H. Green, 1968), *The Family in Search of a Future* (Appleton-Century-Crofts, 1970), and *Ways of Growth* (with John Mann; Grossman, 1968). His own books include *Guide to Developing Your Potential* (Scribner's, 1968), *More Joy in Your Marriage* (Hawthorn, 1969), and *Group Methods Designed to Actualize Human Potential* (Holistic Press, 1970).

ISADORE RUBIN, Ph.D., late editor of *Sexology* and *Luz* magazines, was on the board of the Sex Information Council of the U.S. (SIECUS). He was a Fellow and Executive Board Member of the Society for the Scientific Study of Sex. His articles have been published in the *Journal of Marriage and the Family, Medical Times, Sex and the Contemporary American Scene,* and *Pastoral Psychology.* He has written *Sexual Life after Sixty* (Basic Books, 1965), and edited *Sex in the Adolescent Years: New Directions in Guiding and Teaching Youth* (with Lester Kirkendall; Association Press, 1968), *Sex Freedom in Marriage* (New American Library, 1969), and *Sex in the Childhood Years* (with Lester Kirkendall; Association Press, 1970).

WALTER R. STOKES, M.D., now retired, was a psychiatrist in private practice in Washington, D.C. for thirty-five years. He is a guest lecturer on sex, marriage, and the family at many universities, including University of Maryland, Florida State University, University of Miami, Columbia, Cornell, Ohio State, University of Indiana, and University of South Carolina. He has written articles for *Geriatrics, Psychiatry, Journal of Marriage and the Family, Journal of Sex Research,* and *Professional Psychiatry.* He is author of two books, *Modern Pattern for Marriage* (Rinehart and Co., 1948) and *Married Love in Today's World* (Citadel Press, 1962).

PREFACE

This volume illuminates the varied dimensions of an emergent and dynamic force, the New Sexuality, which is an outgrowth of homo sapiens' quest for self-understanding. Man's thrust to understand the sexual nature of his being gained considerable impetus as a result of the Freudian theoretical frameworks and speculations. The sex research of the forties, fifties, and sixties, including Kinsey's and Masters and Johnson's work, added momentum to this thrust toward increased understanding of sexuality. Inseparable from this surge are the contributions made by the writers of sex manuals and the sex education movement. The result of these confluent streams is the New Sexuality, which in the years to come will have a profound impact on the nature and form of many of our social and interpersonal relationships, and the quality and evolution of life-styles.

I wish to express my appreciation to Elizabeth Garfield for her help in the initial stages of organizing this volume and to my wife Roberta for editorial assistance and ideas. Finally I would like to thank colleagues and members of various facilitator and leadership training groups I have conducted for their suggestions and stimulating dialogue about the New Sexuality.

H.A.O.

PART I

SEX IN
THE SEVENTIES

Chapter 1

THE NEW SEXUALITY: AN INTRODUCTION

By Herbert A. Otto, Ph.D.

We are living in an age of change and flux. Everything is open. All habitual attitudes are being investigated. Labels are being examined, reexamined, thought, and rethought. Everything seems to be more permissible. Everything is on trial, and what is emerging is the desire for every man and woman to see himself whole and free, accepting himself as the unique individual he is. Perhaps this will be known as the humanitarian age, an age of the renaissance of man, characterized by a new and more satisfying relatedness of man to man, with deep caring, concern, and empathy. The search for finding oneself, for self-realization, and for living life fully and in dignity is everywhere.

As part of this search, there is a growing awareness that man is functioning at a very small fraction of his potential and that the actualizing of this potential can be man's most exciting life-long adventure. We are witnessing the emergence of a new attitude—a new feeling and outlook about our sexuality and sexual functioning. One of the pervasive characteristics of the New Sexuality is a sense of growth, of emergence, and of experimentalism. Never before has there been so much experimentation in modes of sexual self-expression. Books on sex techniques—known as "plumbing manuals" in the publishing trade—are selling at an unprecedented rate. A considerable industry is devoted to the production of films explicitly featuring foreplay and coitus within heterosexual, bisexual, and homosexual frameworks. These are shown in special theaters that have mushroomed seemingly overnight and that cater exclusively to "sex films." A rapidly increasing number of American males (the audience in the sex film houses is better than 90 percent male) now enjoy what only a couple of years ago was considered hard-core pornography or "stag movies" without fear of a police raid. Scenes of nudity and coital play have appeared in increasing numbers in feature films and plays, as well.

In both Los Angeles and New York City, sex play and actual copulation between men and women were staged in a number of "legitimate" bars and nightclubs during the summer and fall of 1970. These bars subsequently faced public prosecution, and in many instances they re-opened with the same show. In the context of the sexual liberation movement, at rock festivals and concerts as well as during public meetings of the "radical left" political action groups, there has been considerable public intercourse by couples. With the Beatles' song "Do It in the Road" in the background, public sex has now fully emerged as a form of protest and confrontation, and as a technique designed to underscore or break down sexual attitudes.

In a parallel development, a number of publishers (particularly Grove Press) have made available—in inexpensive paperback editions—many of the classical volumes of erotica formerly known primarily to the collector or sex researcher. Since their advent on the U.S. publishing horizon, these books, especially written to arouse sexual feelings, have sold by the million. Intimate and detailed accounts of sexual experiences and techniques have become a staple article in a wide range of magazines. This communication explosion has included verbal communication. The open discussion of sexual matters has gained momentum not only in the cocktail circuit but in neighborhood backyard communication and mixed social groups. There is also evidence of a greater acceptance of bisexuality and homosexuality.

As a part of this changing climate there has been an increase in the experimentation with modes of sexual self-expression. Inevitably, on reading about varied sexual techniques or seeing them on film, people have been stimulated to try them at home. This willingness to try something new has not been restricted to the technique level of experimentation. A growing number of persons have begun to explore different sexual life-styles in an effort to improve the quality and enjoyment of their level of living. There is a noticeable spreading emphasis on man's sexual potential and on increasing the qualitative aspects of man's sexuality. Awareness of this thrust encouraged me to organize a symposium for the 1969 annual meeting of the American Psychological Association entitled "Sexuality—Regeneration and Self-Discovery." The papers of the symposium participants (Drs. Calderone, Greenwald, Harper, and Rubin) form the core group for this volume.

The goals and aims of the symposium were described as follows:

> The purpose of the symposium is to examine some of the many positive aspects of sexuality. In our attempts to understand the sexual aspects of man's functioning, there has been an excessive emphasis on "sexual pathology," coital techniques, and the techniques of foreplay. A focus on the regenerative aspects of sexuality, from the perspective of the holistic approach, has been generally lacking. We too often tend to view man's sexual experiences as distinct and separate from his life. Yet, sexuality (the recognition of our gender-linked functioning) pervades all aspects of our being and is inseparable from our life-style.
>
> The massive influences of the Puritan heritage directed a strong scientific preoccupation towards so-called "unnatural," "deviant," and "abnormal" aspects of man's sexual functioning. Coupled with extensive conditioning about the dangers and risks of sexual experiencing, the result has been the establishment of highly ambivalent attitudes and feelings about sex in relatively healthy and well-functioning individuals. Deep feelings of guilt, fear, shame, and anxiety in the area of sexual experiencing are, with few exceptions, a part of the burden borne by every participant in our contemporary culture. Possibly as a result of this, the concept of sexual experiencing as an avenue for deepening self-understanding, self-awareness, and self-discovery has received little attention. There is a need for regeneration of the social framework and institutions which contribute to the formation of sex attitudes.
>
> Awareness of our maleness and femaleness can be a source of life affirmation and deep joy, and sexual relations can give us a feeling of vitality and enhance our capacities to offer warmth, love, and sympathy. In this sense, sexuality itself is a regenerative force. The fuller exploration and development of the regenerative aspects of man's sexual functioning can add new dimensions to self-perception and bring greater wholeness to man.

The New Sexuality is life-affirmative and life-enhancing in
its emphasis. It is fueled by the discoveries and speculations of
contemporary sex researchers in the full recognition that as of
now we have only a very narrow and incomplete understanding
of man's sexuality and sexual development. In this sense the
New Sexuality is more of a viewpoint or *Weltanschauung*, a
beginning and developmental dialogue with growth overtones for
all participants in the dialogue.

It is in this light that these chapters, written specifically for
this collection, stand to make a significant contribution. They
are a form of dialogue and invite dialogue by the reader in
identifying dimensions of this unique emergent thrust called the
New Sexuality. The richness of the dialogue is attested by the
many main themes, ideas, and subthemes pursued by contributors. Inevitably some contradictory viewpoints are presented.
This, however, makes for a more exciting and thoughtful dialogue
and indicates areas where more exploration and research is
needed. Not only do many of the papers include ideas that are
on the growing edge of humanistic thought, but there are numerous valuable suggestions for fostering and enhancing sexual
functioning. A brief description of the chapters follows.

In Chapter 2 Ben Ard looks at sex and sexuality as forces
in personal and social regeneration. He believes we need to allow
new forms of sexual relationships to develop and that this calls
for "a pluralistic, democratic stance... one of live and let live."
The late Isadore Rubin has compiled a summary of recent findings from sex research and explores the implications and trends
flowing from this work.

LeMon Clark and Eleanor Hamilton examine emotions and
sexuality in the man and the woman respectively. Both papers
reflect the deep compassion and understanding of the authors,
who are known for their many decades of pioneering work in
the area of human sexuality. The articles contain an unusual
number of ideas for enhancing sexual experiencing.

Jessie Bernard contributes a seminal essay on "Sex as a
Regenerative Force," in which she expounds the basically social
nature of sexuality. Albert Ellis then explores the many ways
in which sexual adventuring can foster personality growth.

Bernard Gunther has contributed a delightful poem on "Sensory Awakening and Sensuality." He invites the reader to

participate in a series of *experience-experiments*. He is followed by a paper on "Enhancing Sexuality Through Nudism" by the research team of William Hartman and Marilyn Fithian. They found that "the most effective way of enhancing sexuality appears to be in the formal socialization process while experiencing one's self in a situation involving social nudity."

In a pathbreaking study, John Cuber finds that human sexual behavior and fulfillments take place within the framework of three sexual life-styles. He has called them the *sexually expressive*, the *sexually non-expressive*, and the *sexually ambivalent* styles. Cuber concludes that "lasting, deep sexual fulfillment is rare in present American society regardless of the particular life-style."

David Mace presents one of the most thorough and stimulating analyses to date of the ways in which sex enriches marriage. Implicit in his presentation are valuable suggestions for the enhancement of a couple's sex life. Spurgeon English, looking at a much neglected side of the affair, utilizes a creative perspective in "Positive Values of the Affair."

Harold Greenwald leads out his brief essay on "Sex as Fun" with the statement: "Enlightened parents now tell their children all about sex except its most important aspect—that it's fun." He is followed by "The New Sexuality and the Homosexual" by Phyllis Lyon and Del Martin, which includes, among other things, a brief historical survey of the Homophile Movement and its relation to the Woman's Liberation Movement and examines the institution of the "gay marriage."

Joel Fort then examines the relationship of sex to health. He questions the arbitrariness and subjectivity that have been used in defining certain forms of sexual conduct as "unhealthy" or pathological. Then, Ethel Nash presents an "intellectual meditation" and examines sexuality in loving vis-à-vis a symbiotic relationship, a triangle, and the adolescent.

Walter R. Stokes traces the history of the control of procreation and examines the effect on today's youth and adult. Jeffrey Garfield, Sander Marcus, and Elizabeth Garfield discuss premarital sex from the existential perspective. They stress the elements of choice, commitment, responsibility, and intimate emotional sharing as important aspects of premarital sexual experiences.

In a challenging chapter entitled "Sex and American Attitudes," Robert Harper points out that in our culture we are anti-sexually conditioned as children. He favors the withdrawal of the right to reproduce and believes the rules governing the *privilege* to reproduce should be worked out by democratic means. Finally, Mary Calderone addresses herself to the question "Sexuality—A Creative Force?" and raises a number of fundamental issues pertinent to this topic.

As an integral part of the emergent New Sexuality, a number of key issues and areas are in the process of receiving considerable attention. Several experts have recently gone on record with the observation that what is currently described as the "Sexual Revolution" is taking place more on a verbal and attitudinal than on an action level. There is no question that a vastly greater number of people subscribe to a sexual liberalism than act it out, but this too is shifting. We have entered an era where profound changes in sexual attitude are taking place. The older generation is, for the most part, still saddled with a sense of guilt about sexuality and the deeply ingrained feeling that sex is somehow "dirty," "sinful," or both. The younger generation has inherited these attitudes to a slightly lesser extent and appears to be less guilt-ridden about sexual experiencing.

A dramatic shift has taken place over the past decade indicating that young women are engaging in premarital sex more often and are losing their guilt feelings about this sexual activity. For example, Dr. Carlfred Broderick, a professor of family relationships at Pennsylvania State University, in 1970 conducted a study of two hundred newlyweds in Pennsylvania. He found that 75 percent of them had sex with each other before marriage, and 30 percent of the women were pregnant before their marriage. Broderick concluded that this marked gain in premarital sex is primarily due to a change in the attitudes of women rather than men. The increase in premarital sex appears to cross all socio-economic groups and is a part of a massive change in social values now under way. Broderick notes that this overall change in social values is in the direction of a "radical existentialism." He noted that "such a life-style does not concentrate on conserving social institutions such as church, family or country but instead centers on heightening and expanding personal experiences."[1]

Although changes in sexual attitudes are under way, the need for sex education has never been greater. In this connection, the work of SIECUS (Sex Information and Education Council of the U.S.) is to be commended. This organization is playing an important role in bringing sex education to our public school system. Unfortunately, the whole sex education effort in this country has centered excessively on "information giving" and providing an understanding of the reproductive processes. It is fallacious to assume that information-giving alone creates healthy sexual attitudes. The development of healthy attitudes toward sexuality and sexual functioning has been almost totally neglected. All too often, teachers of sex education courses convey their own ambivalence, confusion, and unhealthy attitudes about sexual functioning on a nonverbal level. These nonverbal messages in the final analysis leave a deeper residue in the personality than the data imparted. There is a pressing need to help teachers of sex education courses to clarify and work through their own attitudes about sexuality and sexual functioning *before* they work with children. Finally, as author John Fowles so well expressed it, "To teach the physiology of sex without the psychology of love is to teach all about a ship except how to steer it."

Another neglected area that is beginning to receive attention is sex education for adults. I am here referring to the fact that the so-called average healthy adult is functioning at a small fraction of his sexual potential. The quality of total sensual enjoyment—the fuller experiencing and enjoyment of foreplay, intercourse, and afterglow, as well as the quality and quantity of orgasm—all these can be greatly enhanced and intensified. As a part of this process, greater depth, scope, vitality, and zest are added to the relationship between the sexes, coupled with increased feelings of communion, love, and caring.

We need a proliferation of programs that center on attitude regeneration and are designed to help man actualize more of his sexual potential. I am currently at work on such a program that uses dyadic and small group interaction as the medium for growth. The work of such pioneers as Alexander Lowen, Gerhard Neubeck, and contributors to this volume has opened the way for a massive development in the area of actualizing sexual potential. To date, work with small groups has taken place largely within the framework of growth centers of the human potentialities movement. In the foreseeable future, these growth centers, which have grown from fewer than half a dozen to more than one hundred and fifty in three years, will undoubtedly offer an increasing number of small group experiences that focus on the actualizing of sexual potential. (A list of Growth Centers can be found in the Appendix.)

Already noticeable and indicative of a changing climate is the lessening in the tyranny of the *cult of the orgasm*. The new emphasis is on developing a free-flowing spontaneous sensuality, on the erotization of the total body, and the development of all aspects of our sensual being. The focus is on enjoyment, play,[2] exploration and discovery, love and caring, letting it happen—not on producing an orgasm. As a member of one of my Developing Personal Potential marathons put it, "Sex is knowing what the other person feels like and what you feel like." Sex is emerging as an art, as a form of creative expression. Sexual interaction becomes a means of discovering and appreciating each other's fullness of being, a means of expanding and illuminating our identity, a way of revitalizing and adding joy to our lives.

There are numerous signs that a more free-flowing and spontaneous sensuality (and sexuality) is in the process of emerging. The young people (and some members of the helping professions) are now touching, embracing, and stroking each other freely, and there is a clear awareness that touching is a dimension of caring without necessarily having a connotation of seduction or sexual advances. Another straw in the wind: it has taken over a hundred years since the bedsheet came into general usage to change this article from sterile white, where every spot pointed to the user's "dirtyness," to today's sheets of brilliant colors and multi-hued patterns so beautiful we can fantasy ourselves lying amidst fields of flowers.

The emergence of the sexual fantasy from the netherland of shameful concealment into the sunlight of creative communication is another hallmark. We are entering an era where the free sharing of fantasies, flights of imagination, and free association sequences are adding a whole new dimension to interpersonal communication. The unprecedented response to the Fantasy Marathon Experiences I have conducted at Esalen Institute, Oasis, and other growth centers shows a great readiness among segments of the public to explore and expand this capacity.

As a part of my work in the area of developing the capacity for fantasy and imagination, I have worked out a group method called "Sexual Fantasy Sharing"[3] that focuses on the creative use of sexual fantasies. It is my observation that the fantasy that remains too long unshared and uncommunicated may be experienced as an irritant or stands in danger of becoming obsessional. During leadership training workshops in my group methods that I have conducted for facilitators, I have been engaged in a study of men's and women's most frequent sexual fantasies. Preliminary analysis of data indicates that there are some differences in the male's and female's most frequent sexual fantasies. Descriptions of women's fantasies are somewhat less anatomically explicit, have more elements of romance and mood-making, (candles, rich draperies, etc.), and more frequently involve a specific person (husband or lover, past or present) than men's sex fantasies.

The shifting flow of our sexual fantasies and images, like the part of the iceberg above the water, gives us another indication of the deeper topography of our libido and unconscious or pre-conscious processes. I strongly suspect that if we allowed the free and unimpeded flow, through communication, of our sexual fantasies and images, this would not only help the development of our sexual potential but would enhance the flow of our creative potential. This is borne out by reports from participants in the Sexual Fantasy Sharing experience. There are also some indications that the process of verbally sharing sexual fantasies can contribute to the emergence of a sexual magnetism or charisma that is latent in every person in a unique individual form. Helping every person who wishes to do so to uncover this powerful force, as an aspect of bringing greater wholeness to the self, will in the years to come offer one of the most exciting frontiers to the humanistic psychologist, psychiatrist, or group facilitator.

Some writers decry what they describe as "the current unnecessary emphasis on sex and sexuality." I disagree most strongly with this position. We have actually paid too little attention to the development of this aspect of man's potential. To compensate for this neglect of the past, a more concentrated investment of energy and effort needs to be made at this point in time. This will reestablish a balance in what Henry Winthrop calls "the holistic quest for balance in the expression of *all our distinctively human potentials.*"[4]

The New Sexuality faces two major challenges: (1) *How can man be autonomous within the context of intimacy, love and, commitment?* Implicit here are the issues of possession, possessiveness, fidelity, and jealousy. Many young people who are living together in love, married or not, are attempting to come to grips with these issues. As a member of one of my "More Joy in Your Marriage" weekend marathons put it, "I have sex with this third person because of good feelings for that person, not because of reacting to anything in my partner or our relationship. The main question is, are you moving to other sexual relationships out of strength or to patch your relationship? The responsibility I have is to try to be honest about what is going on and talk about it to the one I live with and the other."[5] (2) *How can the development of a new sexuality help to foster the growth of love and caring among all people?* Implicit in this question is the development of approaches and experiences that foster life-affirmative attitudes and help us to enjoy every moment of our existence here on earth. To love people also means to love our environment and the Ground of All Being. It means to allow our own unique creativity and love to grow in fullness with the love and creativity of others. From the holistic perspective, these elements are inseparable from the development of a New Sexuality.

What then are the major characteristics of this emergent thrust called the New Sexuality?

1. There is a new openness of communication about most aspects of man's sexuality both in the media and on the level of verbal communication.

2. There is a new venturesomeness on the part of numerous segments of contemporary American society. This is a developing experimentalism, a willingness to try something new—perhaps to experience sexual functioning as a form of regeneration, self-discovery, joyous play, or to try different sexual life-styles.

3. There is a growing recognition of "the man in the woman and the woman in the man," of man's ambosexual nature and the need for a nonjudgmental acceptance of any sexual practice that takes place in private between consenting adults. Coupled with this is an earnest examination and reexamination of the cultural definition of our gender-linked sex roles and how these impinge on our ways of relating sexually and interpersonally.

4. There is also an increasing awareness that we need to view man from the holistic perspective, that man's creativity, productivity, self-image, and mode of relating to others are bound up with man's sexuality and sexual functioning. Consequently, there is a growing awareness that the development of sexual potential

can make a key contribution in bringing greater wholeness to man.

5. There is a renewed exploration of spiritual elements in the sexual union, of sex relations as a spiritual experience, a means of transcendance and a form of communion with the Ground of All Being, God or the Universe.

6. There is a focus on research into man's sexual functioning with emphasis on making the findings available to people so that they can improve the quality of their sexual experiencing.

7. There is a clearer awareness that the puritan (and Victorian) heritage, transmitted through parental attitudes toward sex, has resulted in a pervasive antisexual conditioning that contributes materially to the lack of lasting, deep sexual fulfillment endemic in contemporary American society.

8. Finally, there is a new emphasis on love, caring, and empathy as a part of the sexual relationship, a new concern for the unique individuality of the partner and his needs, and a focus on the development and exploration of values, and on the qualities of authenticity, intimacy, responsibility, commitment and mutual fulfillment.

By deepening and extending this dialogue of the New Sexuality, we can bring greater wholeness to ourselves, to each other, and to contemporary society. The emergent thrust of the New Sexuality, if adequately nurtured and supported, stands in a position to make a profound contribution to the quality of man's being and the nature of his becoming.

CHAPTER NOTES

1. Los Angeles *Times*, 14 January 1971, p. 4.

2. The concept of growth through interpersonal gaming is gaining increased currency with the publication of *Growth Games* by Howard Lewis and Harold Streitfeld (New York: Harcourt, Brace, Javanovich, 1971).

3. Herbert A. Otto, *Group Methods to Actualize Human Potential: A Handbook*, 2nd ed. (Beverly Hills, Calif.: Holistic Press, 1970), pp. 98 99, 371–404.

4. Henry Winthrop, "The Future of Sexual Revolution," *Diogenes*, no. 70 (Summer 1970) :71.

5. Personal communication.

Chapter 2

SEXUALITY AS A PERSONAL
AND SOCIAL FORCE

By Ben N. Ard, Jr., Ph.D.

Sex and sexuality have for so long been considered in an essentially negative context that it is high time some consideration be given to the *positive* forces for personal and social regeneration that may be found in sex and sexuality. In the immediately following pages an attempt will be made to discuss what the forces are that have heretofore presented sex and sexuality in such a negative light. Then, after the necessity for combating these negative forces has been demonstrated, sex and sexuality may be seen in a much more positive light as forces for personal and social regeneration.

To the average (normal) person, sexual relations provide some of the most significant events in his existence, frequently those most deeply associated with his personal happiness as well. In addition they may provide much of the meaning and zest in his life.

For clarity and better understanding, it is usually a good idea for the basic terms of any discourse to be clearly defined early so that the reader may know just what is specifically intended. This is particularly necessary in the area of sex, where words for too long have been used to confuse and hide rather than to clarify. In practically every area except that of sex, it is taken for granted that the best language is the clearest and most precise language. In the sexual area, euphemism seems to have been preferred to clarity of expression. Here, at least, let us be explicit.

Sex, in the present context, means the whole sphere of inter-personal behavior between male and female human beings most directly associated with, leading up to, or resulting from, genital union.

Sexuality, in the present context, means the condition, potential, or state of readiness of the human organism with regard to sexual activity.

Regeneration as a concept can be used in several different ways. For one thing, it can mean spiritual rebirth or revival, or for another, it can mean the regrowth of a body or part or tissue. The use that is closest to what is intended in the present context is that which means to revive, or to reform, or to become shaped anew, to reestablish on a new, and usually better, basis, to restore original properties, to return energy.

Force, in the present context, means active power, vigor, the power to affect relations or conditions, strength or power of effective action; to make or cause, make to be, or accomplish through natural or logical necessity. *Force* here also means to raise, to accelerate or heighten to the utmost, to hasten the speed, growth, progress, developing, or maturing of, in this case, either the individual person or society (or the institutions thereof).

Having defined the basic terms of our discourse, now we can turn to why sex and sexuality have been heretofore considered in such a negative light. The effort here is to get back to the basic or fundamental factors involved.

Before a scientific approach to sex arose, the dominant stance toward sex was a religious one, and, in our culture, it was the Christian religion. This traditional Christian religious stance was, essentially, that sex was bad, a sin (the "worst" sin, in some eyes), something evil and dirty. Sex, in this view, could (and usually did) lead mankind to hell and damnation. In some religious leaders' views, the sexual act itself was the specific act that led to the downfall of all mankind. While "original sin" may not now seem to have been very original, it was considered the first sin, the act that led to the banishment from the Garden of Eden, to women bringing forth children henceforth in pain, and so on.

Theologians have written extensive treatises on the many minutiae of sex that can lead men and women astray. These books were all about sex that was "unnatural," "deviant," and "abnormal."

We need to counteract this long tradition and teach people the joyous aspects of sex, rather than merely the abnormal. If we are seriously concerned about what is really abnormal regarding sex, we need to assiduously question traditional moralistic views about sex. In fact, one of the commonest abnormal emphases in our culture, the total rejection of joy in sexual experience, threatened at one time to become an official and moral norm, as Alex Comfort has pointed out.[1]

If the traditional religious views of sex and the human condition are correct, then there is essentially no hope, because what makes us bad is what makes us. It is a closed circle of despair. This closed circle of despair determines much of our culture. Good and evil, in this view, are absolutes, one of which, evil, is assumed to be built into us by the way we are made. Every Christian and neo-Christian scheme of redemption is only a mitigation of the original premise that we need redeeming.[2]

That premise needs to be seriously examined, questioned, challenged, and expunged, if we are to free sex from the negative hold of religion and allow it to become the positive force in our personal lives and in our society that it can be. Wayland Young has shown that the basic reason sex (or eros) has been denied in our culture can be traced back to the Christian religious scheme.[3] We must, ultimately, reject this whole religious scheme as inert, sanctimonious, and obsolete. There really is no "original sin" except as people assume without question that there is. We need no "redemption" except as people believe without question that they do.[4]

Hard as it will be to ultimately reject these religious views of sex, it would seem to be necessary if we are to learn to look at sex in a more positive light. These early religious presumptions about sex have not been clearly faced, challenged, and eliminated, so they have crept into the views of those who thought they were being scientific rather than religious.

Hans Reichenbach, in his book *The Rise of Scientific Philosophy,* has said "the ethics of sex relations is filled with so many taboos that it is extremely difficult to overcome habitual prejudice even when psychological considerations have made it clear that we must change some of our traditional valuations if we want happier and healthier men and women."[5]

Even after a scientific interest in sex arose, much of the writing dealt with the abnormal, psychopathic aspects of sexual functioning. The names of some of the early leaders in the scientific study of sex, such as Krafft-Ebing, Magnus Hirschfeld, and Sigmund Freud, need only be mentioned to call forth images that back up this esoteric and still essentially negative view of sex. To this day, if one finds a section of a bookstore wherein books on "sex" are kept, probably the predominant theme of many, if not most, of the books will still be "sexual pathology" (i.e., what is *wrong* with sex, rather than what is *right* with sex).

Freud has had probably the greatest influence on matters pertaining to sex, but the way he felt and thought about sexuality is not an entirely appropriate guide for this present age. To describe the normal, natural development of the sexuality of children as "polymorphously perverse" is not a healthy or even a scientific way to describe normal sexual development. This is merely the doctrine of original sin dressed up in somewhat more modern terms.

With this continuing history of essentially negative attitudes toward sex, it is hardly surprising that many people in this culture still have predominantly ambivalent, anxious, guilty, negative feelings and thoughts about sex. Sex is, unfortunately, for too many people, something that should take place only between lifelong, monogamous, married partners who are always faithful (even in their thoughts and fantasies), and should only take place, it would seem, at night, with the lights out, shades drawn, under the covers, with as many clothes on as it is possible to keep on and still accomplish the act.

Now this foregoing description may sound amusing to some readers (hopefully), but it does (tragically but accurately) represent the views of those people who follow the traditional teachings regarding sex in our culture. The puritan and Victorian influence, derived from earlier Christian teaching, is still with us and even, in fact, pervades much of the recent "scientific" or professional literature on the subject of sex, even though many people today consider themselves to be "modern," sophisticated, and up-to-date on the subject.

As Margaret Mead, the well-known anthropologist, has put it, "Any set of lies that children are told about sex is an important part of the character structure of adults in that society; there are probably few children in America who haven't been lied to magnificently about birth and sex."[6]

Some of the traditionalists have argued that all sexual behavior that precludes parenthood will set up some feelings of frustration.

This is patently absurd. It is the old equation of sex with reproduction, in essence. That is the fatal flaw in the argument. Sex
in human beings cannot rationally be tied exclusively to reproduction. This should be obvious to anyone who realizes that human
females are receptive when they are not fertile and cannot conceive and also throughout the period of pregnancy. One-fourth
of American women reach the menopause having borne no children. These facts should bury the old argument that sex is merely
reproduction.

Sex needs to be considered in something other than the traditional serious, glum, moralistic, reproductive, biological, and religious sense. Even the scientific studies of the subject have tended
to perpetuate this dry, serious aspect of sex. In too many of the
scientific studies, sex is treated as a biological necessity, but practically never is there any suggestion that sex is fun. Rarely is
there any recognition of the pleasure that men and women take
in each other's company, let alone their bodies. Sex relationships
have been described as the cement that has held the world together
for a long time.[7]

Perhaps one of the most outstanding exceptions to the ubiquitous study of the abnormal in sex is the work of Abraham Maslow
in his study of self-actualizing people. These psychologically
healthy people seem to integrate sex in their lives in a context of
love and affection. As Maslow has pointed out, no purpose would
be served in confusing sex and love unnecessarily (as many
so-called "modern" authorities unfortunately tend to do) ; the
facts are that these psychologically healthy people *did* integrate
sex in their lives in a context of love and affection.[8] But, as Maslow
also noted, "We cannot go so far as some who say that any person
who is capable of having sexual pleasure where there is no love
must be a sick man."[9] With regard to this relationship of sex and
love among psychologically healthy people, Maslow is not sure
that they would rather not have sex at all if it came without
affection, but he is quite sure that he had many instances in which
for the time being at least sex was given up because it came without love and affection.[10]

Maslow's self-actualizing people tend to be good and lusty animals, who are hearty in their appetites, enjoying themselves
mightily without regret or shame or apology. They seem to enjoy
their sexual lives and all the relatively physiological impulses
without unnecessary inhibition. *They accept themselves at all*

levels. This shows itself in a relative lack of the disgusts and aversions seen in average people and especially in neurotics, for example, disgust with body products, body odors, and body functions.[11] The animal processes—sex, urination, pregnancy, menstruation, growing old—are part of reality and so must be accepted. Thus no healthy woman feels guilty or defensive about being female or about any of the female processes.[12]

Maslow's finding, which is perhaps most relevant to this present chapter, is that for several of his subjects the sexual pleasures and particularly the orgasm provided, not passing pleasure alone, but some kind of basic strengthening and revivifying that some people derive from music or nature.[13] These healthy people described feelings of great ecstasy; they had the conviction from these orgastic experiences that something extremely important and valuable had happened; they were to some extent transformed and strengthened even in their daily lives by such experiences.[14]

Before some reader begins to assume that these experiences are some sort of mystical or religious experience, let us hasten to add that, as Maslow has stated, it is quite important to dissociate this experience from any theological or supernatural reference. None of Maslow's subjects spontaneously made any such tie-up. These experiences are a natural experience, as Maslow has pointed out, well within the jurisdiction of science.[15] Freud's term for this experience—the oceanic feeling—might be used.

One of the values of separating this oceanic feeling from any religious, mystic, or supernatural experience is that it then becomes not an absolute thing but a relative thing. We learn from Maslow's subjects that such an experience can occur in a lesser degree of intensity. As soon as it is divorced from mystical or supernatural reference and studied as a natural phenomenon, it becomes possible to place this experience on a quantitative continuum from intense to mild. Maslow discovered that this mild oceanic experience occurs in many, perhaps even most individuals, and that in the favored individual it occurs dozens of times a day.[16]

In summing up the portent of Maslow's findings about sex in the lives of psychologically healthy people, we can say that his results show that sex can be a force for personal regeneration. If some people can learn to use sex in this positive way, others can learn this too.

What can one do, basically, to bring about the fullest possible enjoyment and regeneration through sex? Some have suggested that it is better not to do anything special about any of our natural pleasures and functions; it is felt that it is better just to let them operate (the implication being that they will do very nicely if we just let them).[17] This might be true for the psychologically mature person (Maslow's self-actualizing individual), but many people may have to do more than just let their natural functions operate.[18] Before the positive forces within their natural sexual potentialities can come to the fore, they may need to go through the hard task of getting rid of the negative forces within themselves, specifically what they have learned from an anti-sex culture. Deindoctrination through psychotherapy may be necessary for some people before they can achieve this.

Having put considerable emphasis upon psychological maturity, we need to point out that the term has been used elsewhere in other ways, and we do not want the reader to be confused about this matter. Some so-called "modern" writers on sexual subjects have tried to restate what is essentially the orthodox Christian view by dressing it up, so to speak, as "psychological maturity." What has been discussed here in these pages with regard to psychological maturity must be carefully distinguished from the views of the Christian apologists, in whatever disguise. As Wayland Young has so succinctly put it: "Nor do I believe it is any longer interesting to relay the orthodox Christian view, whether in traditional form or dressed up as 'psychological maturity.' It doesn't work, and most people are not interested in trying to make it work."[19]

These writers who restate traditional positions in terms of "psychological maturity" usually lay great emphasis upon the importance of "love" over that of sex. But the net effect of this emphasis on love in sex is to limit sexual experience and make experiment in new sexways (as well as new loveways) more difficult and confusing, as Lawrence Lipton has pointed out in his book on *The Erotic Revolution*.[20] We are back again with the whole romantic love concept, which actually gets in the way of a realistic, straightforward approach to sex.[21] What is the relation of sex and love? When we speak of love here we mean, of course, heterosexual love. Love in this sense is achieved through sex. Sex is a condition of love, not the other way around. In other words, sex may be considered a *necessary* but not a *sufficient* condition for love.

So far we have spoken largely of how sex and sexuality can be a force for personal regeneration within the lives of individuals. Now a few words need to be said about how sex and sexuality can be a positive force in *social* regeneration, through the institutions of society. Of course, it should be rather obvious that we are going to have to reeducate a whole generation if we are to make significant progress in this regard. This can only be done through the schools. As Lawrence Lipton has concluded, "If we are ever to be delivered from the strait-jacket of the Judeo-Christian anti-sexual moral code, it will have to *begin* in the schools."[22] Sex education in the schools, on a scientific basis, is the necessary prerequisite to a fundamental change in our society in its basically anti-sexual attitudes.[23]

Attitudes toward sex are influenced by many social institutions other than the schools, of course. The various mass media portray sex to many millions in ways that are not always healthy, to say the least. Films, television programs, art galleries, museums, advertising in various media, the newspapers, novels, and magazines are constantly providing their various publics with many false ideas, questionable assumptions, and faulty basic values about human sex and sexuality. Censorship is *not* the answer,[24] but scientific sex education and honest discussion in these various media of a healthy attitude toward sex would go a long way toward using our social institutions as a positive force in the needed regeneration of our society regarding its attitudes toward sex.

To take one example of how complex the problem is, and how these factors overlap and intertwine, let us consider the number of unhappy marriages and divorces that arise out of teen-age marriage and divorce.[25] If we can provide better (more scientific, realistic, honest) sex education in the schools that gets through to teen-agers so that they do not marry too early, we will thereby help the individuals involved stay in school and finish their education, get better jobs, bring fewer unwanted babies into the world, keep more people off the welfare roles, and thus perhaps ultimately even lower taxes. The various social institutions involved in such a matter as teen-age marriages and divorces and the problems arising therefrom are obviously many. The social regeneration possible through a better outlook on sex would lessen many social evils with us today because of our past, traditional attitudes toward sex.

The societal choice today is actually between that older system and a newer, more equalitarian, and more permissive system. An individual may choose abstinence as his standard, but he must recognize the fact that for two thousand years the Western world has failed to bring up the majority of even one generation of males in behavioral conformity to this code, as the sociologist Ira Reiss has noted in his recent study, *The Social Context of Premarital Sexual Permissiveness*.[26]

The Sexual Revolution (or renaissance) that is occurring in America today has both positive and negative elements in it. We have argued so far in favor of some of the elements of a positive sexual revolution. It is only fair to comment on some of the negative elements that may be found in the erotic revolution currently in progress.

A segment of the present youthful peer culture operates in the present only, without benefit of history, and it moves on feeling and sentiment rather than logic. It has, moreover, become quite alienated from adult contact and influence. In our society today there is, among some elements, an increasing use of drugs and liquor as devices for making sex more joyful. And there seems to be, among some, a frantic chase after sexual pleasures as measured by statistical frequency charts, length of time spent in sexual intercourse, insistence upon (even demanding) simultaneous orgasm—burning the candle at both ends, so to speak, in this desperate seeking after some sexual Nirvana. But we need to help coming generations of young people see that because they are young and strong, they do not need liquor or drugs. Good sex, in a context of love and affection, is better without liquor or drugs.

The implication of the foregoing pages is, hopefully, quite clear: the anti-sex values of orthodox Christianity should not be allowed to survive in this age of increased scientific knowledge about sex, which we have attained and are attaining. If we can work through the various social institutions to change the traditional ideas about sex, then we can help sex become a positive force for personal and social regeneration in an increasing number of lives. We also need to experiment with new social institutions and frameworks.

Insofar as women achieve true equality, there will be more opportunities for men and women to work out new sorts of sexual relationships within new frameworks. Some indications or forerunners of what the future may hold may perhaps be seen in such new institutional arrangements as the new coeducational dormitories in some universities, the kibbutz of Israel (collective farms where the children are reared by nurses and teachers rather than just parents), the new apartment complexes in Scandinavia where arrangements are made to allow professional women to work and have others do their homemaking tasks, and finally the communal living being tried by some "hippie" groups. If we are to allow new forms of sexual relationships to develop, a pluralistic, democratic stance is needed, one of live-and-let-live. We must even allow people to make some mistakes, if there is a chance for them to learn from their mistakes. We need to get away from the puritanical fear that somewhere, somebody might be having some sexual fun. Perhaps the basic principle needed is one of encouraging people to do their own thing, to try out new ideas and relationships, *as long as they do not unnecessarily interfere with the rights of others and their efforts are not self-defeating.*

To Vance Packard the contemporary upheaval in male-female relationships seems best described as *The Sexual Wilderness.*[27] But Lawrence Lipton has described *The Erotic Revolution* from an affirmative point of view.[28] And Simmons and Winograd, in *It's Happening,* have provided a sympathetic portrait of the young scene today.[29]

Some people (usually conservative right-wingers) confuse "communal living" (or any new ideas about sex) with Communism. While some members of the new communal living groups may have pro-Communist leanings (or revolutionary ideas), there are serious, non-Communist people who are trying to work out new sexual ethics and new relationships between men and women. As a matter of fact, the Communists have become repressive in the sexual area, as they have in many other areas (in Russia many years ago and in China recently).

The new sex scene among some segments of the youth of today is not merely that old bugaboo of "free love" nor mass debauchery, orgies, or promiscuity. More people are becoming more sexually experienced (both in numbers of partners and in varieties of the act), and sex is losing some of its sacred character. The guilts and fears that hounded those who took part in nonmarital sexual behavior are hopefully lessening. People are becoming more aware that guilt is not innate and inevitable but rather created by parents and society whose credo is that you should feel guilt when you transgress the traditional sexual mores (or even fantasy transgressing).[30]

Alex Comfort has described sex as "the healthiest human

sport."[31] But Comfort is not suggesting that sex is a game where one scores points at the expense of the other person involved. The sexual act may be an aggressive act when it is done out of hostility, but sex can be (and ideally is) a tender act, an act with genuine reciprocity and thoughtfulness.[32] In this sense, it is the highest compliment one can pay to a member of the other (never "opposite") sex.

Good sexual satisfaction, at a frequency that is reasonable, can release more love, warmth, and generosity into the world than the traditional attitudes toward sex of withdrawal and self-abnegation engendered by Christian teachings.

As James Hemming has put it, "At long last, sex is becoming a positive value of life, a creative influence in the human search for wholeness, fulfillment, and mutuality, a human relationship amenable to human values."[33] We need to help more people realize this, that sex can be a positive force in their lives, a force that can bring joy, fulfillment, satisfaction, pleasure, ecstasy, and a revivifying effect that adds to the enjoyment of many other areas of life as well.

CHAPTER NOTES

1. Alex Comfort, "Sex: The Healthiest Human Sport," *Sexology* 36 (September, 1969), 26.
2. Wayland Young, *Eros Denied: Sex in Western Society* (New York: Grove Press, 1964), p. 357.
3. Ibid.
4. Ibid., p. 358.
5. Hans Reichenbach, *The Rise of Scientific Philosophy* (Berkeley: University of California Press, 1951), p. 299.
6. Margaret Mead, "An Anthropologist Looks at the Report," in American Social Hygiene Association (Eds.) *Problems of Sexual Behavior* (New York: American Social Hygiene Association, 1948), pp. 60–61.
7. Ibid., p. 68.
8. Abraham Maslow, *Motivation and Personality* (New York: Harper, 1954), p. 241.
9. Ibid., p. 242.
10. Ibid.
11. Ibid., p. 207.
12. Ibid., p. 208.
13. Ibid., p. 215.
14. Ibid., p. 216.
15. Ibid.

16. Ibid., pp. 216–217.

17. Wayland Young, *Eros Denied: Sex in Western Society* (New York: Grove Press, 1964), pp. 333–334.

18. Ben Ard, "Seven Ways to Enjoy Sex More," *Sexology* 35 (March, 1969), 508–510.

19. Young, *Eros Denied*, p. 354.

20. Lawrence Lipton, *The Erotic Revolution: An Affirmative View of the New Morality* (Los Angeles: Sherbourne Press, 1965), p. 157.

21. Ben N. Ard, Jr., "Love and Aggression: The Perils of Loving," in Ben N. Ard, Jr. and Constance C. Ard (Eds.) *Handbook of Marriage Counseling* (Palo Alto: Science and Behavior Books, 1969), pp. 50–60.

22. Lipton, *The Erotic Revolution*, p. 182.

23. Ben Ard, "Do As I Do, Be As I Am: The Bruising Conflict," in Seymour M. Farber and Roger H. L. Wilson (Eds.) *Sex Education and the Teenager* (Berkeley: Diablo Press, 1967), pp. 78–88.

24. *The Report of the Commission on Obscenity and Pornography* (New York: Bantam, 1970).

25. Ben Ard, "Gray Hair for the Teenage Father," in Seymour M. Farber and Roger H. L. Wilson (Eds.) *Teenage Marriage and Divorce* (Berkeley: Diablo Press, 1967), pp. 95–104.

26. Ira L. Reiss, *The Social Context of Premarital Sexual Permissiveness* (New York: Holt, Rinehart & Winston, 1967), p. 176.

27. Vance Packard, *The Sexual Wilderness* (New York: David McKay, 1968).

28. Lipton, *The Erotic Revolution*.

29. J. I. Simmons and Barry Winograd, *It's Happening: A Portrait of the Youth Scene Today* (Santa Barbara: Marc-Laird Publications, 1966).

30. Ibid., pp. 106–107.

31. Alex Comfort, "Sex: The Healthiest Human Sport," p. 22.

32. Ben N. Ard, Jr., "Love and Aggression: The Perils of Loving."

33. James Hemming, *Individual Morality* (London: Panther Modern Society Books, 1970), p. 126.

Chapter 3

NEW SEX FINDINGS: SOME TRENDS
AND IMPLICATIONS

By Isadore Rubin, Ph.D.

The story is told that recently Dr. William H. Masters was driving
a car containing his colleague Virginia E. Johnson; Paul H.
Gebhard, head of the Institute for Sex Research; and several
others. Dr. Gebhard reportedly cautioned Masters to be careful
in his driving: "If you get us all killed, there goes sex research in
the United States."[1] This anecdote suggests that, despite the
volumes on sex that pour out in an unending stream from the
nation's presses, the basic research of our time is still being conducted by the Institute that Kinsey founded at Indiana University
and the Reproductive Biology Research Foundation in St. Louis.
Unhappily, the extent of sex research in this country is very far
from adequate in terms of the unsolved problems still before us.

Obviously, it is unnecessary to tell any body of professionals
at this date what the major contributions of the Kinsey Institute and of Masters and Johnson have been. Suffice it to say at this
point that, with all their limitations, they have furnished us with
the most reliable empirical data we have about the broad range
of sexual behavior in this country as well as the most reliable
laboratory observation of what actually takes place physiologically during human sexual response. More than anything else this
body of empirical and experimental data has revealed the great
limitations of the theoretical concepts of sex that had been derived
from armchair philosophizing, from interpretation of the behavior
of an atypical sample of disturbed patients undergoing psycho-

analytic therapy, or from outmoded biologic concepts that no longer have any place in modern thinking.

Perhaps the major contribution of the new research findings to our thinking should be, not the drawing of hard and fast conclusions, but rather the reopening of many questions that were foreclosed prematurely by psychoanalytic thinking on the basis of hypotheses that hardened into conclusions without being tested by the rigorous methods of science. As our research probes into many areas, it becomes increasingly clear that there are many serious inadequacies in our traditional concepts of sex drive, psychosexual development, male-female differences, sexual deviance, and other key questions of human sexuality. Today, for the first time in history, human sexuality must be considered in terms of the entire life cycle, and for the first time important areas of research have extended not only to the last years of life but also into the highly critical period before birth.

Although the research of Kinsey, Masters and Johnson, and others has left many questions unanswered, their work did destroy a number of myths that had long hindered any real understanding of human sexuality. Perhaps the major contribution of the Kinsey research was that "it provided statistical evidence showing discrepancies between the common assumptions of a moralistic public and the actual behavior of people. Conventionalized deceptions that masturbation, premarital or extramarital coitus, and homosexuality are merely occasional deviations from normal behavior can no longer be maintained."[2]

It is clear from the new research into the range and variety of sexual expression that the concepts of sexual "normality" and "abnormality" have become terms incapable of clearcut, scientific definition. According to Kinsey and his colleagues, current concepts of normality and abnormality represent primarily moral evaluations with little if any biologic justification, and "perversions are simply a measure of the nonconformity between an individual's behavior and the mores of the particular society in which he lives."[3]

The scientific sanction usually given to psychiatric thinking about what is perverse or normal derives from Freud's analysis of perversions and his insistence that genital primacy was "the final outcome of sexual development." A good case has been made for the thesis that Freud's definitions of perversion represented a disguised introduction into psychoanalysis of the Roman Catholic

views prevailing in his day.[4] It is important in dealing with the
value-laden area of human sexuality that we avoid the circular
logic whereby prevailing religious and moral judgments are intro-
duced, in carefully disguised form, into scientific analysis, and
then the conclusions derived from this analysis are used as "scientific support" for the prevailing religious and moral judgments.

As Alex Comfort noted, in contrast to some cultures that tended
to develop the wide range of sexual practice into a social asset
and a source of pleasure and recreation independent of its function of reproduction, cultures dominated by Judeo-Christian concepts repudiated all cultural elaboration of physical sexuality and
severely restricted most of its manifestations.[5] In fact, he says,
"the total rejection of joy in sexual experience threatened at one
time to become an official and moral norm." Our entire culture is
in a process of transition from these limited attitudes concerning
manifestations of sexuality toward a greater acceptance of sexual
relationships as a rich and meaningful interpersonal encounter
completely independent of reproductive needs. It is little wonder
that our society should experience tremendous stresses and strains
in this process of transition. Actually, it is the pleasure or play
aspect of sex that is the motivating force for most sexual relationships; yet, says Nelson Foote, the taboo against valuing sex as
play has been so strong that even the more liberal moralists tend
to boggle when they contemplate the recognition of sex as a legitimate form of play.[6]

A major contribution of the Masters and Johnson laboratory
research was that it laid at least the foundations for an understanding of female sexuality. At long last it cut through the Gor-
dian knot of controversy about vaginal versus clitoral orgasm by
its unequivocal finding that, physiologically, orgasm was orgasm
no matter what the source of stimulation was.[7] Although we still
find some professional counselors and writers continuing to think
in these terms,[8] the theory that "clitoral orgasm" is a more immature response than "vaginal orgasm" can no longer claim scientific
validity.[9]

Today at least we are beginning to arrive at some understanding of the nature of female sexuality. As Waxenberg has well
noted, times *have* changed: "Woman, fifty or even twenty years
ago, was considered by psychologically oriented practitioners to
be a physical and moral inferior of the male. In fact, she was considered to have started life as a deprived, defective travesty on the

male prototype. Castrated before genitality entered her life! And what genitality she was expected to attain despite all her handicaps—namely, vaginal orgasm—turns out to be a figment of the compassionate imagination of a philosopher of sexuality, Sigmund Freud."[10]

Today it is well recognized that the female is biologically and—if our measure is the capacity for orgasm within a given period of time—sexually superior. The psychoanalyst Sherfey, in her perceptive analysis of the nature of female sexuality, suggests the replacement of the biblical and psychoanalytic myth of Eve–out–of–Adam by an Adam–out–of–Eve myth on the basis of her belief that the concept of an initial anatomical bisexuality of all embryos has been shown to be incorrect by recent embryological research.[11] She argues that all mammalian embryos are morphologically female in their early stage. The human male begins to differentiate from the female by the action of fetal androgens; where these androgens are lacking, even genetic males will develop into females. As one author put it, "even if the Y chromosome is present in a tiny foetus, that foetus is still far from home and on the male side of the fence. It has to force its maleness on a body and brain which are only too inclined to choose the path to femininity."[12]

Although the well-known 1939 report of Benedek and Rubinstein, which made a direct correlation between the intensity of the female sexual drive with the height of the estrogenic level,[13] still appears persistently in present-day psychiatric literature, its finding that the highest desire coincided with the period of ovulation, has not been borne out by most following research.[14] Though recent research by Udry and Morris is an exception,[15] most studies have found that only a small minority of women who reported cyclical changes of sexual desire found it highest at the time of ovulation. Studies of adrenalectomized women as well as the research of Masters and Johnson report lack of consistent coincidence in a large majority of women of peak responsiveness at ovulation time, the time of peak estrogen level.[16] There is a growing body of evidence to suggest that it is the androgen (so-called male hormone) originating in the adrenals that supports female eroticism (rather than estrogen).[17]

Recent research has also focused attention upon a number of areas that have all too long been neglected: sexuality in the later years, coitus during pregnancy, and sexual activity after

serious illnesses such as coronary attacks. It is now clear that
physicians and counselors of various kinds have seriously neglected these areas both out of embarrassment and out of ignorance. Certainly, with the growing proportion of aging in our
population, this group cannot be ignored. Further, as Hellerstein
and Friedman emphasize in their study of post-coronary patients,
sex is inextricably woven into all phases of the fabric of life—
biologic, physiologic, psychologic, sociologic, marital, and familial
—and the importance of the sexual act far exceeds that of a mere
physical expression: "It has profound symbolic significance of
the highest order and, for this reason, deprivation or loss of this
function . . . may be catastrophic.[18]

The research of Kinsey indicated that there was no automatic
cutoff to sexual life at any particular age. Though the number
of older individuals in their sample was quite small, their finding
was confirmed by a number of studies among the aging, and
clearly established by the observations of Masters and Johnson.[19]
Particularly important was the longitudinal study of older men
and women by psychiatrists at Duke University, who studied
sexual attitudes and behavior in depth as a part of a larger study
of aging.[20] This group found that in a sizable portion (15 percent) of older males, sexual desire and ability actually increased
rather than decreased with age. Those who have worked in the
field have noted a strong resistance to accepting sexuality in
older persons, in many respects similar to the resistance to
accepting the concept of infant and child sexuality put forward
by Freud. Undoubtedly it will take a considerable length of time
before the normalcy of sexuality in the older years is accepted
by our society as a whole. Unhappily for those moralists who
urged younger and middle-aged men to "conserve" themselves
sexually, it is regularity of sexual expression that seems the best
guarantee for its continued functioning in the later years.[21]

The work of Masters and Johnson focused attention on the
problem of sexual intercourse during the final weeks of pregnancy.[22] These two researchers declared that the usual blanket
interdiction of intercourse during the last six weeks before labor
has no basis in physiology and often leads to marital infidelity
and unhappiness. They suggest that it should be an individual
decision made by the physician in each case and that for most
couples sexual intercourse can probably continue almost until
delivery. At any rate, their finding that orgasm resulting from

masturbation leads to stronger uterine contractions than that resulting from intercourse calls into serious question the advice of physicians who counsel petting or masturbation rather than intercourse during pregnancy, particularly for cases of threatened abortion.

It is interesting to note that in a recently published book, *Sex and the Unborn Child*, the author draws upon Masters and Johnson's findings that orgasm leads to temporary blackout to conclude that intercourse during the first three months of pregnancy leads to serious mental retardation in infants because of anoxia (oxygen starvation).[23] This conclusion, I may say, is a pure conjecture, with no confirmation whatsoever from the data of Masters and Johnson or from any other known data. Leading thought in the field tends in the opposite direction.[24]

A problematic area at this time—sexual functioning following a coronary—awaits more definite data, promised for the future by Masters and Johnson. However, present data leave little doubt that many physicians taking care of coronary patients often ban intercourse much longer after recovery than medically indicated, give indefinite or anxiety-producing advice, or give the patient no advice at all, allowing him to draw his own conclusions. This is hardly surprising since Hellerstein and Friedman, reviewing thirty-three cardiologic text books, found a grand total of less than one thousand words referring to sexual activity and heart disease, with the advice being vague and non-specific when given.[25] Based on their careful study, these two researchers conclude that over 80 percent of post-coronary subjects can fulfill the physiologic demands of sexual activity without symptoms or evidence of significant strain. They add that the heart patient's happiness and successful re-entry into the family dynamics depend in great part on the way in which he fits into his sex role and directs his sexuality.

For a long period of time, particularly after the publication of Margaret Mead's *Male and Female*,[26] the feeling prevailed that the traits exhibited by males and females resulted almost entirely from their environment and upbringing. Work on gender role identity by Money, Hampson, and Hampson led to the conclusion that the adoption of a gender identity as a male or female was the result entirely of the sex to which the individual was assigned at birth, even though this sex of assignment contradicted the genetic, gonadal, and anatomic sex.[27]

However, this view of psychosexual neutrality at birth was challenged by critics who pointed out (among other things) that this conclusion might hold only for individuals of anomalous sex, whose hormonal levels might be quite inadequate[28] and for cases of ambiguous sex, whose gender role development did not follow this pattern. Stoller, for example, reports on cases where the effects of rearing are overturned and where patients are impelled, possibly (he suggests) by an overpoweringly strong biological force, to insist in their thinking, fantasy life, and behavior that they are members of the opposite sex.[29] It must be concluded that whether individuals are born with a psychosexual neutrality or with a sexual predisposition is still in the realm of controversy.

Of special interest are the recent animal studies that have suggested that behavior as males and females in later life might be permanently influenced by the level of hormones circulating at certain critical periods before or just after birth.[30] Although their application to human behavior is purely conjectural, these animal experiments have shown that during certain critical periods of fetal development, changes are taking place in the brain that direct the animal to exhibit male or female behavior when adult, and that injections of male or female hormone at these critical periods could cause a switch in the animal's behavior. It is not outside the realm of possibility that some human individuals are at least made more susceptible to gender role deviations by the failure of male sex hormone to act upon the brain at the critical periods or by some imbalance of hormone circulating at that time. This is given some weight by a small body of human clinical evidence in terms of the masculinization or feminization of genital and other body structures during the prenatal period. As Money and Alexander put it: "These varying lines of evidence from animal experiments and human clinical investigations, from males and females, and from androgen deficiency to androgen excess, indicate that fetal hormones exert an effect, via the central nervous system, on the eventual organization of behavior, sexual and sex-related."[31] At any rate it is quite clear that the old commonsense view that sex and gender were synonymous is no longer tenable.

Unfortunately, much of the area of psychosexual development in the early years also remains conjectural. According to Gagnon and Simon, the original potentiating mechanisms for the development of childhood sexuality do not reside in the specifically sexual things that adults do with children, but in the patterns of nonsexual things that they do with them, a lesson that was well demonstrated for primates by Harlow and his famous cloth monkeys.[32] A major element in this socializing of the child is the degree to which the touching and handling behavior of the mother as she responds to the behavior of the infant is warm and consistent, so that the child learns to be comfortable with his own body and to find it a basic source of pleasure. Thus, they say, the potentiating of sexual development lies not in the instinctual or biological nature of the child, as Freud erroneously believed, but in the manner in which the child is socialized by adults.

Recently, the latency theory has emerged from the area of theoretical speculation into the controversial arena of sex education for younger children. It has been put forward particularly by Rhoda Lorand, a non-medical psychotherapist, to justify her charge that almost any kind of sex education during the so-called latency period (ages of six to eleven) is potentially damaging to psychosexual development.[33] To begin with, the latency theory is a highly controversial one, not only among experts in the field of child development but among psychiatrists themselves, even those psychoanalytically oriented. Ausubel, after reviewing the available empirical evidence in 1954, concluded that the notion of a latency period was neither empirically nor theoretically tenable.[34] Broderick, who has devoted himself to empirical study of the preadolescent period, declares flatly that the latency theory is "a myth."[35] Lidz observes that just as there is no evidence of a physiologically determined increase in sexual drive of the oedipal child, there is no reason to believe that a diminution in sexual drive occurs during the latency period and little if any evidence that the child has less impulsion to masturbation or that sexual curiosity diminishes appreciably.[36]

Money and Alexander, on the basis of a longitudinal study of up to 18 years of the psychosexual development of males with precocious puberty, noted that a change did occur in these boys somewhere between the ages of seven and twelve which resembled the latency period.[37] On the basis of their experience they suggest that "the so-called latency period in normal boys does not represent a negation or loss of sexual urge, imagery, or participation per se—that is, in fact, empirically obvious to anyone who knows anything about the untrammeled sex lives of free-ranging boys." It is rather, they believe, a period in which a boy makes a double leap in maturation: on the one hand rehearsing sexual self-restraint as a sign of the ability to conform to established standards of morality, on the other consolidating his masculine gender identity, separate from and uncontaminated by the feminine, in preparation for his later falling in love.

Clearly, the whole question of the latency period remains hypothetical and controversial. When the hypothesis is utilized, as Lorand and a handful of others do, as a weapon to oppose sex education in our sex-saturated culture, one finds little support for this attempt even among those psychiatrists who accept the latency theory in principle. Certainly this theory has little application to sexual behavior in a black slum area, as studies in St. Louis have made very clear, where "destructive social and economic forces ... often create a situation in which the young child is exposed to sex-socializing influences almost constantly."[38] Although the idea of children as being asexual is a common middle-class conception, the idea of asexual childhood is almost inconceivable to black slum-dwellers. Rather than support the position advocated by Lorand, it is probable that psychiatrists generally will agree with the psychiatrist Ellen Rothchild, who sees latency as "an optimal time in which to complete enlightenment as to the major facts of reproduction."[39]

Gagnon and Simon also make some highly interesting observations concerning the divergent socialization process of males and females.[40] They note that the whole early training process of the boys is concerned with learning the physical experience of sex, while girls are being trained in the language of love, in self-control, and in management of male behavior. It is only in the later part of adolescence that the two sexes attempt to break through the differences and begin to learn to combine the necessary elements of sexual commitments and love, a process most difficult for both sexes and one that poses a profound challenge for sex education. Interestingly, there is some indication in the latest Institute for Sex Research study that the two sexes are beginning to converge somewhat, in the finding that more college-educated boys than in the past are reporting their first sexual experience with someone whom they loved.[41] Although the rise is only from the 1 to 5 percent range to the 11 to 14 percent range in a generation, it does perhaps mark a trend. It does not, of course, yet begin to approach the 70 to 90 percent of girls whose initial experience is with someone they love.

It is fairly well established that women still feel a greater necessity for emotional commitment before they become involved sexually and that masculine attitudes toward the meaning and place of sex in human relationships still carry a fundamentally amoral component, which contradicts the morally supported values of sexuality. Udry sees the polemical point of view taken by Albert Ellis and *Playboy* as an attempt to legitimize the "underworld" values of the male subculture by defining these values as "healthy" and by describing the prevailing values (which are closely patterned from female values) as "sick" and as evidence of an emotionally disordered society.[42]

Although there are more responses commonly shared than formerly believed, there is no doubt about the existence of differential sexual responses and behavior among males and females,[43] as well as continuing controversy concerning the importance of cultural or biological factors in producing these differences. However, some of the differences, as Kagan notes, seem to stretch across cultures and species, suggesting that sex-role standards are neither arbitrary nor completely determined by the social group: "Each culture, in its wisdom, seems to promote those behaviors and values that are biologically easiest to establish in each of the two sexes."[44]

Americans are now in the process of integrating a tradition in which men have authority over women, with newer values that emphasize the equality of men and women. There is a general tendency, Udry says, for equality of rights to be transformed into similarity of rights and then for this similarity of rights to be justified in terms of similarity of needs.[45] This has fostered the belief that men and women are basically similar in their emotional and sexual needs. The fact is that men and women are really quite different in their sexuality, and sex has different meaning for each, probably deriving from the different contexts in which men and women experience sexual learning. Kagan warns that the effect of the reach for independence and autonomy on the part of American women need not necessarily lead to a more satisfying and egalitarian relation between the sexes; it could also make each partner so reluctant to submerge his individual autonomy and admit his need for the other that each walks a lonely and emotionally insulated path.[46]

The Institute for Sex Research has now embarked on a large-scale investigation of homosexuality that will hopefully provide a real basis of fact for this highly controversial area. More and more, the concept of homosexuality as a "disease" or as a symptom of mental illness—though it still dominates psychiatric thinking—is under sharp attack by a number of behavioral scientists.[47] There is also a growing consensus that early conclusions about homosexual behavior as a characterological disorder were premature generalizations that went far beyond the facts, and were based on atypical, distorted samples limited to disturbed psychiatric patients or to a prison population.[48] Greater unanimity exists around the belief that homosexuality is not a clinical entity and that its etiology must be sought in a far greater complex of factors than earlier thinking allowed. Few careful observers are content to believe that the close-binding, dominating mother and the absent or hostile father relationship that Bieber and his colleagues made so much of is sufficient to explain all, or even most, cases of male homosexual behavior, and the ongoing studies of female homosexuals by Gundlach and Riess show how difficult it is to support by empirical evidence the traditional generalizations made about lesbians. For example, they noted, "in no question regarding parental attitudes toward the daughter was there a significant difference in the frequency of female homosexual and heterosexual responses."[49]

Alan Bell, psychologist at the Institute for Sex Research, disputes the notion that a heterosexual commitment reflects a resolution of issues that is not even dared, much less accomplished, in a homosexual commitment.[50] He suggests that neither orientation can be considered more or less mature than the other and that each may be determined by equally severe but different anxieties that arise inevitably from the father-son relationship.

Simon and Gagnon have warned that, whenever we view any role in which the sexual element stands out—as is usually the case with sexual deviations—we tend to impute more extreme and intense sexuality than is really the case.[51] They suggest that it is important to refuse to make judgments about the meaning of specific sexual activities in isolation from the larger context of the social life of the deviant actor. It is possible, they say, that a broader perspective will aid us in seeing deviant behavior as less exotic when we view it in terms of the realities of everyday existence. They suggest that we treat with suspicion all dangerously simplified presentations that offer to provide us with a description and/or analysis of *the* homosexual or *the* lesbian. Although the homosexual commitment in itself has a profound impact upon behavior, there are many different ways of expressing homosexuality. They argue, further, that homosexual behavior is "unnatural in the way that all human behavior is unnatural; that is, it is without an absolutely predetermined and fixed shape and content, and it is a complex condition which derives from man's unique abilities to think, act, and remember and his need to live with other humans."

Studies in the past of unwed mothers suffered from the same defect as studies of homosexuals: from highly selective, unrepresentative, and skewed samples. As Clark Vincent pointed out, the result was a popular notion that the illegitimate child was conceived in a relationship based primarily on force, moral depravity, and exploitation, and that the mother was a socially, morally, psychologically, and mentally inferior woman.[52] Vincent's data showed that, when a representative sample was studied, unwed mothers were fairly representative, socioeconomically, of all females of equivalent age, race, and marital status. The majority reported either a love relationship or a close friendship with their sexual mates, and the majority showed little evidence of subnormal mentality or emotional instability. Vincent also showed the importance of studying the unwed fathers, who also represent a cross section, if we are to understand the whole problem and contribute to its solution.[53] Later studies have given suport to Vincent's findings.[54]

The term "Sexual Revolution" has been used as a cliché both by the standard bearers of sexual freedom and by the prophets of doom who would gladly take us backward to "the good old days of sexual morality." Actually the popular conception of the Sexual Revolution as a complete and thoroughgoing change in sexual attitudes and behavior, supposedly created by the revelations in the Kinsey report and by technological developments in contraception (mainly "the pill") is a myth. To begin with, every careful study has shown conclusively that the contraceptive pill and other developments have played a very, very minor role in premarital sexual behavior of adolescents or of the college population.[55] In the majority of cases, initial intercourse has taken place without the use of any contraceptives whatever and only a very small minority have used the pill.

Although the findings of studies vary concerning the extent of premarital coitus—and our information is still very scant for non-college groups—the extent of change since the first Kinsey report makes very dubious the fitness of the term "revolution" to describe it, if we judge the country as a whole. The most reliable index of change—the most recent Kinsey report of first coitus on the college campus—indicates an increase of perhaps 25 percent in premarital intercourse over the original Kinsey sample (studies published in 1948 and 1953). According to Gebhard, there has been comparatively little change in the enormous differences between how males and females view their initial partner: "Females surrender their virginity to males they love whereas males are much less emotionally involved."[56] The age at which intercourse begins has not changed too greatly; however, for college males prostitution has become "quite insignificant" as a source of initial intercourse (2 to 7 percent).

There is a marked trend toward greater enjoyment of first intercourse by girls and an increase in the number reporting orgasm. "All of this," Dr. Gebhard concludes, "sounds like a continuation of the trend toward sexual equality, with the female being regarded both by males and by herself less as a sexual object to be exploited and more as a fellow human with her own needs, expectations, and rights."

Thus, the basic change is that taking place in middle-class women. It represents a continuation of the great change in female sexual attitudes and behavior that took place after World War I as an accompaniment of the movement to establish equality for women in all areas of life. There are still few indications that female promiscuity has become the norm, and most female sexual behavior still occurs within the context of affection and impending marriage. The behavior of males, far from moving in the direction of greater promiscuity, has been slowly moving toward the female norm.[57]

The real revolution that has occurred has been a revolution of openness.[58] When one recalls that as late as 1937 it took tremendous pressure for the surgeon general of the United States to win the right to use the term "venereal disease" on the radio, one can see how fast and how far this kind of sexual revolution has moved. But to interpret the sudden revelation of sexual behavior as an actual change in behavior or to equate the increase in overtness with an increase in the behavior itself is to make a very serious error. We have no way of knowing, for example, whether homosexual behavior has in fact increased, although the tremendous increase in public discussion and expression of that behavior is a clear matter of public record. The famous poet who wrote "When

I was one-and-twenty" carried his secret to the grave; when Somerset Maugham died, his homosexual proclivities appeared on page one of the *New York Times*.

In the past, the values held by individuals were neglected in assessing the effects of any kind of behavior. The work of Kirkendall[59] and particularly Christensen[60] has shown that it is dangerous to do so, since the values of an individual are important intervening variables that influence the effect of any kind of sexual behavior. Christensen's cross-cultural data have indicated that it is not so much the behavior itself that is damaging but behavior that goes contrary to a person's value system.

In the area of premarital sexual standards, the work of Ira Reiss has begun to lay a solid basis of data and of sociological theory. His analysis of the four types of standards—abstinence, double standard, permissiveness without affection, and permissiveness with affection—is a well-known part of the literature.[61] In his later studies, Reiss sees the growing sexual permissiveness among young people as basically the result of two factors: the decline of the influence of the family, which is an institution of relatively low premarital permissiveness, and the growing assumption of responsibility by young people for their own sexual behavior under a system of participant-run courtship, an institution of relatively high premarital permissiveness.[62] The relative strength of the influence of these two institutions varies in accord with the role position of the individual.

Reiss's data show that the general notion that diminishing permissiveness usually attributed to older persons is a function of the growing conservatism and rigidity of age or an indication of a sex revolution among their more permissive offspring is not correct. Even though older persons do tend to be less permissive, the difference is not too marked, and Reiss suggests that the lower permissiveness shown by parents is a function of the responsibility that they have and the role that they must play. Thus, Reiss found, childless couples indicated greater willingness to accept premarital intercourse than comparable couples with children of courtship age; even first-born children who are responsible for their siblings are less permissive than the youngest children. As the individual participates in courtship, he is led to a breakthrough of the adult taboos. Later, participation in the family leads him to at least a partial return to these adult taboos. Reiss also disputes the belief of the Kinsey investigators that the differences in sexual behavior

and attitudes between Negroes and whites were basically social-
class differences. When he controlled his data for social class, he
found large variations in the way whites and blacks viewed premarital permissiveness, with Negroes generally being more permissive. He is careful to note that the differences do not suggest
racial superiority or inferiority.

No doubt there are deep changes in attitudes that are beginning
to take place, even though there are many stabilizing influences
that prevent too rapid change from occurring. The new phenomenon of mass dropping-out from society on the part of young people,
their insistence on immediate satisfaction, and their existential
disregard for the future indicate that we are beginning to reach
the end of the Protestant ethic, which placed its premium on the
values of work, saving, future-orientation, and asceticism. Interestingly, many of the sexual values formerly associated with puritanism are now being most strongly espoused by such socialist
countries as the Soviet Union and China, which apparently also see
in these values important social norms for rapidly building up the
industrial bases of their society.[63]

CHAPTER NOTES*

1. T. Buckley, "All They Talk About Is Sex, Sex, Sex," *New York Times
   Magazine,* April 20, 1969.
2. C. C. Bowman, "Social Change as Reflected in Kinsey Studies," *Social
   Problems* 1 (July 1954) : 1–6.
3. A. C. Kinsey et al., "Concepts of Normality and Abnormality in Sexual
   Behavior," in P. H. Hoch and J. Zubin, eds., *Psychosexual Development in
   Health and Disease* (New York: Grune & Stratton, 1949), pp 11–32.
   See also I. Rubin, "Concepts of *Sexual Abnormality and Perversion in
   Marriage Counseling,*" in H. L. Silverman, ed., *Moral Issues in Marriage
   Counseling.* In preparation.
4. M. Hoffman, "On The Concept of Genital Primacy," *Journal of Nervous
   and Mental Disease* 137 (December 1963) : 552–556.
5. A. Comfort, *Sex in Society* (London: Gerald Duckworth & Co., 1963),
   pp. 42–44.
6. N. N. Foote, "Sex as Play," in J. Himelhoch and S. F. Fava, eds., *Sexual
   Behavior in American Society* (New York: W. W. Norton & Co., 1955),
   pp. 237–243.
7. W. H. Masters and V. E. Johnson, *Human Sexual Response* (Boston:
   Little, Brown & Co., 1966), Chapter 9.

*Editor's note: The reader may note a few omissions in the Chapter Notes.
Regrettably, Dr. Rubin was killed in an automobile accident before he had an
opportunity to complete them.

8. See, for example, E. Fried, "The Fear of Loving," in G. D. Goldman and D. S. Milman, eds., *Modern Woman—Her Psychology and Sex* (Springfield, Illinois: Charles C. Thomas, 1969), pp. 48 and 50.

9. M. J. Sherfey, "The Evolution and Nature of Female Sexuality in Relation to Psychoanalytic Theory," *Journal of the American Psychoanalytic Association* 14 (January 1966) : 28–128. See also S. J. Kleegman, "Clinical Applications of Masters' and Johnson's Research," in P. J. Fink and V. B. O. Hammett, eds., *Sexual Function and Dysfunction* (Philadelphia: F. A. Davis Co., 1969), pp. 23–33.

10. S. E. Waxenberg, "Psychotherapeutic and Dynamic Implications of Recent Research on Female Sexual Functioning," in Goldman and Milman, eds., *Modern Woman*, pp. 3–29.

11. Sherfey, "The Evolution and Nature of Female Sexuality."

12. G. Chedd, "Struggling Into Manhood," *New Scientist* (June 5, 1969) : 524–526.

13. T. Benedek and B. B. Rubinstein, *The Sexual Cycle in Women*, Psychosomatic Monographs, 3: 1–2 (Washington, D.C.: National Research Council, 1942).

14. Waxenberg, "Psychotherapeutic and Dynamic Implications."

15. J. R. Udry and N. M. Morris, "Distribution of Coitus in the Menstrual Cycle" (Paper presented at the annual meeting of the Population Association of America, Cinn., Ohio, April 1967).

16. Waxenberg, "Psychotherapeutic and Dynamic Implications"; J. L. Hampson and J. G. Hampson, "The Ontogenesis of Sexual Behavior in Man," in W. C. Young, ed., *Sex and Internal Secretions*, 3rd ed., 2 vols. (Baltimore: The Williams and Wilkins Co., 1961), 2: 1401–1432.

17. S. E. Waxenberg, "Psychotherapeutic and Dynamic Implications"; J. Money, "Sex Hormones and Other Variables in Human Eroticism," in W. C. Young, ed., *Sex and Internal Secretions*, pp. 1383–1400.

18. H. K. Hellerstein and E. H. Friedman, "Sexual Activity and the Postcoronary Patient," *Medical Aspects of Human Sexuality* 3 (March 1969) : 70–96.

19. For a summary of this research, see I. Rubin, *Sexual Life After Sixty* (New York: Basic Books, 1965) and I. Rubin, "Sex After Forty—and After Seventy," in R. Brecher and E. Brecher, eds., *An Analysis of Human Sexual Response* (New York: New American Library (Signet), 1966), pp. 251–266.

20. E. Pfeiffer, A. Verwoerdt, and H. S. Wang, "Sexual Behavior in Aged Men and Women," *Archives of General Psychiatry* 19 (December 1968) : 753–758; and "Observation on a Biologically Advantaged Group of Individuals" (paper presented at Gerontological Society, Denver, Colorado, Oct. 31–Nov. 2, 1968).

21. Masters and Johnson, *Human Sexual Response*, chapters 15 and 16.

22. Ibid., Chapter 10.

23. R. R. Limner, *Sex and the Unborn Child* (New York: Julian Press, 1969).

24. See L. Israel and I. Rubin, *Sexual Relations During Pregnancy and the Post-Delivery Period*, SIECUS Study Guide No. 6 (New York: Sex Information and Education Council of the U.S., 1967).

25. Hellerstein and Friedman, "Sexual Activity and the Postcoronary Patient."

26. M. Mead, *Male and Female*. (New York: William Morrow and Co., 1949).

27. J. Money, J. G. Hampson, and J. L. Hampson, "Hermaphroditism: Recommendations Concerning Assignment of Sex, Change of Sex and Psychologic Management," *Bulletin of the Johns Hopkins Hospital* 97: 284–300.

28. M. Diamond, "A Critical Evaluation of the Ontogeny of Human Sexual Behavior," *The Quarterly Review of Biology* 40 (June 1965): 147–175.

29. R. J. Stoller, *Sex and Gender* (New York: Science House, 1968).

30. W. C. Young, R. W. Goy, and C. H. Phoenix, "Hormones and Sexual Behavior," in J. Money, ed., *Sex Research—New Developments* (New York: Holt, Rinehart and Winston, 1965), pp. 176–196.

31. J. Money and D. Alexander, "Psychosexual Development and Absence of Homosexuality In Males With Precocious Puberty," *The Journal of Nervous and Mental Disease* 148 (February 1969): 111–123.

32. J. H. Gagnon and W. Simon, "Sex Education and Human Development," in Fink and Hammett, eds., *Sexual Function and Dysfunction*, pp. 113–126.

33. R. Lorand, Brief No. 35322 filed in case of Cyndy Becker, et al. vs. the Board of Education, et al., Superior Court of the State of California for the County of San Luis Obispo, Oct. 4, 1968.

34. D. P. Ausubel, *Theory and Problems of Adolescent Development* (New York: Grune & Stratton, 1954), pp. 24–29.

35. C. B. Broderick, "Normal Sociosexual Development," in C. B. Broderick and J. Bernard, eds., *The Individual, Sex, & Society* (Baltimore: The Johns Hopkins Press, 1969), pp. 23–39 and also C. B. Broderick, "Is the 'Latent Period' Really Latent?" in I. Rubin and L. E. Kirkendall, eds., *Sex in the Childhood Years* (New York: Association Press, 1970).

36. T. Lidz, *The Person—His Development Throughout The Life Cycle* (New York: Basic Books, 1968), pp. 265–266.

37. Money and Alexander, "Psychosexual Development and Absence of Homosexuality."

38. B. E. Hammond and J. A. Ladner, "Socialization into Sexual Behavior in a Negro Slum Ghetto," in Broderick and Bernard, eds., *The Individual, Sex & Society*, pp. 41–51.

39. E. Rothchild, "Emotional Aspects of Sexual Development," in S. R. Homel, ed., "The Physician and Sex Education," *The Pediatric Clinics of North America* (Philadelphia: W. B. Saunders Co., 1969), pp. 415–428.

40. Gagnon and Simon, "Sex Education."

41. Reported in *Sexology*, 34 (June 1968): 780–781.

42. J. R. Udry, "Sex and Family Life," *The Annals of the American Academy of Political and Social Science* 376 (March 1968).

43. W. B. Pomeroy and C. V. Christenson, *Characteristics of Male and Female Sexual Responses*. SIECUS Study Guide No. 4 (New York: Sex Information and Education).

44. J. Kagan, *Psychology Today*.

45. Udry, "Sex and Family Life."

46. Kagan, *Psychology Today*.

47. See, for example, E. Hooker, "The Adjustment of the Male Overt Homosexual," *Journal of Projective Techniques* 21 (1957) : 18–31.

48. J. Marmor, ed., *Sexual Inversion* (New York: Basic Books, 1965), Introduction, p. 16.

49. F. Riess, Discussion of paper on female homosexuality, in Goldman and Milman, eds., *Modern Woman*, pp. 268–271.

50. A. P. Bell, "The Scylla and Charybdis of Psychosexual Development," *The Journal of Sex Research* 5 (May 1969) : 86 89.

51. W. Simon, and J. H. Gagnon, "The Lesbians: A Preliminary Overview," in J. H. Gagnon and W. Simon, eds., *Sexual Deviance* (New York: Harper & Row, 1967), pp. 247–282.

52. C. E. Vincent, *Unwed Mothers* (New York: The Free Press of Glencoe, Inc., 1961).

53. C. E. Vincent, "Spotlight on the Unwed Father," *Sexology* 28 (March 1962) : 538–542.

54. See for example, C. V. Von Der Ahe, "The Unwed Teenage Mother," *The American Journal of Obstetrics and Gynecology* (May 15, 1969).

55. E. H. Pohlman, *Psychology of Birth Planning* (Cambridge, Mass.: Schenkman Pub. Co., 1969), pp. 29–30, 352–355.

56. Reported in *Sexology* 34 (June 1968) : 780–781.

57. Ibid.

58. J. H. Gagnon, "Talk about Sex, Sexual Behavior, and Sex Research" (Paper presented at 32nd annual meeting of the Groves Conference on Marriage and the Family, Kansas City, April 18-20, 1966).

59. L. E. Kirkendall, *Premarital Intercourse and Interpersonal Relationships* (New York: Julian Press, 1961).

60. H. T. Christensen, "Scandinavian and American Sex Norms: Some Comparisons, with Sociological Implications," *Journal of Social Issues* 22 (April 1966) : 60–75.

61. I. L. Reiss, *Premarital Sexual Standards in America* (Glencoe, Illinois: Free Press, 1960).

62. I. L. Reiss, *The Social Context of Premarital Sexual Permissiveness* (New York: Holt, Rinehart, and Winston, 1967).

63. J. Bernard, "Technology, Science and Sex Attitudes," and E. Kostyashkin, "Sex Morality and Sex Education in the Soviet Union," *Impact of Science on Society* (Unesco), 18 (Oct.–Dec. 1968) : 218 and 249–258; also, J. Bernard, "The Fourth Revolution," *The Journal of Social Issues* 28 (April 1966) : 86–87.

PART II

SEX AND
INDIVIDUAL DEVELOPMENT

Chapter 4

EMOTIONS AND SEXUALITY
IN THE MAN

By LeMon Clark, M.D.

Writing about another subject, entirely unrelated to the one we are to consider here, Bertrand Russell made a statement that applies very pertinently. "Anything that one says on this is sure to be wrong! It is difficult to find a form of words, and the difficulty is due to linguistic problems." Nowhere is the difficulty due to linguistic problems greater than when one is trying to discuss the subject of sex, since the feeling tone connected with any given word can be so different for different individuals.

All words relating to sex or sexual activity are emotionally charged. What does "sexual intercourse" mean to you? Does it bring up a concept of a delightful, emotionally thrilling, deeply satisfying, enjoyable experience? Can you, in contemplating it, plan a time, place, and setting for it? If you can "make a production" out of an attempt at coital activity, you are fairly well emancipated from the feeling of guilt that has troubled the human race for generations.

But how do you react to the little Anglo-Saxon word meaning "to plant or sow" and by implication for those early forebears meant coitus—the word "fuck"? It isn't the meaning of the word that triggers your emotional reaction; it is the circumstance under which you learned it, the feeling tone that surrounds it. Acceptable words carry an aura of niceness, of consideration, cooperation, social acceptance. Unacceptable words convey a sense of baseness, coarseness, mere physical appetite as contrasted with spiritual values.

I recall a prayer book definition of marriage as the legitimate indulgence of concupiscence. A dictionary definition of "concupiscence" is: 1. "sensual appetite; lust; 2. eager or illicit desire."[1] The dictionary definitions confuse the picture. We certainly cannot class "sensual appetite" as undesirable. But *lust* is defined as "passionate, overmastering desire; unbridled or lawless sexual desire or appetite, all emotions of the baser kind." *Lustful* means "full of, or imbued with lust." But *lusty* means "full of, or characterized by healthy vigor, robust, strong, sturdy." A lusty individual is quite acceptable. A lustful individual is not.

"Eager desire" is certainly permissible, even very desirable, within the framework of marriage. A wife "eagerly desiring" her husband's lovemaking contributes a great deal to the experience. "Illicit desire" implies a very undesirable direction. Why couple the two meanings in one definition?

Roget's famous Thesaurus recognizes and separates the two concepts. Under "concupiscence" there are two headings: *desire* as one and *impurity* as the other. Clearly the prayer book has in mind only the normal acceptable aspects of desire, with no derogatory implication. Roget, having separated the two aspects, lists a whole host of words and phrases under each.

The prayer book's statement contributes still more towards covering the experience with something of a cloud. "Indulgence" has at least a slight implication of doing something that we might better get along without. Supposing the prayer book statement read "the legitimate *enjoyment* of concupiscence"? The whole feeling tone of the statement would be improved.

Choice of words can create issues. In 1871, Charles Darwin published his *Descent of Man*. This was answered in 1894 by an English clergyman, Henry Drummond, in a book *The Ascent of Man*. One can only wonder how differently Darwin's book might have been received had he entitled his *The Ascent of Man*. His thesis would have remained unchanged.

In talking about sex, one must use words. In trying to express how one feels to a loved and loving person, words must be used. The words used may connote one thing to one but have quite a different feeling tone to the other. This undoubtedly is the cause of many misunderstandings between couples trying to adjust their different backgrounds to a mutually satisfactory sexual understanding within the framework of marriage. A word used by one may arouse a totally unexpected emotional reaction in the other.

One may find the use of the little four-letter words sexually exciting; the other may find them at least distasteful, possibly disgusting, and so a definite sexual depressant.

Emotion is "an effective state of consciousness." It is not something that one can experience with his sensory equipment—the nerve endings of the five senses, touch, taste, sight, hearing, and smell. And yet stimulation of any end organ of sense may beget an emotional reaction—for example, the sight of a shapely leg (especially in this day of mini-mini-skirts), the odor of a perfume, the sound of a special musical piece, the taste of real homemade bread, having someone caress your hair, or your own caress of a smooth velvety cheek.

"Sexuality" is defined in Dorland's Medical Dictionary as "the constitution of an individual in relation to sexual attitudes and activity." The American College Dictionary defines it as "the recognition or emphasizing of sexual matters."

A considerable constellation of emotions center around the sexuality of any individual. On the positive side, some of them are sympathy, kindness, thoughtfulness, forgiveness, affection, passion, ecstasy, rapture, and love. On the negative side, some of the emotions are worry, fear, regret, feeling of a lack of self-control, self-criticism, sense of wrongdoing, guilt, and sin.

Two questions may be asked: How does emotion affect sexuality in man? How does sexuality affect one's emotions?

A. Moll, writing in 1897, used the term the "impulse of contrectation"[2] to describe the impulse to approach another individal, generally one of the opposite sex, with the desire for physical contact. But he also felt it applied to the psychic inclination to become generally interested in such a person. Such interest is dependent upon certain physiological processes in the individual. Prior to the onset of puberty, the beginning of function in the gonads, the young of the species do not have much interest in each other—at least as a sexual object. With the onset of puberty and the developmental period of adolescence, all this is changed. People of the opposite sex become interesting, because they are of the opposite sex. The sexuality of the individual thereafter does affect his emotions.

G. V. Hamilton, in his pioneer study of sexual research, noted that the tendency for amorous emotion appeared earlier in the development of the individual than genital sex desire.[3] It was experienced quite independently of such sexual desire after puberty. In past generations, teen-agers commonly developed the sense of amorous emotion, the ethereal love of the troubadours, for months—sometimes for years—before the advent of strong genital sex desire. One of the important questions of our day is, is this still true? With the advent of mini-skirts, with constant sexual confrontation in TV and advertising of all kinds, does the attention of the teenager focus upon the sexual-genital aspect of the contrectation impulse at an earlier age? My own feeling is that it does.

One other factor could contribute to such change. During the last century the onset of puberty has come at a progressively earlier age. This has been measured by the age of menarche, or onset of menstruation, in girls and the age of first seminal emission and the age of the attainment of maximum growth in adolescent boys. With glandular maturity occurring earlier, genital sex desire may also give further evidence that sexuality does affect the emotions.

The most important sexually-based emotion, we could possibly agree, is love. How may we define it? On the purely idealistic side, Dr. Paul Johnson of the Boston University School of Theology has defined it as "a growing interest in, appreciation of, and responsibility for another person." This leaves out the real motivating force that generates love—genital sex desire. Another definition recognizes the two aspects, the physical and the spiritual: love is the desire to possess and the desire to serve. Under different circumstances these two aspects of "love" can be quite separate. A man can feel a very strong desire to seize a woman and carry her off to bed with no element of wishing to do anything but to have intimate physical contact with her. But in another case, he may have a desire to do things for a woman, to try to please her and serve her with little desire for intimate sexual contact. A successful marriage is most firmly based when there is a perfect blend of these two emotions, centered on the marital partner.

Whatever the basis of the man's interest in the woman, ethereal love or genital-based sex desire, there must be some inclination towards the woman for him to function in coitus. His emotions vitally affect his sexuality. A woman may be unconscious, she may have a feeling of loathing for the man, she may be held down by others while he wreaks his will upon her, but an erect penis can be inserted into her vagina. But if the penis does not become erect, a man cannot perform the act of coitus.

If a man fails once, fear of failure may become a serious problem. Such fear may be a vital factor in affecting later performance. He may fail again and again. When this is complicated by other emotional factors, his ability to function—to develop an erection sufficiently firm to permit insertion of the penis into the vagina— may be impaired.

I have received many letters from middle-aged men wanting to know why they are impotent with other women when they are quite normally potent with their wives. The important influence of habit is well demonstrated in such a case. A man has formed the habit of having intercourse with his wife; with her, he is relaxed and confident, since he has performed quite capably many times before. But in addition, she knows what he likes as a part of pre-intercourse play, what is for him the most effective type of stimulation. With another woman, he misses the customary pre-intercourse play, but, in addition, there may be seriously inhibiting factors—a sense of wrongdoing, of guilt, even of sin for attempting such activity outside of the framework of marriage. His guilt may be compounded by the sense of "cheating" on his wife.

Another important element contributing to failure may well be the fear of venereal infection. With his wife, a man feels safe from such a possibility. With another woman, there is always the nagging doubt.

A man may feel that he would most dearly love to have a very passionate woman who would literally sweep him off his feet. Faced with just such a situation, he may find himself impotent. If he feels that the woman is leading him rather than he leading her, subconsciously he may feel demeaned, or he may doubt his ability to satisfy such a woman and, as a consequence, fail completely.

Another cause of difficulty is a rigid attitude toward what is permissible or proper in the process of lovemaking. A small woman felt overwhelmed during intercourse with her two-hundred-pound husband above her, but he felt that that was the only right way and could not reach orgasm with her above him. Such an attitude demonstrates quite vividly the influence of emotion on sexuality. Primitive peoples have laughed at the man-above position as "the missionary position." The big man's difficulty had nothing to do with anatomy or physiology. Variety is the spice of life and, as Disraeli said, the mother of enjoyment. Emotional fixations of any kind that limit one's ability to experiment will lessen one's ultimate pleasure and satisfaction.

Another example of the effect of emotions upon sexuality is

seen in the objections to the use of a contraceptive such as the vaginal diaphragm. It takes a matter of seconds to put in place, yet men and women may object to the interference with the process of the buildup of tension, although in almost every other social experience we accept delay when something is being done to enhance the pleasure later. Time spent in preparing an item of food in a special way is an example. Such reluctance actually may stem in part from a lingering sense of guilt over the enjoyment of sexual activity. To indulge in it when driven by desire, we can accept. But to plan it, to look forward to it, in my generation, was almost totally unacceptable. If we could accept the proposition that such sexual activity should be regarded as play at the adult level and that anything and everything that can be done to increase the pleasure of such play is not only permissible but desirable, the sum of pleasure and satisfaction resulting from sexual activity, freed from the gnawing fear of possible unwanted pregnancy, would be greatly increased.

This thought raises the question of what generation we are talking about and what generation we are trying to talk to. I am certain that great progress toward a more rational attitude regarding sexual expression has been made. I am just as certain that there is a long way yet to go to win complete freedom from the attitudes inherited from the Judeo-Christian, puritan-Victorian sexual ethics.

For a young man, attainment of an erection is not commonly a problem. For a young adult, sex desire arises spontaneously in the male. This, of course, presupposes that there are none of the possible inhibiting factors already mentioned. In middle and later life, however, desire may be present but the capacity to generate a spontaneous erection may not be. Whereas, at young adult ages, actual tactile contact, gentle petting, caressing, and manual stimulation helped arouse a woman, this was ordinarily unnecessary for a young man, granted that it was nevertheless very pleasurable. At middle and later age, such tactile stimulation may be essential for his physiological function.

In addition to actual tactile stimulation, a warm, accepting, cooperative, eager female companion is most helpful. A wife who tries to do her "wifely duty" in a mechanical, uninspired fashion fails to give the emotional stimulation so essential. The story is told of a prominent Washingtonian who was distressed to meet his nephew entering a famous "house" as he was leaving. Constrained to give at least some semblance of an explanation, he remarked to the nephew, "The simulated interest and cooperation of these young women is vastly more stimulating than the dignified acquiescence of your auntie."

Once having failed to gain an erection or to maintain it long enough to permit his partner to reach orgasm, a man is beset with fears that it will occur again. If he could accept the proposition that his partner could help, granted that he suggested to her what would help, real improvement in the situation could be achieved fairly quickly. He could, if he would, suggest that she flex one thigh and then passing her hand around her own buttock gently stimulate the whole sexual area, perineum, scrotum, and the shaft of the penis itself. Only the emotional reaction of fear of being misunderstood, or of feeling degraded in her eyes as something less than a normal male, prevents such suggestions.

Fear and embarrassment may prevent an older man from using a simple device that helps generate an erection and helps to maintain it through a sufficient period of time to permit both partners to achieve orgasm and release from sexual tension. An ordinary rubber band about two inches long, doubled to give the right amount of tension (which must not be too tight or too loose) can be placed around the base of the penis near the pubic bone. In many cases this will help solve the problem of gaining and maintaining an erection.

Willingness to consult a physician and seek help for middle and later age difficulties can prove rewarding. Physicians are becoming aware of some of these problems now, and one can be found who should prove helpful. One should never let embarrassment or shyness keep him from seeking help in overcoming sexual problems.

At any age, premature ejaculation may be a problem. In a young man, it may be due to excessive tension because of infrequent sexual experience. If this becomes a habit, it may take much longer to overcome the difficulty. But here again, the cooperation of an understanding partner and the *emotional acceptance* of the necessity for such cooperation on his part is essential. He must be willing to suggest what may be done to help, and she must cooperate willingly, eagerly. If she will manually stimulate him to the point where he feels orgasm approaching, and he then asks her to stop all stimulation, the tension will subside somewhat. Stimulation can then be renewed, and the sequence repeated through a period of many minutes. Ultimately, the same technique can be

carried over into the act of intercourse, he asking her to lie perfectly quiet and doing so himself when the tension approaches the
point of orgasm. Emotional acceptance of such cooperation and
training is essential.

In a middle-aged or older man, premature ejaculation may develop. A low-grade prostatitis, a posterior urethritis, or an overly
sensitive verumontanum may cause it. Fatigue or worry may contribute to it. The important thing to remember is to seek help. Do
not let such troubles become habitual.

Fear of the physical strain of intercourse and orgasm can be a
real factor in lessening desire or inhibiting its expression in middle
and later life. One does not have to carry it on through the greatest
possible length of time, and the motions of intercourse do not have
to be so vigorous as to create undue physical strain. But if "jog-
ging" can exercise the heart beneficially, the experience of intercourse carried on with moderation can do the same, and the relief
of emotional tension as a result will confer real benefit. Very, very
few men die during the act of coitus. (Our statistics on this are, of
course, grossly inadequate since, our emotional attitudes being
what they are regarding the sex act, a wife would hardly admit
that the man found dead in bed died while making love to her. But
one of my old professors years ago hoped he might die that way,
since he would certainly die happy.)

Negative emotions undoubtedly cause most of the difficulties in
carrying on a satisfactory sexual act, but what might be called
positive emotions when carried to the extreme can do the same.
For example, a young man married a very beautiful young woman.
He was absolutely impotent with her. Why? Because he worshiped
her, idolized her, and "nice girls" don't do such a thing. Only the
fact that his wife was a sane, well-balanced person made it possible to overcome an unfortunate situation.

A middle-aged man feared something serious must be the matter
with him. Practically invited by a pretty blond to take her to bed,
when he did so he was completely incapable of having an erection
and having intercourse with her. She was young enough to be his
daughter and was the daughter of lifelong friends. He had watched
her grow up and was fond of her in, one might say, an "uncle-y"
way. She had been married and divorced, so he was not "violating"
a young girl; but in Kipling's words, he "couldn't do such 'cause he
loved her too much."

In younger men, fear of excessive coitus and its possible adverse effects may inhibit even normal sexual expression. What is normal? The limits are so broad that they cover a wide area. I have known couples who averaged intercourse twenty-five times or more a week; others who averaged two or three times a month. Whatever is satisfactory to the pair, with due consideration for the needs of each, may be considered "normal." It is physiologically impossible to have intercourse too much. It is not truly exhausting; it is relaxing. If a man had intercourse so many times that it was almost impossible to get out of bed, there would be no danger of him starving to death; ultimately, enough nervous tension would be generated so that he would be moved to seek food.

One of the great influences upon the sexuality of man and, through his sexual inclinations, upon his emotions is unquestionably the change in working hours during the last fifty years. A twelve-hour day was common in the steel mills fifty years ago. Judge Gary in those days defended the twelve-hour day on the grounds that the workers wanted to make the extra money. Farmers commonly worked from dawn till dark, literally. The laborsaving machinery, now considered a necessity on a modern farm, was only beginning to be used.

Now we have the eight-hour day—or less—and the five-day week —or less. With greater reserves of energy seeking outlets, sexual activity and interest in men is unquestionably greater today than fifty years ago.

Modern methods of birth control or contraception, freeing both men and women from the fear of unwanted pregnancy resulting from sexual union, have also made a greater interest in sexual activity possible.

With the increasing industrialization of the country, a vast number of married women are working outside the home. When they get home, there is the housekeeping to be done, meals to be prepared, and a thousand-and-one things that still seem to be regarded as "women's work." Men, with the shorter work day, may have more nervous and physical energy to devote to sexual activity. Women may have less. Fifty years ago, when "a woman's place was in the home," she could relax several times during the day. Grandma, in her rocking chair beside the stove, might deny vigorously that she took a nap, but she probably did. A woman in industry can get no time off for a nap, even with a coffee break.

Equal rights for women, the feeling that, after all, she does not have to submit to the sexual advances of her husband if she doesn't want to, has brought still another area of change.

These four factors, the shorter working day, contraception, women in industry, and equal rights for women, have probably brought about a greater change in sexuality within the framework of marriage than outside it. But because of these changes, emotional problems connected with sexuality became very real. There is still a long way to go to solve some of the emotional problems these changes have brought about.

The beginning of function in the testicles brings about the physiological changes of puberty. This ushers in the sense of sexual interest that is something more than mere curiosity that may be present in an eight-, ten-, or twelve-year-old. There is a drive back of it, a genital-based sex desire. In later middle life, there is a waning of gonadal function. In the female this is dramatically evidenced by the cessation of menstruation. Does the human male go through a climacteric, a period of physiological change, similar to that of the menopause in women? Personally, I am convinced that he does. The sexuality of the individual changes, and with such change, his emotions are affected. He may be more irritable, restless; he may sleep poorly. There may be a decrease in his physical energy, his sense of well-being. All this, it must be admitted, is a moot question. Some authorities disagree with this position.

Where a middle-aged man does suffer any of the above symptoms, it is a simple matter to administer sufficient testosterone to give him the therapeutic test. Two hundred milligrams of an aqueous suspension of testosterone may be given once a week for five or six weeks. If this helps, as it very well may, further administration can be given as indicated.

If it proves helpful, he should sleep better, be more relaxed, but have greater drive in his work. Libido will increase, and the satisfaction in coitus will improve. He will be less irritable. The sexual decline will be reversed, and his whole emotional makeup improved.

One of the most shocking things to an older man's emotional makeup is the possibility of a prostatectomy. His fear that having such an operation will render him impotent is very real. The possibility of such a result depends upon at least two important factors, the sexual situation before the operation and the type of operation.

If he enjoyed a reasonably active sex life prior to such an operation, he should be able to resume sexual activity afterwards in the majority of cases. The type of operation, however, may influence this result. If the perineal type of operation is necessary, the interference with the nerve and blood supply to the area may be sufficient to militate against the possibility of ever again generating an erection sufficient to permit vaginal penetration. But where the most common operation is performed, a transurethral resection, done by a skilled operator, the chances of continued sexual ability should be good.

Kinsey is authority for the statement that a young man reaches the peak of sexual desire and performance in the late teens.[4] From this peak he slowly declines in sexual activity until senescence and impotence set in. A young woman, however, does not reach the peak of sex desire and ability until twenty-nine or thirty and then stays at that high level for twenty-five or thirty years. Havelock Ellis made the same observation fifty years or more earlier. If a man reaches the age of impotence but his wife is still sexually active, what can be done? This change in his sexual ability may generate a very real emotional turmoil for him.

Where a couple has maintained a sense of real rapport and where they are free from sexual inhibitions, it is still possible to work out a satisfactory relationship. He can stimulate her either manually or with the help of such a device as a vibrator-massager to the point of orgasm and release from tension. If something in the vagina contributes to her satisfaction, any smooth cylindrical object may be employed in addition to the clitoral-vulvar stimulation. Artificial penises of various types are available that can be attached in such a way as to make actual vaginal penetration and the normal actions of coitus possible.

Where a couple is free from all sexual inhibitions and such activity is indulged in, even the husband may achieve a considerable degree of emotional release and satisfaction. The fact that he sees his wife enjoying the sexual activity is in itself a satisfying experience.

Masturbation, despite the progress that has been made in saner attitudes during the last decade or two, still ranks as a very great bugaboo. In my boyhood, everything that possibly could be was attributed to the sin of masturbation—poor health, poor physique, poor memory, acne, lack of self-confidence, failure to achieve one's goals. Worry about masturbation may cause emotional troubles, but the act itself, used to relieve sexual tension, is harmless. This needs to be repeated over and over until it is finally accepted as the true fact that it is.

Masturbation after marriage in both men and women is common. One of the pair may not be sexually inclined when the other is. Rather than bother the other, it may be much easier to gain such release through masturbation. But it is also true that masturbation may give a quite different sensation. In the short run, it may be a more intense, specific, localized sensation. In the long run, it does not give the complete satisfaction gained from coitus on a loved and loving basis, but it can satisfy a specific need. Masturbation may be carried on throughout adulthood and during long years of marriage. When we can free ourselves from all the bugaboos connected with it and accept it as the safety valve it should be, we shall have advanced still further along the road of a sane attitude towards sexuality in man—and woman.

A widowed adult need have no sense of guilt whatever over gaining relief from sexual tension through masturbation. Older men certainly do not have the opportunity to find a female companion who might be sexually stimulating and attractive. Many considerations may make it unwise or difficult for him to try to find a female partner. If masturbation helps, he should certainly have no hesitation in using it.

At the human level, because we have a cerebrum that remembers and foresees, we cannot separate our sexuality from our emotions. The moment that, as humans, we began to appraise our actions and even our very thoughts, sex and emotions were inseparably intertwined. As a man "thinketh in his heart, so is he."[5] What the individual finds in the sexual activity of life depends entirely upon his emotional approach to sexual activity. You remember the story of the search for the Holy Grail. It turned out that anyone could find it who had it within his own heart to find it.

Just so, the union of sexuality and emotions within the individual can be a most satisfying, pleasant, truly recreative experience. When we free ourselves from any sense of guilt or sin in relation to sexual feelings, when sexual activity can be regarded as play at the adult level, human life and living will be much more satisfactory.

But sexual activity still remains only sexual activity. The union with one of the opposite sex for the purpose of establishing a home and the rearing of children, with the great satisfactions that the establishment of such an institution can give, still remains perhaps the outstanding human emotional experience.

CHAPTER NOTES

1. *The American College Dictionary*, s.v. "concupiscence."
2. Quoted in Havelock Ellis, *Sex in Relation to Society* (Philadelphia, Pa.: Davis, 1925), p. 38.
3. G. V. Hamilton, *A Research in Marriage* (New York: A & C Boni, 1929), p. 360.
4. Alfred C. Kinsey, Wardell Pomeroy, and Clyde E. Martin, *Sexual Behavior in the Human Male* (Philadelphia, Pa.: W. B. Saunders Co., 1948), p. 219, ff.
5. Prov. 23:7.

Chapter 5

EMOTIONS AND SEXUALITY IN THE WOMAN

By Eleanor Hamilton, Ph.D.

The longing for emotional fulfillment is most fully realized by woman when she is deeply in touch with her own sexuality and from this magnetic base she exchanges love energy with a male.

Michael Faraday is quoted as saying, "Electricity and magnetism are the male and female elements in the universe." If so, when they are joined, the love energy generated is transforming to both. Concepts of physics derived in Faraday's world are not to be taken literally today, however, particularly since magnetism and electricity cannot be considered so distinct as Faraday thought, anymore than male and female can be considered so distinct as we once thought them to be. Today we know that men and women are no longer poles apart but are infinitely enmeshed, the basic sexuality of both being more alike than different.

When love exchange occurs between man and woman, it is necessary for each to give and for each to reveal Self. In other words, each can really be fulfilled only in the act of fulfilling.

Though there are few thinking women who would disagree with this premise, there are many who find that they are either seriously blocked when it comes to expressing its reality, or that they exhibit what psychologists call "the leaky bucket syndrome." The latter is exemplified in the story of the man who prayed to God thus: "Oh,

---

Some of the material in this chapter appears in Dr. Hamilton's new book, *Sexual Fulfillment* (New York: Hawthorn Books, 1971).

Lord, fill me with Thy spirit." Whereupon he heard a Voice answering, "I do, but you leak."

A leaky-bucket personality cannot be filled for long, nor can it be fulfilling, for out of emptiness nothing overflows. You cannot give away what you do not have. This premise brings us to the matter of *giving* as the primary element in sexual love.

Unfortunately, our culture teaches girls to believe that it is better to *get* than to *give*. A girl is encouraged to focus on the material advantages that may accrue to her through her future partner —position, prestige, wealth, security, and so on. Such things, while pleasant enough in themselves, have never been known to yield deep emotional fulfillment. Yet from dating days onward the social milieu encourages the girl to raise such debasing questions of herself as "Where can he take me? How much money can he spend on me? What will people think of me when I go out with him?" Such focus has the deleterious effect of making a girl insecure. Insecurity works this way: when any individual concerns himself with what someone else can give to him, he knows very well that that someone must necessarily love him less, for he himself would love another less if the tables were reversed. So in the end he—in this case, she—ends up with loss of self-regard, which quickly leads to lack of self-confidence.

The focus on acquisition produces insecurity in another way also, for no matter how much anyone accumulates, it is always possible for someone else to pile up more. If these piles are used for the benefit of others, the owner can take pleasure in ownership; but if they are used as a source of status or of competitiveness, they create insecurity rather than security. In other words, if the focus is on *having* more than her neighbor, a girl misses the boat.

Women have still another cultural influence working against them in their progress toward exchange of love energy with a male. This has to do with self-revelation. Girls, even modern girls, are taught to conceal rather than to reveal. I am not talking about bodily concealment, of which there is very little these days, but the concealment of honest emotion. Girls are told, "Don't show what you really feel—especially if what you feel for a man is love—or you will lose him"; or, "Keep secret to yourself your likes and dislikes"; or, "Learn to control others by keeping them guessing"; or, "Don't expose your hand or you will be vulnerable."

However, concealment leads to fear, and fear leads to hostility. Hostility and love cannot survive in the same room, so automatically women are led to shut themselves off from emotional fulfillment through concealment. Even worse, this leads to isolation, which is something no one can stand.

Young people today are making all manner of experimental attempts to break loose from such cultural liabilities—group therapy, sensitivity training, meditation groups, and group living are evidences of the need of woman as well as man to *connect* emotionally with others, to relieve the loneliness in which they find themselves.

A third negative environmental influence of which women are victims lies in the world of work that separates a man from his woman during the most creative hours of each day. This plays terrible havoc with both, but especially with homemakers. So squeezed is their time for sexual and affectional contact that both partners may be turned away from intimate relations with each other. This creates loneliness for both, of course, but the impact falls most heavily on the woman. Many a girl has chosen the life of secretary rather than wife so that she could be with a man all day. Even her sexual life may be superior to that of her sister at home, for if she and her comrade at work are in love, they have many daytime opportunities for lovemaking, while a wife may enjoy sexual intimacy only at night or on weekends.

Thus it is that modern woman suffers three major blows from the cultural milieu in which she lives—encouragement to conceal, encouragement to *get* rather than to *give,* and isolation from her man throughout the creative hours of the day. Fortunately, modern women are beginning to appreciate the disadvantage of these negative influences and to find ways to counteract and overcome them.

In sexuality, a woman is more like man than she is different, yet there are some variations that need to be understood. One of the few real sex differences between them seems to lie in the fact that men are stimulated more from *seeing* than women are. There are few voyeurs among women, although this is not at all uncommon among men. However, a woman is taught early that while the female body, properly appareled, is beautiful, the naked one, at least from the waist to thigh, is neither beautiful nor lovable. Nor is she taught that her own senses can take delight in the male body. The consequent fear of revealing herself genitally to the male and her steady rejection of the male organ as an object of beauty can become a serious detriment to her own sexual fulfillment as well as to that of her lover. There are very few acts that endear a woman to a man more poignantly than her expressed enjoyment of his penis, such as her willingness to fondle it, kiss, it, take it in her mouth, as well as in her vagina. All of these acts have deep meanings of acceptance, and the ability to enjoy them stems from an attitude that believes that the body is beautiful and clean all over; furthermore, that it is meant to be shared, used, and enjoyed.

Embarrassment itself is really nothing but *anticipation* of the disqualifying tendency of people around one. But since this anticipation has been often enough realized by a girl during her growing-up years, embarrassment is reinforced for her. The undoing of such conditioning is vital to a woman if she wishes full exchange of love energy with a man.

Another difference between men and women is that women set high store by verbalization during lovemaking. A woman likes to be talked to when she is made love to. Perhaps this is her need to be reassured. Perhaps it may be the engrossing hypnotic effect of positive suggestion that helps her to focus her mind on lovemaking rather than on the distractions of pleasure anxiety or the fear of failure; but whatever the undercurrent of her need, she is likely to say, "Talk to me."

It is strange how few men are able to appreciate and act upon this need. Though men, by nature, are the talkers of this world, in bed they become strangely dumb, as if embarrassed to make the words of love.

Another problem that many women face is the cyclical nature of their sexual desire. Some women are as wildly sexual part of the month as a cat on a hot tin roof, and at other times are as cool as cucumbers and couldn't be less interested in sex. This is often just as bothersome to them as it is to their partners.

The reverse can also be true. A highly sexed woman, ready to jump into bed at any time of the month, can be distressed beyond measure by a mate who wants sex but once a month. It is too bad that the level of sexual eagerness of each is not more carefully explored before marriage rather than waiting until after, when it can become a matter for a divorce court. A good principle to remember, one that marriage counselors are very familiar with, is that two people trying to work out a love relationship need to pay attention to the sexual needs of the *most eager* partner. This does not have to be accomplished through intercourse, however. In fact, intercourse should not be forced on anyone. But petting a partner to orgasm need be no more demanding of the less eager partner than rubbing his back or doing any one of a number of other personal acts of love. Without release of sexual tension, frustration can build up to volcanic proportions. This is one aspect of sexuality that requires the utmost frankness. Couples need to communicate their needs to each other without fear of rebuff.

One quirk of female nature is the irrational assumption that the man who loves her ought to *know* her sexual needs, to anticipate them in every detail, and that she ought never to have to verbalize these to him. A man's usual reaction to such an assumption is "I'm no mind reader. I would love to satisfy you if you ask outright for what you want, but I can't be expected to guess your wants." He might well like to add, "And I'd like you to act pleased when I *do* give you what you want."

The fear of asking goes very deep for both men and women, for when one asks, one risks. The fear of rejection is irrationally terrifying to men as well as to women, but women have had much less experience with it than men have. For example, from adolescence onward boys get used to being turned down by girls and prospective employers. Furthermore, they get an early and consistent training in reaching for what they want, fighting for it if necessary, and in being a good sport about it if they lose. But most women have had no such training. They come into adult life with a large-sized, infantile fear of rejection still in operation. The result is that they don't ask, they just expect and then go underground in moodiness if they don't get.

In sex the woman's usual pattern is to say, "I asked him once and he refused," or, "He forgets what I like even after I have told him once." And then such a woman goes on to assume that forever after it doesn't pay to ask for what she wants, or she concludes that her man doesn't love her.

Women have many other problems relating to orgasm potential which, if not unique to their sex, at least are particularly distressing. I am thinking especially of the relationship of a person's ability to express anger to his ability to move sexually. Let me explain: If we accept the premise that emotion by definition is "feeling in movement," we shortly observe that the movement of certain feelings involve specific musculature. For example, an angry person needs to let his body move aggressively. Certain sets of muscles tense for action; namely, those involved in hitting, scratching, kicking, biting, pounding, and screaming. If tension is not discharged physically through some substitute but similar movement, the result is a tightening of the muscles involved. Boys are expected to draft off anger tensions through aggressive sports or even through aggressive action, but girls are never expected to move aggressively or even to get angry. "Nice little girls don't get angry" is hurled at the girl-child growing up; yet she is just as prone to feelings of irritation and anger as her brother. So she tightens the muscles that control the movements we know as aggressive anger. Furthermore, she doesn't fully relax them afterward, and so they tend to remain chronically tight. All this would not be so serious except for the fact that it is impossible for sexual feelings to move through the muscular blockade of held-onto anger. If the large muscles that control hitting, kicking, pounding are in a state of chronic contraction, they will not permit the soft flow of tender feeling to move easily, if at all. This cuts off genital feeling and tends to result in the problem that so many women face, namely, that of being sexually aroused and yet unable to relieve sexual tension through orgasm. They come up against what they usually describe as "a wall," through which they cannot move. Furthermore, the more excited they become without release, the more distressed, for the closer a woman is brought to orgasm the greater the pelvic congestion and therefore the more uncomfortable she becomes when there is no release. There is no use in working on more and better techniques of stimulation for such a woman. The first job is to teach her to discharge anger in physical terms. Beat a couch, pound a pillow, scream, bang pots and pans around. All of these are useful discharge mechanisms. They hurt no one, and they relieve the tension that the woman is holding onto for dear life—indeed for fear that if she lets go she jolly well may kill someone.

Most women are terribly frightened of their own anger. Largely this is because they don't know what will happen if it is released. It is as if the world might fall apart. The unfortunate truth is that when such women expressed anger as small children, they did pay an exorbitant price for it. Now, they are defended against even *feeling* anger, and this creates a block against the free flow of sexual feeling.

The emotion of sadness is more acceptable to women, though it becomes something of a problem to men. Many a woman releases not only her sadness but her anger by the route of tears, and many a man, distressed by female tears, will say, "There, there, don't cry, dear, don't cry." What a woman wants is just the reverse. She needs a man who can say, "Come and have a good cry on my shoulder, dear; it will make you feel better." This helps her to release the tension of held-onto sadness and opens up her whole organism to a freer flow of sexual love energy. In other words, it makes sexuality more accessible. Men, by the way, have exactly the same problem expressing sadness as women do in expressing anger, though without quite so devastating an effect upon their sexuality. The reason for this is that the muscles that control expressions of sadness are not those large muscles that, when tensed, are hard to break through. Incidentally, stiff-mouthed kissing is one of its results. Held-onto sadness does tend to hold back somewhat the flow of sexual feeling, yet sexual feeling is not entirely immobilized and *can* move through it. In such instances, a woman may start to cry at the moment of orgasm as well as to enjoy sexual feeling, to the great surprise of her partner. She is not sad, she is simply relieved of long-stored sadness.

Fulfilling sexuality releases creative energy in women as few other experiences can. While a man may feel "spent" after a sexual encounter, many a woman may be floating on air and ready to dance right into a day's work. The exchange of love energy seems to act for her as an inspiration to creative action, courage, and self-confidence.

Perhaps the commonest question about sex that women ask marriage counselors is, "How can I learn to come to orgasm?"

Many books have been written in response to this question alone, so obviously any answer I give here will be grossly oversimplified, yet the outlines of an answer seem indicated.

The first thing a woman must learn, of course, are the facts of stimulus-response. Consider the analogy of an electric lamp. To have light, one must connect a plug and turn on the switch. If you pull out the plug, the light goes out. Much the same thing happens in sexual excitation. If you stimulate the nerve endings surrounding the clitoris, you get mounting sexual pleasure that eventually results in orgasm. If you remove that stimulus, the response generally stops. Many men utilize excellent stimulatory techniques until a woman becomes excited. Then they mistakenly "pull the plug" by removing clitoral stimulation and substituting penile penetration without clitoral contact. This is the equivalent of disconnecting the power source. The same men wonder why the woman's sexual excitation "turns off." Quite naturally, the woman loses sensation and her near-orgasm recedes, leaving her with congestion and discomfort in her entire pelvic area. She is then in a mood generally described as "bitchy." Had her lover continued his foreplay right on to the point of no return, to the very start of her orgastic release, she would have, no doubt, experienced orgasm. Furthermore, she could comfortably enjoy and tolerate *his* coming to orgasm through penetration thereafter—perhaps sharing a second orgasm with him. Once the orgasm reflex is well established, a woman may learn to undulate her own hips in response to his pelvic thrust so that her clitoris gets sufficient stimulation from the penile thrust alone. However, most women continue to need considerable manual stimulation.

Women can do much to train themselves to come to orgasm. Learning to masturbate successfully is an important first step. Many girls refuse to do this, explaining indignantly when the suggestion is made to them, "I'm married, why should I do this to myself when I have a husband to do it for me." The fact remains, however, that most men tire after forty-five minutes or so of continuous clitoral stimulation, and this may very well be the time that it will take an untrained girl to reach climax. Her own willingness to educate herself may make the difference between a woman able to come to orgasm with her husband and one who cannot.

Another great aid to the woman in orgasm ability is learning how to breathe with full exhalation so that no muscular tension in the groin, the pelvis, or the buttocks exists at the end of an exhalation. Tension begins with inhalation but completely releases with exhalation, producing a sense of aliveness in the pelvis, which leaves a woman warm and tingly right to the bottoms of her feet and to the tips of her fingers. Women can also learn to contract and relax their vaginas, doing this simple exercise fifty or sixty times a day. Fantasy is another aid; a woman can encourage her own mind to dwell on erotic subjects, casting all other thought to the wind. Sexual imagination is one of the keys to sexual heaven.

Women often fear that they will not remain sexually attractive to their mates as they grow older. Such fear itself is responsible for much of the action that later does indeed occur. However, a woman who develops her sexual skills, along with other aspects of her nature, becomes more attractive as the years go by. This means, of course, that emotional components do form greater and greater parts of the sexual act. It also means that the woman must pay attention to the care and grooming of her body, though without elaborate efforts to simulate youth. Most of all it means that she continues to find surprising and delightful aspects of her *husband's* body and personality to admire and to express appreciation about, and that she can develop her own imagination and spontaneity in sexual expression. Of such women, men do not tire. Women need to hear more about this aspect of maturity.

Sometimes it comes as a surprise to some women that they can love more than one man. Human beings are not monogomous by nature, though we live in a society that has monogomy as its ideal. People have many sides to their natures, and while one man may be fulfilling to one part of that nature, another may be equally fulfilling to a different part. Of course, if a woman wants to live comfortably within our culture, she must generally decide which man most fully meets her needs and limit herself to that male— unless she has an unusually liberating partner who does not hold to the notion of exclusivity in sexual experiences. Most women, however, feel more secure if their sexual relationship remains exclusive between themselves and their partners.

I might conclude with the statement that I have never known a woman who thought of herself as "bad" at the moment of orgasm. On the other hand, many women describe this moment as a time when they have sensed oneness with God and with the creative principle of life. Perhaps the greatest of the gifts sexuality confers upon us is this preview of at-one-ness, the merging with "God" while we are still encased in bodies on this earth.

Chapter 6

SEX AS A REGENERATIVE FORCE

By Jessie Bernard, Ph.D.

"A healthy sexual relationship is always the result of a healthy interpersonal relationship," says Milton R. Sapirstein.[1] That spells out the basic thesis of this paper, namely, that it is not the biology or the physiology of sexual relationships that determines their quality but the social, interpersonal matrix in which they occur. This has been well documented in the researches of Masters and Johnson,[2] who found, for instance, that not the physiological experience but the social context was the important variable related to subjective satisfaction; that although female orgasm produced by self-stimulation was more intense and more frequent than that produced by coitus, the women themselves preferred the latter.

If the physiology of sexual response is the same, regardless of kind of stimulation, varying only in intensity, it must derive the different meanings from other sources. Whether it is pleasurable or unpleasurable, exciting or dull, will depend on the social context in which it occurs; the intimacy, tenderness, and warmth of the relationship between partners will be more important than the orgasmic experience itself.

In terms of the social-psychological context in which they occur, sexual relations vary as widely as do other interpersonal relationships. A relationship between a man and a woman may be—on the part of one or both—punitive, defensive, sadistic, masochistic, domineering, appeasing, trusting, or what have you. The outcome may be, for one party or both, either destructive or constructive. Since our concern here is with the positive, and not with the pathological, abnormal, or the destructive aspects of sexuality, no attention will be accorded to them here.

Omitted here also is the excited sexuality associated with the chase, and finally, the form of sexuality in which the social context is empty—one in which there is no danger, fear, guilt, or other meaningful relaionship but only a dull, vacuous, boring blank.

REGENERATIVE SEXUALITY DISTINGUISHED FROM EXCITING SEXUALITY

A distinction is made here between regenerative and exciting sexuality. The difference between them may be epitomized by male responses to two women: "I'd like to make that dame!" or "I'd like to fall asleep in that woman's arms." The first implies adventure, excitement, conquest, victory; the second, security and peace. The potential tie between violence and sexuality is very near to the surface in exciting sexuality; it is remote, if present at all, in regenerative sexuality.

In rather sharp contrast to Dionysian exciting sexuality is the Apollianism of regenerative sexuality. Here we might enlist such terms as: warmth; intimacy; gentleness; tenderness; gaiety; playfulness; full acceptance; security; serenity; freedom from inhibiting tension, anxiety, threat, defensiveness, hostility, or achievement-drive. Sapirstein's statement of its nature is one in which the "general tone . . . is one of comfort, relaxation, feeling 'at home,' 'the chase is over,' and relief from the strain of living up to the former self-protective social facade."[3]

Among the young, the exciting form so dominates popular thinking and mass media presentations that anything else is viewed as inferior. Some young people look with dread at the thought of its passing with marriage. It does tend to pass and be replaced by regenerative sexuality in a good marriage, but rather than lose its significant quality it may actually gain greater significance by enriching rather than limiting the total relationship.

SEX RELATIONS AND SEXUAL RELATIONS

Before proceeding to a consideration of the functions of regenerative sexuality a word is in order on the wide gamut of behavior included in the concept of sexual relations.

In *The Sex Game*,[4] I distinguished between *sex* relations and *sexual* relations, the first referred to any kind of relation—work, play, whatever—between the two great collectivities known as men and women; the second, to relations that are specifically sexual in nature, from simple handholding all the way to genital contact. Not all sexuality has to be genital in order to be regenerative, just as not all genital sexuality is necessarily regenerative.

A ten-level gradient of sexual relations between the sexes might be usefully distinguished: (1) presenting one's self as a woman or a man, proclaiming one's sexuality by clothes, make-up, stance, and/or recognizing another's sexuality; (2) sex-related talk; (3) handholding; (4) touching of bodies, including a light hug; (5) superficial kiss of any part of the body; (6) body exploration and caressing; (7) deep kissing; (8) strong body pressure, close embrace; (9) external genital contact; (10) intromission. All are sexual relations; all may be regenerative. Some forms seem more suitable at one time, some at another; some may be regenerative at one stage in the life cycle but not at another. A gentle caress may pack more regenerative wallop in one setting than intromission in another.

There is a tendency in thinking about the forms of sexuality to concentrate attention on the intromission end of the continuum. This is an overly simple point of view and leaves out an enormous range of sexuality, every point along which has regenerative potentiality. The mere sight of the other sex may be regenerative in the sense of reassuring, enlivening. Restriction to one-sex activities becomes oppressive. Living alone is hard to like if no provision is made for contact with members of the other sex. The importance of simple touch in all human relations has long been recognized, or as Ernest Crawley wrote:

> ... the ultimate test of human relations ... is contact ... Ideas of contact are at the root of all conceptions of human relations at any state of culture; contact is the one universal test, as it is the most elementary form, of mutual relations. ... Desire or willingness for physical contact is an animal emotion, more or less subconscious, which is characteristic of similarity, harmony, friendship, or love. ... More interesting ... is the universal expression by contact of the emotion of love.[5]

The importance of touch has recently come to be recognized in the form of "touch therapy."

There can be great physical consolation in simple body contact. Lying quietly together, body to body, can be regenerative even without genital relations, as young people demonstrate to us in parks all summer long. Eugene O'Neill in his play, *Moon for the Misbegotten,* describes a moonlit quasi "therapy" session in which a disturbed man achieves catharsis and relief in the arms of a woman who hears him out in the night as he expiates his guilt vis-à-vis his mother. It is an almost clinical scene. There is no coital relationship—the man is too disturbed—and scarcely even kissing. But there is infinite comfort and reassurance in contact with the woman's body.

Eric Berne has reminded us of the importance of physical stroking in the developing infant, and he has extended it to include psychological or social "stroking" beyond infancy. Stroking constitutes a major form of regenerative sexuality. Genital relations may even be viewed as mutual stroking, literally, of the most sensitive erogenous areas of the body.

At the coital end of the continuum, sexuality may or may not be regenerative. Overemphasis on orgasm, for example, may militate against the regenerative aspects of the relationship. If orgasm is viewed as the sole objective, anxiety may preclude regeneration. Any failure to achieve climax is seen as complete failure, as unworthiness, as inferiority. Most women have always known what Masters and Johnson spelled out for us, namely that orgasm was secondary to the emotional "stroking" in sexual relations. Only in recent years has the idea of orgasm-at-any-cost been made the major objective of sexual relations. If absence of climax is viewed as a defeat, then blame must be assessed. Blame means criticism— of technique, of anatomy, of functioning—and criticism means the end of regeneration. If sexual relations are to be regenerative, the point of view must be: if climax comes, well and good; if not, well and good anyway. Further, coital experience is not regenerative if the aftermath results in depression, *la tristesse de l'amour,* guilt, or regret.

A woman in therapy once noted that "after a while my body 'closes shop' and I can't do it any longer. It's involuntary. I just close up. My first husband used to hold it against me. He made me feel there was something wrong with me. But my present husband never did. The first time it happened all he said was 'there's nothing wrong with the apparatus so the control must come from some other part of the system.' No ill will. No anger. No resentment. No blame. No making me feel awfully inferior. Just a scientist's witty and tender acceptance of the inevitable. It made me feel so grateful that it hardly ever happens any more."

SEX AS WORK

The deadly seriousness with which sexuality is currently approached has led one team of sociologists to analyze sexual relations, in only a half-satirical manner, as work.[6] In their analysis, based on an examination of fifteen marriage manuals, they note that partners are instructed to invest great effort in the enterprise. "The orgasm is portrayed as the product of marital sex. Other aspects of a job deemed necessary in sexual behavior are a work schedule and special techniques and equipment."[7] Input, technical know-how; output, orgasm. Preparation and training for this kind of job—including reading and studying—are viewed as just as essential as for other kinds of jobs. "That sex involves effort is a pervasive theme in the fifteen manuals."[8]

Among the work-oriented points they refer to are: marital sex should not be an impromptu performance or be approached with a casual mien; good sexual relations are a goal laboriously achieved; sexual relations are something to be worked at and developed; women especially should work at sex since sex is, in effect, another chore in the housewife's burden; rigorous practice is a must, as is experimentation; proper technique is absolutely essential, including knowledge of timing of the phases of arousal and climax; some equipment is necessary or desirable, ranging from lubricating jellies all the way to such anti-pleasure devices as anesthetics applied to the glans to control sensitivity.

The authors explain their conclusion that "sexual play in marriage has . . . been permeated with dimensions of a work ethic" in terms of the necessity Americans feel to justify play by transforming it into work. "Through this transformation of play, the dignity of consumption is seemingly established; it is now work, and work is felt to carry with it a certain inherent dignity"[9]—though hardly regeneration.

THE FUNCTIONS OF REGENERATIVE SEXUALITY

Regeneration as used here should be distinguished from so-called "tension release." It is true, as Sapirstein notes, that sexual activity can serve as a way of escaping many kinds of tensions related to many kinds of causes, that it can act almost anesthetically to allay anxiety, for in the throes of sexual excitement other drives are for the time being suspended. Without such a channel of even temporary escape, tensions may mount and anxieties proliferate.[10] But Sapirstein is referring to "effective erotic experience," to "fulfilling sexual experience." In such cases tension release may be regenerative. But it is the context in which the release takes place that renders it regenerative, not the simple physiological response. Sometimes it may have precisely the opposite result.

More meaningful for our purposes is the concept of regenerative sexuality in terms of the psychological functions it performs. We have become accustomed to the old bon mot that sexual relations used to be for reproduction but now they are for recreation. One of the dictionary (Oxford) definitions of *regenerate* is, precisely, "to recreate," and *recreate* means "to invest with fresh vigor or strength, to refresh, to reinvigorate, to enliven by some sensuous or purely physical influence, to affect agreeably, to cheer by giving comfort, consolation, or encouragement, to gratify." The discussion here, then, will focus on sexuality that provides "fresh vigor or strength"; that cheers, gives comfort, consolation, encouragement; that conversely does not hurt, reject, diminish, punish, degrade, or make invidious comparisons. The partners feel complete security in one another, and know they can be completely, deeply, wholly themselves.

A caveat is in order at this point. Sexuality is not the only form that regeneration in the sense of restoration can take. Other forms include religious worship, religious exaltation, artistic creativity, scientific achievement, music, and even mystic experience.

Lest the discussion of "needers" that follows be misinterpreted, it should be made clear at the outset that the concern here is not clinical; regenerative sexuality is not viewed as performing a therapy or treatment function. Nor is it assumed that the people discussed are in any sense sick, pathological, or abnormal if they need regenerative sexuality. It is conceivable that a physician or therapist or counselor might "prescribe" some form of sex-related activity for therapeutic reasons. But such a "medicinal" view of sexuality is not implied here.

What, one may ask, is regenerative sexuality regenerative *against*? What kinds of restorative functions are they performing? Who needs this regenerative solace? Sex and sexuality are regenerative against lack or loss of sexual self-confidence, an aspect of self-confidence referring to the sexual component of self-feeling.[11] And who needs it? You, I, and all those around us do.

THE SEXUAL SELF

The self, as social psychologists have been teaching us for a long time, is a complex phenomenon, a product of social interaction, never complete, never wholly achieved, always susceptible to deflation, vulnerable to all the myriad responses it is subjected to in its contacts with others. It arises originally in the response of others to us, flourishes or wilts as they approve or disapprove of us. Few people can retain their self-feeling when confronted with continuing rejection.

The sexual self may be thought of as the core of the total self. In current psychological and biological research a great deal is being learned about the nature of this sexual self. We know that it is susceptible to aberrations, that gender and biological sex may not coincide, that a person may have a male sexual self but a female body, or vice versa. In some cases there are biological anomalies; but in other cases gender and biological sex do not coincide because of early childhood experiences. The social world has not properly identified the child's sex.[12]

Our concern is not with pathologies or abnormalities. The sex-gender researchers are mentioned only to highlight the social-psychological nature of the sexual self. We need social validation of our masculinity or femininity, our maleness or femaleness. Each sex needs the other in order to achieve its own sexuality—and to maintain it, for the sexual self must, like other aspects of the self, be constantly reinforced, shored up, supported. Social neglect of one's sexuality is one of the ways of desexing, even psychologically castrating, human beings.[13]

Sexual self-confidence is, therefore, as important as confidence in any other aspects of the self, confidence in one's ability to achieve professional success, to play tennis, to earn money, to win friends and influence people, to do any one of the thousands of things that people want to do. And it is the generation and regeneration of confidence in this sexual self that invites our attention here.

NEEDERS

In the sense of maintenance and restoration of sexual self-confidence, it may be said that everyone needs regeneration to some extent at some time. In general, anyone who is feeling blue or depressed or discouraged needs regeneration. Such periods of depression seem to have rhythmic recurrence to most people. A generation ago a study of such individual cycles was reported in which:

> ... remarkable regularity was observable in all the subjects; they all had regular periods when they tended to feel at their best, organic and bodily functions seemed to be speeded up, and fatigue was easily resisted or overcome. With equal regularity came periods when the reverse conditions tended to prevail. A man who was usually open and talkative would, in these periods, tend to be silent and withdrawn or more irritable than otherwise; fatigue was harder to resist or overcome.... These cycles in men and women, with their sometimes profound influence on the whole personality, have important repercussions in the marital relationship that may show up anywhere.[14]

Unfortunately, just when our need for the regenerative solace of sexuality is greatest, we are least likely to attract it. When we are low, depressed, frightened, anxiety-laden, uncertain, or denigrated, we are often disagreeable, repellant, rejecting, and hence rejected; we thus put would-be suppliers of regenerative sexuality off. We are defensive, querulous, even hostile. Resentful of our great need, we do not allow anyone to assuage it. We repulse suppliers precisely because we need them so much. If our energy level is low, it may not be genital sexuality we crave, but primarily the gentle reassurance of warm, understanding physical contact.

In addition to the universal need for sexual self-validation, there is a category of human beings for whom the problem of such validation is especially serious, namely those whom Erving Goffman has labeled the "stigmatized."[15] Stigmas vary both qualitatively and quantitatively, and some have less serious implications for sexual-selfhood than others. Disfigurements, mutilations, or serious skin blemishes may revolt potential suppliers of sexual regeneration, a fact that scarcely requires documentation. The nature and significance of stigmas vary with the life cycle. Skin blemishes in youth, operations in the middle years—especially any, like breast removal, having to do with sex characteristics—and the evidences of age itself in the later years, all act as stigmas and may seriously interfere with the securing of regenerative sexuality.

It is, therefore, worth breaking down the category of "needers" according to stage in the life cycle. Youth, the middle years, and the later years—each deliberately left unspecified as to precise boundaries—are sufficiently distinct for the broad brushstrokes applied here.

Youth

Judging by popular myths about youth today, need for regenerative sexuality is the last thing one would associate with them. In the case of men, tension release, excitement, sometimes even violence, aggression, or conquest, are popularly considered the hallmarks of male sexuality in youth. Such characteristics may persist in lower socioeconomic levels, but they no longer predominate in the higher, at least college, levels.[16] The need for regenerative sexuality is as great in youth as at any other stage of the life cycle, however different the form it may take. Much of the "search for identity" is a search for sexual identity, a goal by no means easy to achieve.

Even in an age when a great deal of permissiveness with respect to sexual relations prevails, it is almost inevitable that young men will approach their first sexual encounters with apprehension. There is uncertainty of how their advances will be received, fear of rejection, fear of not succeeding, fear generated by ignorance. Sexual self-confidence has not yet been achieved, or if achieved, it is still vulnerable.

Young women are also vulnerable. It is difficult for men to believe that, even at the height of their youthful beauty and appeal, most women do not have great sexual self-confidence; that they need reassurance of their desirability. Many accept, even if they do not necessarily welcome, sexual intercourse as validation of their sexuality.

So much of the interaction between young men and women has taken on the characteristic of a battle that all too often each sex is rendered incapable of suplying the reassurance and validation both so badly need. Young women may think, "If you let men know that you want them, it gives them an advantage over you.

They take a sort of taunting, conceited, condescending attitude toward you, even when you know you are better than they are." Such disparagement can be anxiety-generating; it is certainly not restorative.

In addition to the battle setting of so much interaction between the sexes in youth, there is a host of conventional patterns that interfere with the development of regenerative relationships. Illustrative of some of the social, including class, impedimenta is the case of this young woman:

I was liberated along with a group of others when we took over a campus building when I was a sophomore. Here, all together, the games I had always felt I had to play with boys fell away. My mother had always directed my life, including who to date. And since my parents are the upper-middle-class suburban type who have really made it, they wanted me to date the men who were on the make and who would also become successful upper-middle-class suburban types. There weren't too many that my parents considered good enough for me to date. And the others were afraid of me. I got better grades than almost all of the men in my classes. I looked down on most of them because, according to my parents' standards, they weren't in my class. The others, who weren't afraid of me, were the aggressive type, and dates were just one sparring match after another. I hated it. They had to be clever to outwit me. I was too proud to give in to their aggressive tactics so I fought back. Both verbally and physically. Well, during our occupation of the campus building, there was none of that. We were all in it together. I found that I was attracted to one man who, according to my inbred standards, would never have come to my attention. Under normal conditions I wouldn't even have looked at him; but here, cut off from everything my family stood for—even fighting it —I found I could make a normal, outgoing, affectionate connection with him. I saw him just as a human being—male human being— and the relationship with him was independent of the fact that he would probably never amount to much careerwise. But he was a loving, tender human being. And, after my experience with men on the make, this was new and wonderful. At one time I would have been insulted if he had aspired to my attenion. Now I was grateful that he wanted it. I was, as we say nowadays, liberated. I could relate to a man as a human being, without having to calculate whether or not he was suitable for me. I asked him how come I had not intimidated him, and why he wasn't afraid to approach me, since I did better than he did gradewise and came from a higher-class background. It had never occurred to him. He knew what and who he was; his self-feeling didn't depend on doing what the world told him to do. I loved that independence. I loved his being my "human" equal, unintimidated by either my brains or my class background.[17]

In addition to those whose sexual self-identity has been impeded by class, ethnic, and racial restrictions, there is a whole category of young people—so-called alienated youth—seriously in need of regenerative sexuality but incapable of accepting it. Sexuality for them is especially fraught with difficulty. Kenneth Keniston in his study of these alienated young people notes that "central to alienation is a deep and pervasive mistrust of any and all commitments, be they to other people, to groups, to American culture, or even to the self. Most basic here is the distrust of other people in general— a low and pessimistic view of human nature."[18] He quotes one young man as saying, "Emotional commitments to others are usually the prelude to disillusion and disappointment"; and another, "It is generally advisable to avoid close personal attachments to others."[19]

These alienated youth desire yet fear intimacy; they are attracted to totally dependent or to forbidden partners. They must constantly reassure themselves of the trustworthiness of the other and the harmlessness of the relationship to themselves.

The "Hurricane Years" and the Transitional Cohort

Needers of regenerative sexuality in the period of life that we call maturity—roughly the twenties through the fifties—include, of course, the alienated, but also their opposites, the overly involved. These are men who, in our society, find themselves in incessant and unrelenting testing, for maturity is the time of the rat race. It is a time for making it, a time of constant challenge, of having to prove oneself.

This period reaches a sort of crescendo in, let us say, the forties —which novelist Cameron Hawley has called the "hurricane years"—when the accumulated strains reveal themselves in heart breakdowns of one kind or another. It is a time when, having made it, one begins to wonder if the prize was worth the effort; or when one has to recognize that one is never going to make it and is going to have to come to terms with this almost intolerable fact; and when, in either case, one begins to notice the beauty of youth with peculiar poignancy and, with a shock, to recognize that one's own is gone. It is an age when the need for regenerative sexuality is perhaps the greatest.

In the case of women, the fear of waning sexual selfhood with menopause has been an analogous source of need for regenerative sexuality, a fact mercilessly played upon by advertisers. For example, the skin is perhaps the "sexiest" organ of the body and the first to show signs of aging. To retain a skin that men will love to touch —to create "touchables"—a formidable industry of cosmetics has developed. A skin that renders one untouchable can be traumatic at any age.

Along with career tensions for men and menopause fears for women in the middle years, the men and women who happen to be in their forties and fifties at the present time are subject to another set of difficulties peculiar to their generation, which adds considerably to the stresses. Today's middle-aged men and women belong to what might be called a transitional cohort, whose life career spans the so-called sexual revolution. They were born into a world with its own pre-revolutionary myths, collective representations, and preconceptions with respect to sexuality; but they are living their mature years in a world with post-revolutionary standards. Two kinds of cultural discontinuities mark their middle years: one has to do with female sexuality, the other with the propriety of sexuality in the years beyond youth.

With respect to the first, members of this transitional cohort were socialized into a world that denigrated female sexuality, that prescribed inhibited propriety, that made sexual behavior a male prerogative. Still, they were the first sexually emancipated generation. Both men and women of this cohort bear the scars of the transition from the older to the newer approaches to sex. The persisting old standards may be devastating to men; the encroaching new ones may be devastating to women.

The unleashing of female sexuality upon modern society for which neither men nor women were prepared has had, as M. L. Sapirstein reminds us,[20] unanticipated consequences. It led to a democratic rather than, as in the past, a male-oriented definition of the sexual relationship, or it even turned sexual leadership over to the woman. Since successful intercourse rests ultimately on the male's readiness, anything that interferes with that readiness can have disturbing effects. And at least for the transitional cohort, female sexual leadership or pacesetting can have such effects.

In a world that still retains the old concepts and standards of masculinity, men in this cohort cannot honestly say they are not sexually interested when they are not; they are ashamed to expose themselves so honestly. Facing women who have taken over the new leadership or pacesetting role, these men become subject to anxiety, loss of self-esteem, and hence lose their erections, or they ejaculate prematurely. They may resort to marriage-manual "techniques" to cover lack of genuine response, but the result is hardly likely to be regenerative.

The new standards of female sexuality have had untoward effects on many women also. For some it has led to expectations of the unattainable and hence to inevitable disappointment. Others feel they must express constant readiness, or they feel they can no longer say in a world of new concepts and standards that they sometimes do not experience orgasm, that it really is not that important; it does not matter as long as he enjoys it, and she's sure he loves her. She fears this admission would disturb her husband or make her look old-fashioned and submissive, since her husband has been taught to feel responsible for her reaching climax. As a matter of fact, "such an admission would be closer to the biological facts, and would restore the man's self-esteem."[21] His wife's willingness to grant him satisfaction without herself experiencing orgasm "might restore the man's feeling that the sex act was something he had the right to enjoy for himself, and not always a means of proving himself to his wife."[22] In the current ambience, such admissions on the part of husband and wife appear inadmissible. Impotence and anxiety may result.

The time will undoubtedly come when this problem will no longer remain, and men and women will communicate with each other more honestly about their sex needs and times of little or no desire. It will become possible for men to admit that they do not feel erotic at a particular moment and for wives to admit that achieving climax is not always important. But for the present, members of the transitional cohort do have to struggle with a sexual bind. Succeeding cohorts should not be confronted with this difficulty for, little by little, we are beginning to come to terms with the nature of female sexuality, and future generations will be socialized into a world that understands it better.

A second cultural hang-over which wreaks havoc on the transitional cohort is the attitude toward sexuality in the mature years.

The prevailing attitude in the past often was: "They ought to know better." In some cases love between mature people seemed so shocking that critics invoked psychiatric explanations. It represented a "last fling" of aging men and women who could not bear to think that youth was over. It was a menopause phenomenon traceable to glandular dysfunction. It was a regression; it was an escape; it was a symptom. It was, in fact, anything but a normal reaction. . . .

Observers tended to deny love in the middle years, in part, no doubt, also because love between a man and a woman implies a sexual relation, and many people . . . are revolted at the idea that people of their parents' generation should have sexual interests. In addition, because its role in the psychological economy of human beings in the middle years has been ignored, love has often had to be sought outside of marriage, in illicit relationships. Thus, our shock at the violation of the mores frequently involved in love in the middle years may be transferred to the love relation itself. Because we disapprove of the violation of the mores, we disapprove of the emotion that causes the violation—we must debase love. Further, even if the love is not illicit, it is sometimes considered reprehensible, beneath the dignity of mature men and women.[23]

We are coming to recognize that the need for reassurance in the middle years is as great as, if not greater than, at any time after childhood. Regenerative sexuality is a major source for such reassurance. Hopefully, in time we will also come to take it for granted that regenerative sexuality is as appropriate for the middle years as for any other.

The Later Years

If sexuality were rejected for men and women in the middle years, it has been positively tabooed for those beyond sixty. We still almost automatically reject it as, in effect, shameful. We have tended to deal with older people categorically rather than individually, although we know that

people vary physiologically, and also in the extent to which they continue to learn [and retain sexual interests]. Adjacent cohorts tend to permeate one another as the pattern of life chances works itself out. Definitions of age become predominantly social rather than biological categories; they change with time, and with the groups one joins and leaves. The intrinsic aging process may be variously accelerated or retarded by many different institutional arrangements.[24]

Nevertheless, those who retain their sexuality into the later years are, on the basis of years alone, in effect read out of the sexual world.

Because of the myths we have inherited from the past we tend to look at the world through a distorting lens. We react to a stereotype rather than to actuality. One man looks at a sixty-year-old woman and sees her age; another looks at her and sees a still-alluring woman:

> I knew, of course, that she was not a young chick. She made no pretense to be. But she had sex appeal anyway. Her skin was still clear, slightly lined, but far from wrinkled. The flesh was still firmly anchored to her bones. In fact, her flesh was still soft but firm. No dowager's hump. Warm smile. Welcoming eyes. Understanding. Receptive. A sort of glow about her. Naturally I was attracted. We were a good fit, psychologically I mean. We approached the sex part exactly the same way. No fencing, no fending off, no coquetry, no chase. None of the kid stuff. Just two congenial people finding one another. It went on like that for a couple of months. Then I accidentally learned how old she was. I was incredulous. It didn't seem possible. But just the same it affected me. All of a sudden she repelled me. It was the *idea* of her age. She was just the same as before, but I was not. I can't explain it except that it didn't seem right for a woman of that age to be sexy. No wonder women don't like to give their age.[25]

The sexual deprivation of the elderly is not, however, wholly a matter of being read out of the sexual world by myths, collective representations, and cultural taboos. The evidences of aging serve as stigmas; they may repel. The falling away of "sex appeal" may occur at any age. For some women, at twenty-five; for others, not until the sixties. Some extraordinary women like Colette, for example, or Marlene Dietrich, or any one of a number of enchanting women—retain sexual desirability until seventy or beyond. But if any woman lives long enough, her appeal will fade. Men lose physical sex appeal also, to be sure, but women are willing to accept them on other than sexual bases until they are doddering.

Still, regeneration is needed as much if not as urgently as in the earlier years, as one of several grafitti—"dirty old men need love too"—recognizes. Now the destructive forces that have to be fended off or protected against are those of the deprivation that results from rejection, from ridicule that produces shame, and from guilt. Masters and Johnson note that many older sexually deprived women seek substitute validation in religion, business, social work, overzealous mothering of children or grandchildren. "Deprived of normal sexual outlets, they exhaust themselves physically in conscious or unconscious effort to dissipate their accumulated and frequently unrecognized sexual tensions."[26] Self-stimulation may be a satisfactory substitute for the purely physiological aspects of sexuality, but it is hardly likely to be sexually regenerative in the sense that we are using the term here. But for women whose deprivation results from infirm husbands, manipulative activity by the mate may well be sexually satisfying and regenerative, largely because of the social-psychological qualities of the relationship.

So far as actual sexuality is concerned, Masters and Johnson report clear-cut differences in both sexes with age. Among men, "a major difference exists between the response patterns of the middle-aged male (41-60 years) and those of men past the 60-year landmark."[27] As defined by levels of sexual tension, ability to engage in coitus, and ability to ejaculate, there is a marked let-down. Coitus per se is possible as long as erection is possible, well into the higher age brackets, even when climax itself may be difficult or impossible. Of special relevance for our interest here is the fact that male sexuality can be literally regenerated—"reconstituted" is the Masters-Johnson term[28]—even in the later years. The critical factor is someone who can supply the regenerative sexuality, namely "a partner interested in sexual performance."[29]

Still some men in the later years unnecessarily deny themselves the solace of their sexuality because in our society sexual relations are conceived only in terms of intromission and climax. Fearing to disappoint their partners and uncertain of their prowess, they inhibit all expressions of sexuality, the comfort of close body contact as well as more demanding forms. It may even happen that in the peaceful, reassuring touch of a complying body, an impetus may come for more active response. In any event, the simple expression of sexual closeness inherent in body contact can itself be regenerative.

Investigating female sexuality in the later years has not seemed worth the investment of research time and energy until very recently. As a consequence, Masters and Johnson note, our knowledge is still most inadequate. Two important findings of their work, however, deserve special comment here. One has to do with the effect of hormonal treatment for steroid starvation,[30] which does not compensate for all the changes resulting from age, but overcomes many of them and often renders full and satisfying relations possible far into the later years.

Far more important is the second relevant finding:

> Even more necessary [than endocrine-replacement therapy] for maintained sexual capacity and effective sexual performance is the opportunity for regularity of sexual expression. For the aging woman, much more than for her younger counterpart, such opportunity has a significant influence upon her sexual performance. Three women past 60 years were repeatedly observed to expand and lubricate the vagina effectively despite obvious senile thinning of the vaginal walls and shrinking of the major labia. These women maintained regular coital connection once or twice a week for their entire adult lives.[31]

Even a woman who shows the symptoms of sex-steroid starvation "will retain a far higher capacity for sexual performance than her female counterpart who does not have similar coital opportunities."[32]

Masters and Johnson conclude that "the psyche plays a part at least equal to, if not greater than, that of an unbalanced endocrine system in determining the sex drive of women during the postmenopausal period of their lives."[33] Other commentators have noted that once fear of pregnancy has been eliminated, many women show increased interest in coital relations. When all the factors, physiological and social-psychological, are toted up, Masters and Johnson arrive at the conclusion that "... a woman who has had a happy, well-adjusted, and stimulating marriage may progress through the menopausal and postmenopausal years with little or no interruption in the frequency of, or interest in, sexual activity. Additionally, social and economic security are major factors in many women's successful sexual adjustment to their declining years."[34]

But the ability to perform well sexually may be a disadvantage rather than an advantage if opportunity for sexual companionship is not available. Masters and Johnson cite work by Newman and Nichols on the effect of male attrition in the higher age brackets.

They add the further comment that even the men who survive may
be incapacitated by age:

> Many of the older husbands in this age group are suffering from
> the multiple physical disabilities of advancing senescence which
> make sexual activity for these men either unattractive or impos-
> sible. Thus, the wives who well might be interested in some regu-
> larity of heterosexual expression are denied this opportunity due
> to their partner's physical infirmities. It also is obvious that extra-
> marital sexual partners essentially are unavailable to the women
> in their age group.[35]

Although there is no doubt, then, that "there is no time limit drawn
by the advancing years to female sexuality,"[36] this is not the same
as saying that there is no such time limit on her ability to find
sexual partners. "It is very humiliating to retain an interest in sex
long after any physical appeal has disappeared," says one woman,
adding "it was better in my mother's day. She never had an interest in sex. So there was never any break in her life. She never
had to face the fact that she desired a man who did not desire
her." Another woman commented that for a time after her husband's death she had felt dropped from membership in the female
sex; after inviting and accepting the overtures of a younger man,
she felt she had once more entered the human species.

SUPPLIERS

Sexual self-confidence in men can only be supplied by women,
and in women, by men. The aphorism attributed to Madam de
Stael, "the desire of the man is for the woman, but the desire of the
woman is for the desire of the man," is only half true. The desire
of the man also is for the desire of the woman, and of the woman
for the man. Both sexes desire the other and desire to be desired by
them. It is the desire to be desired that is especially relevant in
regenerative sexuality; not merely to be desired physically—
women interpret this as lust, depersonalizing, dehumanizing, "you
only want me for my body"—but as sexual beings.

We make provision for a limited degree of such sexual self-
validation in social life, where a certain amount of flirting is permitted.[37] Women are allowed to play up to men in a sexy way, and
men are permitted to respond in a sexual self-enhancing way.

Each gets an answer to the question, am I attractive, appealing, or even just acceptable to the other sex? On a simple level, such behavior may be viewed as regenerative sexuality. The partners go home reassured of their sexuality, validated by persons outside the marriage. But for the most part, we limit the supplying of such sexual validation with rather severe restrictions. And understandably so, for it can be dangerous. If a man reassures a woman that she is lovely, she may read more into the statement than he meant to convey, or vice versa.

In the past, women have supplied sexual self-validation to men more than men have to women. The building up of the male ego has been one of the components of the feminine role—even of the prostitute's. One of the most durable clichés is that of the prostitute with a heart of gold, a supplier par excellence of regenerative sexuality. Similarly, the geisha girl—whose sole profession is to supply sexual self-feeling, to please, to restore, to build up—is almost the archetype of a supplier of regenerative sexuality. In Latin America and, according to Polly Adler, also in some circles in the United States in the past, it was customary for well-to-do families to hire older women to perform the teaching function for sons. Under the gentle tuition of these women, the sexual education of the young men could proceed without fear; sexual self-confidence could be built up, and at least some of the fear associated with initiation obviated. Sapirstein interprets the feudal lord's right of the first night as a recognition of the fact that defloration is intrinsically fraught with fear and anxiety, and that it was better to have them associated with the lord of the manor than with the husband.[38] Ideally, of course, needing and supplying are complementary processes, the supplier receiving as well as giving, the needer giving as well as receiving.

Ideally, regenerative sexuality is supplied in a secure marital bond. Actually, however, this is often not the case. At the present time the sexual self-regenerative function is increasingly transferred to the burgeoning professions of counseling and therapy. The regeneration of sexual selfhood has become professionalized. It is no longer supplied freely by women socialized into this role; it is, in fact, rather expensive.[39]

Of special relevance is the positive, aggressive, sometimes hostile rejection of the role of supplier of sexual regeneration by many young "liberated" women today. It is always hazardous to try to interpret nascent movements such as the currently mushrooming

"women's liberation movement." They may be aborted and amount
to little, or conversely, they may gain momentum. Nor is it safe
to characterize a whole movement by the opinions of one segment.
In any event, however, it is not wise to ignore them either.

There is explicit rejection by these women of the "traditional
supportive role as comforter for the . . . male exhausted from the
competition and energy-consuming rat race. . . ."[40] These young
women are not simply replaying worn-out records. They are applying modern research, paradigms, and experience to an analysis of
the modern sexual predicament and are thus powerfully armed.
Like the Jesuits, who were so invulnerable in argument or debate
because they knew their opponents' position better than the opponents did themselves, these young women have answers for every
weapon that has been used against feminists in the past. They are
immune to the devastating weapon so powerful in the past—threat
of loss of sex appeal and attraction for men. They are willing that
men "cease to be attracted to you, even despise you, that they cease
to admire you, even find you unnatural and warped and perverted
sexually."[41] Whether or not "liberation" in this extreme form
comes to prevail, the growing insistence by women on the right to
psychological and emotional independence can hardly fail to affect
their performance of the traditional sexual rejuvenation function
for men.

The inverse aspect of this movement is that liberated women
will also themselves cease to have their own sexual self-validation
provided by men. It is for this reason that they are called to deny
any need for it. But whatever the future holds, for the present the
great majority of both men and women look to one another for
supportive sexuality.

SEEKERS, FINDERS, AND THOSE WHO
DO NOT FIND

In at least a thousand rooms in city hotels across the country
tonight, a man and a woman who met one another for the first time
only a few hours before will seek solace and comfort in the close
physical contact of their bodies. It will not be a wholly random or
chance relationship. Both were in the same place at the same time
—cocktail lounge, restaurant, airplane—which meant that they
were probably of approximately the same income class. They

talked at least a few minutes; if their educational backgrounds, as shown by their voices, vocabulary, and grammar, had been too different, they would have gone no further. They found one another at least minimally attractive, or she would not have signalled accessibility, and he would not have picked up her signal. Neither is likely to be a virgin. He is likely to be in his thirties and married, she in her twenties, perhaps divorced.[42] A rough kind of sorting has therefore weeded out the obvious kinds of incompatibility that can be caught by such external indices. The deeper kinds of incompatibility have not, however, been touched. And this, of course, is the crucial kind, which is going to determine whether or not the rendezvous succeeds. Some will have needs, and will be unable to supply; the other needing one will depart as bereft as ever.

If both are suppliers as well as needers, the rendezvous will succeed. It will not remove the crisis that created the need; that still has to be faced. But it will have tided them over, restored them, given them the margin of support they needed to pick up the burden again. They have been regenerated, rendered whole again, restored. They believe in their worth again, because they have found someone who believes in them.

Others will find their loneliness as terrifying as before, perhaps even more so because this desperate calling out has not been answered. Two needing people have been unable to supply each other the regeneration they were seeking. Each faced from the other an outpouring of fears, hostilities, resentments, not a needing human being. A feeling of revulsion, of degradation overcame them. This was not what they were looking for.

REGENERATIVE SEXUALITY AND THE MARITAL VOWS

A review of the nature of the promises incorporated in marriage services in our society reveals, in all denominations, some version of the concept of regenerative sexuality as it is defined here.[43] The partners promise to comfort and cherish one another, and "comfort" means that one will impart strength, that one will cheer, encourage, gladden, as opposed to dispiriting, distressing, discouraging, saddening, or nagging. Nor is this frivolously or superficially intended. The regenerative aspects of sex are built into the very fabric of marriage as institutionalized in our society. We are reminded of the young bridegroom who comes "out of his chamber and rejoiceth as a strong man to run a race."[44]

The husband whose self-confidence has been strained by less than complete success in the competitive work world has his sexual self-confidence replenished by his wife; the wife whose self has been all but sucked dry by lack of adult companionship and the demands of children has her sexual self-confidence similarly replenished by her husband. Regenerative sexuality in marriage is not limited to coital relationships; it can also take the form of simple reassurance. Two studies of marriage offer some insights into this phase of regenerative sexuality, one by Robert Blood, Jr., and Donald M. Wolfe, and one by Harold Feldman.

Blood and Wolfe speak of therapeutic responses of husbands to the mental-hygiene needs of their wives, and vice versa. "If the boss thinks a man is expendable, what about his wife? Does she agree, plunging him into deeper gloom? Or does she see in him values the boss overlooked? ... Any wife can appreciate her husband as a father, a sexual partner, a good companion."[45] Blood and Wolfe found that practically all the wives they studied, at some time or other, regularly or irregularly, turned to their husbands with their troubles.[46] In more than one-fourth of the cases (28 percent) the response of the husband was sympathy and affection (the nearest response that can be interpreted as regenerative sexuality). The effect on the wife—making her feel better—was greater than that of any other "therapeutic response" except "help in withdrawing from the situation," which was the husband's response in only 3 percent of the cases.[47] Blood and Wolfe conclude:

> Sympathy provides the most explicit ego repair as such. It is the commonest form of therapy ..., unusually common in the most satisfactory marriages (40 percent, compared to 28 percent for the total sample). Getting sympathy or affection in return for a recital of troubles proves for sure that the wife is still loved and appreciated—a vigorous tonic for a wilted ego.[48]

Harold Feldman found that talking with one's spouse about the spouse's feelings, about one's own feelings, about the children's problems, and about sex itself had a marked effect in making the partners feel closer to one another,[49] a finding which may be interpreted as reflecting the benign effects of regenerative sexuality.

We may well conclude that the kind of support that we have included in regenerative sexuality is being supplied in a sizeable proportion of marriages. But, there is a widely recognized hazard in marriage stemming from the boredom that results with long familiarity, and there is a considerable research literature documenting the fact that extramarital sexual relationships are sometimes resorted to for the regenerative sexuality no longer supplied in marriage. In some instances the result is to revivify the regenerative aspects of the marital sexuality.[50]

CHAPTER NOTES

1. Milton R. Sapirstein, *Emotional Security* (New York: Crown Press, 1948), p. 162.

2. William H. Masters and Virginia E. Johnson, *Human Sexual Response* (Boston: Little, Brown & Co., 1966), p. 133.

3. Sapirstein, *Emotional Security*, p. 169.

4. Jessie Bernard, *The Sex Game* (Englewood Cliffs, N.J.: Prentice-Hall, 1968).

5. Ernest Crawley, *The Mystic Rose* (London: Macmillan, 1902), p. 76.

6. Lionel S. Lewis and Dennis Brisset, "Sex as Work: A Study of Avocational Counseling," *Social Problems*, Summer, 1967, pp. 8–18.

7. Ibid., p. 8.

8. Ibid., p. 11.

9. Ibid., p. 17.

10. Sapirstein, *Emotional Security*, pp. 106–107.

11. An alternative approach to this problem might be in terms of dependency needs. This approach is developed by Sapirstein, *Emotional Security*.

12. Robert J. Stoller, *Sex and Gender, on the Development of Masculinity and Femininity* (New York: Science House, 1968).

13. Henry Seidel Canby, *The Age of Confidence* (New York: Farrar and Rinehart, 1934), pp. 173–175.

14. Jessie Bernard, *American Family Behavior* (New York: Harper, 1942), pp. 488–489.

15. Erving Goffman, *Stigma, Notes on the Management of Spoiled Identity* (Englewood Cliffs, N.J.: Prentice-Hall, 1963).

16. Eugene J. Kanin, "An Examination of Sexual Aggression as a Response to Sexual Frustration," *Jour. Mar. and Fam.* 29 (August 1967) : 428–433.

17. Personal interview.

18. Kenneth Keniston, *The Uncommitted, Alienated Youth in American Society* (New York: Delta, 1964), pp 56–57.

19. Ibid., p. 57.

20. Sapirstein, *Emotional Security*, pp. 153–155.

21. Ibid., p. 157.

22. Ibid., pp. 157–158.

23. Jessie Bernard, *Remarriage, A Study of Marriage* (New York: Dryden Press, 1956), pp. 119–120.

24. Norman Ryder, "The Cohort as a Concept in the Study of Social Change," *Amer. Sociol. Rev.* 30 (December 1965): 859.

25. Personal interview. See also Ingl Powell Bell, "The Double Standard," *Transaction* 8 (November–December 1970): 75–80.

26. Masters and Johnson, *Human Sexual Response*, p. 246.

27. Ibid., p. 262.

28. Ibid., p. 263.

29. Ibid.

30. The hormone deficiency that may arise post-menopausally is analogous to the deficiency that produces diabetes. Diabetic men have higher vulnerability than well men to impotence. Isadore Rubin summarizes the research on this in *Sexual Life After Sixty* (New York: Basic Books, 1965), pp. 85–86, 165, 210–213.

31. Masters and Johnson, *Human Sexual Response*, pp. 240–241.

32. Ibid., pp. 241–242.

33. Ibid., p. 242.

34. Ibid., p. 245.

35. G. Newman and C. R. Nichols, "Sexual Activities and Attitudes in Older Persons," *Jour. Amer. Med. Assn.* 173 (1960): 33–35.

36. Masters and Johnson, *Human Sexual Response*, p. 247.

37. See Sapirstein, *Emotional Security*, p. 173; Bernard, *The Sex Game*, Chapter 13; and Leslie H. Farber, "My Wife, the Naked Movie Star," *Harper's*, June, 1969, pp. 49–55.

38. See Sapirstein, *Emotional Security*, p. 150.

39. See Bernard, *The Sex Game*, p. 160.

40. Maureen Davidica, "Women and the Radical Movement," *Journal of Female Liberation*, no. 1 (1968), p. 42.

41. Dana Densmore, "On Celibacy," *Journal of Female Liberation*, no. 1 (1968), pp. 22–25.

42. Julian Roebuck and S. Lee Spray, "The Cocktail Lounge: A Study of Heterosexual Relations in a Public Organization," *Amer. Jour. Sociology* 72 (January 1967): 388–395.

43. Jessie Bernard, "Infidelity: Some Moral and Social Issues," in Jules H. Wasserman, ed., *The Psychodynamics of Work and Marriage*, Vol. 16 (New York: Grune and Stratton, 1970), pp. 100–101.

44. Ps. 19:5.

45. Robert Blood and Donald M. Wolfe, *Husbands and Wives* (New York: Free Press, 1960), pp. 177, 178.

46. Only 9 percent never turned to their husbands with their troubles; 3 percent did not answer (ibid., p. 206).

47. Ibid.
48. Ibid., p. 208.
49. Harold Feldman, "Development of the Husband-Wife Relationship," offset research report (Cornell, undated), p. 17.
50. A. C. Kinsey et al., *Sexual Behavior in the Human Male* (Philadelphia, Pa.: Saunders, 1948), p. 593; A. C. Kinsey et al., *Sexual Behavior in the Human Female* (Philadelphia, Pa.: Saunders, 1953), p. 433.

Chapter 7

SEXUAL ADVENTURING AND PERSONALITY GROWTH

By Albert Ellis, Ph.D.

To define *sexual adventuring* is not very hard. But who really knows what *personality growth* is? A lot of words have, to be sure, been spoken and written on this subject during the last quarter of a century—the cynical say *too* many! But the results are hardly definitive. One authority's "growth" is another authority's poison. In recent years, for example, leaders of the existentialist movement in the field of psychotherapy, such as Sidney Jourard, Ronald Laing, and Rollo May, have stressed such personality virtues as openness, authenticity, caring, and acceptance of man's basic irrationality. Those in the forefront of the encounter movement, such as Herbert Otto, Bernard Gunther, and William Schutz, have emphasized physical contact, sensory awareness, expression of deep feelings, and relatedness. Those on the reality therapy level, such as William Glasser and O. Hobart Mowrer, have seen personality growth largely in terms of ruthless reality-facing and self-discipline. And those in the vanguard of cognitive therapy, such as Aaron T. Beck, George Kelly, E. Lakin Phillips, and myself, have insisted that fundamental personality growth rarely takes place without conscious and concerted philosophic restructuring. Quite a kettle of theories!

What, therefore, for the purpose of the present chapter, shall personality growth be deemed to be? I have already given a great deal of thought (not to mention clinical practice) to this topic and have come up with what seems to me to be some reasonably satisfactory answers. In two rather famous (there are those who would say, infamous) papers on the subject of religion,[1] I have outlined what I consider to be the main goals of emotional health or personality growth; and it seems to me that these are at least as good as those outlined by various other theoreticians, researchers, and clinicians.

The most important elements of personality growth—or what I sometimes call rational sensitivity—are probably the achievement of enlightened self-interest, self-direction, tolerance, acceptance of ambiguity and uncertainty, flexibility, acceptance of reality, commitment, risk-taking, and self-acceptance. It is my thesis that just about all these goals are abetted and enhanced by sexual adventuring. And by sexual adventuring I mean the individual's engaging in a good many sex-love relationships before he (or she) settles down to any form of monogamous mating and also, if the spirit moves him (or her!), continuing to engage in some further sex-love experimentation and varietism even after living together, in a one-to-one relationship, with a fairly permanent mate.

Let me now go through the traits that I listed above as being associated with personality growth, define them more precisely, and indicate why I think each of them is usually aided by sexual adventuring.

Enlightened self-interest. The individual who is well-adjusted to himself and to the social group with which he lives is primarily devoted to existing and to being happy (that is, to gaining satisfactions and avoiding truly noxious, painful, or depriving circumstances) and, at the same time, is secondarily devoted to seeing that his fellow humans also survive and are reasonably happy. He is most interested in his own life and pleasure, but he realizes that he is not likely to be maximally creative and enjoying while he is needlessly stepping on others' toes and unduly restricting their living space. Consequently, he tries to be non-harming to practically everyone, and he selects a relatively few individuals (since his time is limited) to actively care for and help. But he is non-injurious to many and devoted to a few mainly because he enjoys that kind of activity and because he does not want to be unnecessarily frustrated and restricted by others and by the environment in which he resides. He does not dishonestly pretend to be purely altruistic; he is authentically and realistically self-interested—and therefore imposes certain social restrictions on himself.

Sexual-amative adventuring encourages and aids enlightened self-interest because the adventuring person keeps asking himself: "What do *I* really want in regard to this relationship I am having or this potential connection that I might have? I realize that she (or he) wants to begin or maintain this affair, but is that what *I* really desire? How much time is likely to be involved? What will I probably learn about myself and others? What alternative satisfactions could I get if I select another relationship, or even no relationship, instead? Granted that the union may or may not work out well, what, in either eventuality, is likely to be in it for me?"

Adventuring of any kind tends to be healthfully self-seeking. I travel, climb mountains, search a library for new books to read, go to a party to find new friends mainly because *I* am curious, venturesome, absorption-bent. If someone will accompany me on these experiments, and especially if that someone can share my delight and converse with me about it, that is great—sometimes truly glorious. But essentially I go for me and not for the sake of my companion. And sometimes I deliberately want to go alone, since that makes the outreaching still more adventurous.

In sex-love adventuring, I almost always require a partner (for the limits of masturbatory experimentation are usually quickly reached!). But I still don't know what is going to happen with and to that partner—and that's one of the main reasons why I find the relationship, as long or as short as it lasts, exciting. I do know, however, that almost anything can happen; that I (and she) are taking some real risks; that the final outcome of the affair—whether it be a one-night stand or marriage—is pretty much in doubt. I often recognize, therefore, that sex-love adventuring is one of the main remaining major explorations of life that is left to me, now that it is pretty difficult to hunt big game in Africa, scale Mount Everest, or fight Indians in the wild West.

I therefore decide to take my chances on having, or not having, an affair. If I decide yes, then I recognize that I am choosing to relate to another human being and that even though she has voluntarily agreed to become enmeshed with me, she has her own desires, ideals, and vulnerabilities. Moreover, because she may be emotionally involved with me and her wishes may very much be father to her thoughts, she is likely to be particularly exposed and subject to disappointment and disillusionment. Consequently, out of empathy and enlightened self-interest, I do not wish to needlessly mislead her. So I lean over backwards, if I am ethical, to be honest with her: to define the kind of relationship, whether it be mere sex or grand passion, that I would like to have with her; and I honor her acceptance or rejection of my offer. I may very well, as I point out in some of my writings,[2] try to "seduce" my partner into having an affair with me. But I try to do so by persuading her that it is probably for her own best interests, as well as for mine, for her to give up any arbitrary, puritanical ideas about refraining from affairs and to make her decision on the basis of true choice rather than compulsion. In any event, I want to engage in some kind of sex-love adventuring, and I in one way or another arrange to do so. Consequently, I am truly self-interested, and the more adventuring of this kind I do, the more I tend to practice having enlightened self-interest.

Self-direction and independence. The individual who has a mature and growing personality assumes responsibility for his own thinking and living, is able independently to work at most of his problems, and while at times wanting or preferring the cooperation and help of others, does not need their support for his well-being or his inner sense of worthiness. The sexually adventuring person tends to fall in this self-directed framework in several ways:

1. He rarely accepts traditional and conventional sex-love views merely because he was taught them during his childhood or because they are the majority views in his culture. He intently considers, weighs, and asks for the evidence backing these opinions and only accepts them when he has come up with some good reasons why he should personally follow them.

2. He enters into relationships knowing full well that he may easily fail at them and that he has no one but himself, really, to fall back upon in case he does fail. By being adventuresome, he gives himself plenty of practice at failing and sees in practice (in addition to theory) that he can easily survive such mishaps.

3. He usually spends some amount of time, in between relationships, in being on his own. He does not convince himself that he absolutely must have a date every weekend (and therefore maintain a long-term relationship with a partner whom he really considers rather inferior) nor that he must not sleep alone during weekday nights (and therefore often has to be with someone who actually bores him). Because of his relative independence, in spite of his desire to keep having interesting and absorbing sex-love relationships, he remains distinctly selective rather than cowardly compromising in his choices.

4. He usually, because of his independence and selectivity, is able to pick partners on the basis more of real interest and love rather than of sheer sexuality. Knowing that he can be happy though alone, and knowing that he can afford to break with a safe and steady partner whom he no longer finds exciting, he tends to select and to remain with those whom he truly cares for and to have deeper and more profound relationships rather than affairs that he merely tolerates.

Tolerance. The emotionally stable and growing individual is highly tolerant of the desires and behaviors of other human beings, even though these differ significantly from his own tastes. Even when they behave in a manner that he considers to be mistaken or unethical, he acknowledges that, because of their essential fallibility, they have a right to be wrong. While disliking or abhorring some of their acts, he still does not condemn them, as persons, for performing these dislikable acts. He tends to accept the fact that all humans are remarkably error-prone, does not unrealistically expect them to be perfect, and refrains from despising or punishing them even when they make indubitable mistakes.

When an individual is sexually audacious, he tends to forgive his own failings and to concomitantly accept those of others. He tries a variety of sex-love behaviors, including some that are often considered deviant or aberrant, and consequently can understand and tolerate the idosyncracies of his fellows. If he is a male, he freely and fully has sex-love relationships with a number of women and consequently tends to adopt a single rather than a double standard of morality and to avoid being a sexist. If this individual is a female, she is more likely to allow herself—and others—to have sex affairs in less restricted and less arbitrarily inhibited ways: to have them, for example, quickly or after knowing her partner for a period of time, with or without love, within or outside the institution of legal marriage. Relatively few sex-love adventurers maintain the rigid, puritanical, damning codes of sex practice that have been so foolishly prevalent in Western civilization for many centuries. And even in nonsexual ways, few of them tend to be as moralistic and proscriptive as individuals sexually unadventurous.

Acceptance of ambiguity and uncertainty. The individual who keeps a growing edge to his personality tends to accept the fact that we all live in a world of probability and chance, where there do not seem to be nor probably ever will be any absolute certainties. He demands no surefire predictions about the future and realizes that it is not at all horrible—indeed, it is in many ways fascinating and exciting—to live in a distinctly probabilistic, variable environment.

The sexual adventurer clearly does not demand that he meet some perfect girl early in his life, that he immediately get into a fine relationship with her, and that this remain intact forever. Nor does he demand that one mate be everything to him and that because he mainly likes her traits and finds it beneficial to be with her that she completely fulfill him, sexually, companionably, emotionally, and otherwise. He realistically accepts the point, which Brian Boylan incisively exposits, that infidelity is the natural desire, if not the actual habit, of the average person, and that giving in to this desire, preferably in an honest and above-board manner, is not horrible.[3]

Just because he is a varietist, the sexually adventurous individual is able to accept the imperfections of each of his partners, to be unterrified by their inevitable ambivalences (knowing full well that he has his own), to face the fact that even the most intense loves may be somewhat ephemeral, and to be unhorrified at the thought of his losing a beloved through her moving away, becoming ill, dying, or otherwise being unavailable. Since, through accepting ambiguity and uncertainty in sex-love areas and resolving to live happily in spite of these realities, he can hardly be thrown by anything that happens to him in these aspects of his life, he generally tends to take an equally realistic attitude toward other aspects of living and to tolerate ambiguity there.

Sexual adventurousness, moreover, almost by definition leads to maximum experiencing. The unadventurous, incurious individual of course exists; but in many ways he hardly lives. The venturesome one, on the other hand, does many more things, has a greater number of relationships, both enjoys himself and suffers more, and in many ways is more alive. By so being, he can hardly help realizing that existence is many-faceted, that everything does not fit into one neat-niched arrangement, and that practically nothing is utterly certain. In this manner, again, he tends to accept uncertainty and to stop upsetting himself when things do not rigidly conform to some of his preconceived notions.

Flexibility. The opposite of the need for certainty and of intolerance is flexibility. The emotionally growing individual consequently tends to be intellectually and emotively labile, to be open to change at all times, and to unbigotedly view the infinitely varied people, ideas, and things that exist in his world. The disturbed person, on the other hand, tends to be exceptionally narrow, rigid, and overly constrained. Personality growth, in particular, would seem to be almost impossible to achieve if the individual is not quite open and flexible: for how can growing and remaining utterly bound be compatible?

Sex-love varietism and pluralism obviously abet human flexibility. The person who thinks that he must only go with one member of the other sex at a time before marriage, that he must remain absolutely faithful to his wife after marrying, and that he must never contemplate divorce, remarriage, communal forms of marriage, or any other diversion from strict monagamic ways is not likely to be marked by flexibleness and openmindedness. The chances are that, like the members of the John Birch Society and similar ultraconservative groups, he is going to be just as uptight about general as he is about sexual "license," and his nonsexual and sexual views are going to be significantly correlated. Similarly, there has usually been found to be a significant relationship between sexual liberalism and social-personal liberalism. Not that this is always true. Many of the members of the Rene Guyon Society, which is in some ways unusually liberal sexually and which espouses full sex relations between young children, are very conservative politically and socially. But in general, sexual adventuring is itself a form of open-mindedness that encourages other forms of flexible thinking and emoting, and that thereby enhances personality growth.

Scientific thinking. The longer I practice intensive psychotherapy, the more I am convinced that what is usually called emotional disturbance and interference with personality growth is the direct result of an unscientific, magical way of thinking— thinking that is particularly involved with irrational, nonempirical, unvalidatable hypotheses such as, "My deeds are not only wrong and inefficient, but I am an awful person for performing them"; "You shouldn't have treated me so unfairly, and you are a thorough louse and should be eternally condemned for doing so";

and "The world is not only a rough place in which to survive and live happily, but it is too hard for me to get along in, and I can't stand its being so hard!"[4] If people would completely follow the scientific canons of thinking in their personal lives, and would stop theologically "awfulizing," "devilifying," and "catastrophizing" about the many kinds of hassles and frustrations to which, as fallible humans, they are inevitably heir, they would not only rid themselves of virtually all their deep-seated feelings of anxiety, depression, guilt, and hostility, but they would also give themselves leeway to discover, with lack of prejudice, what they really enjoy in life and how they can truly, as human beings, grow.

Reason is indeed a limited faculty and may never quite solve all the mysteries of life. But for maximum emotional functioning, the individual would better be fairly consistently objective, rational, and scientific, and be able to apply the rules of scientific method and the laws of logic, not only to external people and events, but also to himself and his interpersonal relationships. Sexual adventuring, though hardly a guarantee of rationality, abets scientific thinking in several important ways:

1. The sexual varietist, as noted above, is nondogmatic and non-conventional. Like the scientist, he is out for discovery, for satisfying his own curiosity, for devising new solutions to old problems.

2. He is, above all, an experimentalist. He does not know what will occur when he leaves an old love or takes on a new one, but he is more than willing to find out. Although he cannot, like the typical physical or social scientist, normally do a well-controlled study of his behaving first one way and then another, he usually does less rigorous, less controlled studies of his own thoughts, feelings, and experiences as he samples first one affair and then another. He may not, thereby, come up with startling truths about sex and love in general; but he frequently does arrive at profound truths about his *own* sex and love propensities.

3. The sexual adventurist is relatively objective and nondefensive about his and others' amorous ways because he has a good deal of first-hand information about love at his disposal, he uses larger rather than smaller samples to observe, and his latter-day knowledge serves to correct more erroneous earlier impressions.

4. He is usually more rational and nonmagical about sex-love affairs than are those whose sex lives are much more restricted, because he strives for greater human pleasure and less pain, and

not for fictional, super-romantic visions of what sex and love presumably should be like in some hypothetical heaven. He tends to be more of a realistic and hardheaded empiricist than a soft-headed visionary.

Commitment to a large plan or goal. Emotionally healthy individuals are usually committed to some large life plan or goal—such as work, building a family, art, science, or sports. When they have steady personality growth, they tend to be vitally absorbed in some large goal outside of themselves, whether it be in the realm of people, things, or ideas. And they frequently have at least one major creative interest, as well as some oustanding human involvement, which is highly important to them and around which they structure a good portion of their lives.

At first blush, many monogamists would seem to do better, in terms of vital absorbing interests, than do sexual varietists, since they so frequently absorb themselves to a considerable degree in finding one mate and then for thirty or more years building a strong sex-love-family relationship with her. I think that this is one of the strongest points about monogamy, and one of the principle reasons that it has survived over the centuries. Sexual adventuring, however, is not necessarily incompatible with this kind of a marriage-building goal, because, today, it is very possible for the varietist to agree with his mate, when he is first settling down to a long-term relationship with her, that they will devote most of their time and energy to remaining attached to each other and perhaps to the children they bear and rear, but that they will also allow each other a reasonable amount of sexual adventuring on the side. In this way, they could reap the main advantages of security and novelty, and fulfill themselves maximally in their sex-love relations.

Sexual commitment, moreover, need hardly be to a monogamous marriage, as there are other possibilities. Thus, two or more couples could decide to live in a communal or tribal marriage and to dedicate themselves to building, on quite a long-term basis, that kind of sex-love relationship. And even varietist adventuring in its own right can become a vital absorbing interest—as indicated by a well-known writer who has spent a large amount of his time during the past fifteen years arranging mate-swapping affairs for himself and his wife to participate in while, at the same time, they have reared three healthy, happy, highly creative children.

Monogamous commitment, moreover, often has its severe limitations, since it is done on an obligatory rather than a truly voluntary basis in innumerable instances. Thus, a man sexually and amatively devotes himself exclusively to his wife and children not because he truly enjoys doing so but because he believes, for conventional or religious reasons, that he ought to do so. In so doing, moreover, he frequently prevents himself from being committed to art, to science, to his work, or to something else (such as a string of intense love affairs) to which he would have been much more genuinely and intensely attached had he not believed that he had to be absorbed only in a monogamous marriage.

The question is: If people were more honest with themselves and their sex-love partners, would there be much fewer obligatory absorptions in a single relationship and many more voluntary absorptions in various kinds of non-monogamous or quasi-monogamous relations? I am inclined to think that there would be. And I am also inclined to think that such a state of affairs would be considerably more emotionally satisfying and healthy.

Commitment, while a most important part of human existence, would better be to one's own individuality than to any kind of pairing. It is questionable whether devotion to a coupling arrangement is often very good or healthy if it is not based on the premise that each of the partners is truly devoted to himself and finds, because of this very self-interest, that he can be authentically and logically devoted to the union. As Herbert A. Otto has noted, "The lack of commitment to self-realization, together with the lack of framework and opportunity for self-realization, are responsible for much of what is labeled as pathological or asocial behavior."[5] For those who enjoy sexual adventuring, therefore, commitment to realizing themselves through this kind of activity may be one of the most healthy and self-actualizing acts they can do.

Risk-taking. The emotionally sound person is able to take risks: to ask himself what he would really like to do in life and then to endeavor to do this, even though he has to risk defeat or failure. He tries to be adventurous (though not necessarily foolhardy), is willing to chance almost anything once to see how he likes it, and looks forward to some breaks in his usual life routines. It is interesting to note, in this connection, that even some of the most self-actualizing and creative individuals, such as Abraham H. Maslow, spend so much of their time in routine, unadventurous pursuits that it takes something drastic, such as near-death from a heart attack, to jolt them into a new sense of vital living and a greater degree of risk-taking savoring of their existence.

Sexual adventuring almost by definition is one of the major, and I would say one of the most exciting and pleasurable, forms of risk-taking. In my own life, for example, I have found that no matter how sorry I was about the breakup of an affair or a marriage (and, contrary to silly rumors that circulate about me, I have had many of the former but only two of the latter), my sorrow was always significantly attenuated by the adventurous thought: "Ah! I wonder with what kind of a person I shall become involved next. How great to look forward to a relationship that is almost certain to include several important elements that I have not yet experienced!"

Venturesomeness in sex-love affairs virtually forces the individual to take notable risks of defeat or failure. For the security-minded individual cannot possibly be truly adventurous; and the adventure-headed individual cannot possibly be terribly security-bound. Sexual varietism, moreover, normally proves to the adventurer that he can definitely survive defeat; that he need not crack up when he is rejected; that even a host of love failures generally end up with a few outstanding successes; and that the loss of a potential or an actual beloved is indeed an *inconvenience,* but it is never truly *awful.* This often-experienced contradiction of his foolish notions that sex failure is horrible may not necessarily generalize to his dire fears of other kinds of failure, but it certainly helps!

Concern and caution are wise and valuable human characteristics. But humans, alas, are born as well as reared with an enormous tendency to escalate these feelings into those of over-concern and panic, and thereby they cruelly emasculate a vast amount of their potential living space. Sexual risk-taking occurs in a lovely area where the individual, unless he is incredibly foolish, will rarely suffer bone-breaking physical injury or death (as he will, of course, in highly respectable sports like skiing and auto-mobiling!). The main thing he risks, sexuo-amatively, is rejection and loss of approval. But it is precisely by taking these emotional gambles that the individual learns how to stop caring *too* much about what others think of him and to start truly accepting himself. If sexual adventuring can give him, as it often can, repeated practice in this important area of his personality growth, it may render him one of the most valuable services of his lifetime.

Self-acceptance. Above all, the emotionally healthy and sane individual is glad to be alive and to fully accept himself just because he is alive, because he exists, and because (as a living being) he invariably has some power to enjoy himself. If he assesses or rates himself at all, he does so, not on the basis of his extrinsic achievements or his popularity with others, but on the basis of his own existence: on his ability to think, feel, and act, and thereby to make an interesting, absorbed life for himself. Preferably, as I have shown in my more recent writings, he does not rate his self, or give his total being a report card, at all.[6] Instead, he only rates his deeds, traits, and performances, and refuses to play any of the usual self-rating ego games. Consequently, instead of deifying himself (saying that he has self-esteem, self-love, or identity and otherwise appraising himself as being better than others) and instead of devilifying himself (saying that he has self-hatred, worthlessness, or lack of identity and otherwise appraising himself as being worse than others), he more modestly strives for self-acceptance. Self-acceptance, which is much less noble and ego-inflated than self-esteem or self-confidence, merely means that the individual accepts the facts that (1) he is alive for a certain length of time, (2) he is able, while alive, to experience pleasure and pain, (3) he chooses, merely on the basis of his bias in favor of living and enjoying, to stay alive and to have a hell of a good and growing time.

The individual who has full self-acceptance lives without any absolutes, without any should's, ought's, must's, have-to's, or got-to's though with a whale of a lot of it-would-be-better's. He ceaselessly experiments and explores to try to discover what he truly likes and dislikes, and he uses this knowledge for his own maximum growth and enjoyment. Although, as Alan Watts indicates, he is not likely to experience sheer ecstasy for more than a few moments a day,[7] he does his best to have those moments and to make them count. He is totally unashamed of his own hedonism, though he often strives for long-term and well-disciplined rather than short-range and kicky types of satisfaction.

What better helps the person to achieve unconditional self-acceptance than realistic sexual adventuring? Practically nothing that I can see. For in the realm of experimentally and spontaneously embarked-upon sex-love affairs, he is likely to find almost innumerable harmless and knowledge-amassing intellectual, emotional, and physical delights. Sigmund Freud, who in spite of his overemphasis on the presumable sexual origins of emotional disturbance was something of a prude and a sexist, and who invented one of the most inefficient and erroneous systems of psychotherapy still extant, was wise enough to see that the two main sources of personal stability and growth are love and work.[8] Occasionally, maximum sex-love fulfillment can be achieved by the bright and cultured individual within a strict monogamic framework; but if we are ruthlessly honest about it, this seems to be far more the exception than the rule. Consequently, if many (though not necessarily all) of us are to grow and grow and grow, it is most unlikely that we will achieve our maximum personality potential, especially in terms of our loving and being loved, in a lifetime setting of minimum sexual adventurousness.

Maximum openness, tolerance, and self-acceptance, in other words, are much more likely to be achieved when the individual truly acknowledges all of his thoughts, emotions, and physical urges and when he refrains from condemning himself for *any* of them. This includes, of course, his pluralist as well as his monogamous, his ephemeral as well as his lasting, his inconstant as well as his steady sex-love inclinations and experiences. Not that all sexuality, nor even all feelings of love, are wise and good for every individual. Both sexing and loving can in many instances interfere with what some persons find are, for themselves, "deeper" and "better" pursuits—such as artistic and scientific endeavors or philosophic contemplations. But no one really knows what he wants and what will be best for him until he widely experiments and experiences. No one knows what his own potential for personal growth is until he takes many risky bypaths of life and wrongly enters quite a number of blind alleys. Trial and *error* is still the road to maximum self-knowledge and growth; and that goes for sexuality as for virtually every nonsexual aspect of living. Sexual adventuring, therefore, is at least to some degree an almost necessary step to greater personal and personality advancement.

Does sexual freedom have its disadvantages and limitations? Of course it does! In an essay on "Group Marriage: a Possible Alternative?," I point out that this form of varietistic relating is, at the present time, "a logical alternative to monogamic and to other forms of marriage for a select few."[9] In another essay,

"Healthy and Disturbed Reasons for Having Extramarital Relations," I show that what I call "civilized adultery" (that is, honest adultery engaged in with the consent of one's marital partner) is highly beneficial to some individuals, but that there are as yet not too many couples who can undisturbedly accept it.[10] For all new and less limiting forms of mating tend to be very difficult for people, especially those reared in contemporary society, to follow, and require a good deal of emotional stability and intellectual wisdom on the part of those who attempt to engage in these sex-love modes.

Herbert Otto, in commenting on my somewhat cautious approach to group marriage, notes that "jealousy and interpersonal conflict in the group are some of the main reasons why Ellis believes group marriage faces great difficulties. Unfortunately, nowhere in his paper does Ellis make any reference to group dynamic techniques, or to the encounter group approach which, with the help of competent professionals, might go a long way toward resolving some of the problems inherent in a group marriage structure."[11]

Otto is right about my omissions, but he forgets to note that my essay on group marriage was written several years before it actually appeared between book covers, and that at the time I wrote it group dynamics and encounter methods had not yet contributed very much to the resolving of marital difficulties. Since that time, I have developed what I call a marathon weekend of rational encounter and find that it works quite successfully in helping some couples to resolve their marital problems and to live successfully with each other in various kinds of unconventional unions.[12] Moreover, the general principles of rational-emotive psychotherapy, which I originally devised in 1955 and have been adapting to a wide variety of sexual and nonsexual problems ever since, are uniquely designed to help couples live together successfully in both traditional and untraditional ways.[13] Although I take a somewhat dim view of the effectiveness of group dynamics and encounter methods per se, particularly when they are employed by leaders who are not specifically trained to be therapists, I believe that they can work almost wonderfully well when combined with a hard-headed cognitive approach (especially, naturally, that of rational-emotive therapy!).

I agree with Otto, therefore, that efficient group (and individual) therapy procedures can help couples be saner and happier in both regular and less regular forms of mating. Quite so! But humans are still human. They are and probably always will remain incredibly fallible. They tend to be enormously different from each other and variable in their own right. Practically all kinds of sex-love relations, moreover, have their intrinsic difficulties and their unideal aspects. Even the healthiest personalities, consequently, are going to have to work their way through various kinds of sexual arrangements until they individually find what is better or best for themselves. Perhaps this is not an inevitable fact of life, but it certainly seems to be one that is highly probable.

Because of the above-mentioned human fallibilities and widespread individual differences, personal experimentation and risk-taking in sex-love affairs is still highly desirable. Sexual adventuring, as noted in the body of this chapter, gives maximum leeway for this kind of experimentation. I therefore contend that it is one of the sanest and most enlightened paths to sex, love, marital, and personal growth.

CHAPTER NOTES

1. Albert Ellis, "The Case Against Religion: A Psychotherapist's View," *The Independent* 126 (October, 1962) : 4–5; and Ellis, "The Case Against Religion," *Mensa Bulletin* 38 (September, 1970); 5–6.

2. Albert Ellis, *Sex and the Single Man* (New York: Lyle Stuart and Dell Books, 1965); Ellis and Roger O. Conway, *The Art of Erotic Seduction* (New York: Lyle Stuart, Ace Books, 1969).

3. Brian Boylan, *Infidelity: The Ways We Live Today* (New York, Putnams, 1970).

4. Albert Ellis, *Reason and Emotion in Psychotherapy* (New York: Lyle Stuart, 1962); Ellis, J. L. Wolfe, and S. Moseley, *How to Prevent Your Child from Becoming a Neurotic Adult* (New York: Crown Publishers, 1966); Ellis, *A Casebook of Rational-Emotive Therapy* (Palo Alto, Calif.: Science and Behavior Books, 1971); Ellis, "Psychotherapy and the value of a human being," in *Value and valuation: essays in honor of Robert S. Hartman*, ed. J. W. Davis (Knoxville, Tenn.: University of Tennessee Press, 1971); Ellis, "Rational-emotive Therapy," in *Directive Psychotherapy*, ed. R. M. Jurjevich (Miami: University of Miami Press, 1971).

5. Herbert A. Otto, ed., *The Family in Search of a Future* (New York: Appleton-Century-Crofts, 1970), p. 112.

6. Albert Ellis, *A Casebook of Rational-Emotive Therapy*; Ellis, "Psychotherapy and the Value of a Human Being"; Ellis, "Rational-Emotive Therapy"; Ellis, *Emotional Education* (New York: Julian Press, 1972); Ellis and J. M. Gullo, *Murder and Assassination* (New York: Lyle Stuart, 1971).

7. Alan Watts, "The Future of Ecstasy," *Playboy*, January 1971, 183–184.

8. Sigmund Freud, *Collected Papers* (New York: Collier Books, 1963).

9. Albert Ellis, "Group Marriage: A Possible Alternative?", in Herbert A. Otto, ed., *The Family in Search of a Future* (New York: Appleton-Century-Crofts, 1970), p. 97.

10. Albert Ellis, "Healthy and Disturbed Reasons for Having Extramarital Relations," in Gerhard Neubeck, ed., *Extramarital Relations* (Englewood Cliffs, N.J.: Prentice-Hall, 1969), pp. 153–161.

11. Herbert Otto, ed., *The Family in Search of a Future*, p. 7.

12. Albert Ellis, "A Weekend of Rational Encounter," in Arthur Burton, ed., *Encounter* (San Francisco: Jossey-Bass, 1969).

13. Albert Ellis, *Reason and Emotion in Psychotherapy* (New York: Lyle Stuart, 1962); Ellis, *A Casebook of Rational Therapy*; Ellis, "Rational-Emotive Therapy"; Ellis and Robert A. Harper, *A Guide to Successful Marriage* (original title: *Creative Marriage*) (New York: Lyle Stuart; Hollywood: Wilshire Books, 1968); Ellis and Harper, *A Guide to Rational Living* (Englewood Cliffs, N.J.: Prentice-Hall; Hollywood: Wilshire Books, 1970).

Chapter 8

SENSORY AWAKENING
AND SENSUALITY

By Bernard Gunther

love
not two
grab push
force squeeze
restrict power
hinder devour

but
two open
kiss touch
caress flow
sensitive care
tender grow

love
two know
to come
together

The bright
newness delight
of courtship
and love
often becomes
in too soon time
lost in
routine
habit
overfamiliar
familiarities

ultimately
the situation
the other person
is taken for granted
and experience becomes
roles
rules
responsibilities
the holding back
of needs
desire
understanding
feeling for one another

the two
no longer
experience-feel
their newness
aliveness
uniqueness
the process change
that is living
flowing growing
together

much of the problem
can be traced to
an over balance
of excessive
verbalization
tension
goal-ego motivation
a lack
of touch-contact
communication
in an over
simplification

   words
   sin
   taxing
   experience

sense
feeling
experience
is always different
and nothing ever
taste smells
sounds looks
exactly the same
but when you talk
think word experience
they become frozen
subject to the laws
rules of language
which impose
all kinds of
restrictions that
are not real
but can become

post-hypnotic
so that after a while
concepts replace
what is
and your existence
self-husband-wife
becomes a static
thing

our culture trains us
to over think
focus on thought and
visual process
almost to the exclusion
of feeling our
other senses
the rest of the body

the tightening
of muscles
against feeling free
can be a
way to avoid
intense emotional
conflict
pleasure-pain
by depressing
desensitizing
deadening
your being
sensation
life

automatic behavior
is a rigid
impersonal

efficient way
to deal with the world
so that things get done
machine-like
but lacking the
natural rhythm of being
sensitive
selective
personal

perpetuated by
goal-ego motivation
manipulation
stressing ends
ignoring means
working against time
nature pleasure joy
the desire to
get a-head
at the expense
of the body
anybody
everybody

touch in our culture
is largely taboo
and after you
are no longer
a small child
you're not supposed
to touch or
need to be touched
by anybody
unless you're going
to have sex with them
and even this

ultimate
intimate contact
is often limited
to caressing
only certain
body parts

this lack of contact
produces
a touch deprivation
which plays a significant
role in the total
emptybody-less
depersonalization
that is so predominant
in our culture

excessive words tension
automatic behavior
goal orientation
and a lack of touch
create a wall of
separateness
which keeps people
from being
close together
a restricting constricting
non-relationship
in which couples
deal with ideas
surface impressions
of the other person
rather than actually
relating seeing
experiencing feeling

sensory awakening
is a method designed to
undercut the words
tension
habitual behavior
goal orientation
to let you relax
non-verbally communicate
make sense
experience touch be
the open joy us
you we

the following
are some meditation-like
experiences which
can help you to
allow recapture
uncover rediscover
the constant renewness
of each other

the experiences here
center around feeling touch
physical contact
sensuous delight in beauty
color sound form
texture rather than
sensual sexual indulgence

this is not a put-down
of sexuality
one of nature's
most divine sharing
caring experiences
but only an attempt to

put into perspective
its narrowed distortion
in our culture
physical contact
of all kinds
on many different levels
releases warmth
energy
tension
a more sensitive
human dimension

when doing
the following experiments
remember
love is care
care for one another
carefully

generalized instructions
for experience-experiments

1. all times are approximate
   subject to feeling-circumstance
2. don't talk unless
   specifically instructed to
3. to increase inner sensitivity—
   decrease visual bias
   keep your eyes closed
   when asked to
4. be sure to let your partner know
   if he/she is slap-touching
   too hard or soft
   too fast or slow
5. After each experience allow
   30 seconds to digest-experience

how you feel
before opening your eyes

being is now
when you allow
time slows down
and everything
becomes timeless

take your time

describe your partner
sit in a chair
or on the floor
knee to knee
and for three to five minutes
look at your partner
and describe
what you are seeing
start each sentence with
I see
after reverse roles
for the same
amount of time

feed your partner
one of you
closes his eyes
and is fed
a meal or some snacks
by the other partner
there is no talking
during the experience
after switch roles
don't discuss
your experience until

after both of you
have been fed

give each other a shampoo
during the process
close your eyes and feel
play with the scalp suds
after pour warm and
cool water over
his/her hair
towel dry and comb

wash your partner's feet
individually
first with warm soap
and water
then with lots
of table salt
dry off and
oil rub them well

feeling for each other
both partners close
their eyes during this
experience and without
talking one of the partners
with both hands explores
the entire body
of the other person
who is passive for five minutes
then the roles are reversed
for five minutes
after open your eyes
see one another
and express how you feel
non-verbally

wash your partner
from head to toe
with a wash cloth
and a bowl of warm
water
take your time and
after doing both sides
change places

play master/servant
for one hour
or a full day
one partner's the servant
and in every way
accepts all commands
that his/her master
wants to convey

close being
without talking
and moving as little
as possible
lie in each other's arms
for five to ten minutes
and feel what's happening
the energy between you

the foregoing
are hints
reminders
experiences
in awareness
of a sensual
rather than
a sexual direction
that you can

learn to allow
become
a continuous part
reflection
of your love life
together

after
laughter

still

touching
you

Chapter 9

ENHANCING SEXUALITY
THROUGH NUDISM

By William E. Hartman, Ph.D.
and Marilyn A. Fithian

Does nudity in any sense enhance sexuality? Our data indicates that it does in every way we have used and studied it.

Social nudism usually refers to individuals of both sexes in interaction without the wearing of clothing for the purpose of concealment. We use it here in this sense, as well as in several restricted senses. It always refers to one or more individuals without clothing but in a limited number for therapeutic purposes only.

Enhancing sexuality increases one's awareness of, and comfort with, one's sex assignment, identification, and function. It operates on both a covert level of feelings and an overt level of relationships with other sexual beings. This phenomenon may be viewed on a continuum of intimacy from one pole, representing little or no ability to feel or relate deeply, to the hypothetical nth degree, usually represented by coitus in our culture. Actually, it may be questionable to suggest that coitus represents this degree of intimacy between two human beings since the enhancement of sexuality may make it possible for individuals to relate more deeply and intimately with others in non-coital ways that may be regarded as more profound in their nature and impact than those experienced through coitus.

We have four main sources of information about the ways in which nudism may enhance sexuality. Our primary source is from

Nudist Society by William E. Hartman, Marilyn A. Fithian, and Donald Johnson.[1] This book reports questionnaire, interview, and personality test data based on four years of field research in nudist parks in America, primarily in California. It also contains a second main source of information about nudism and how it may enhance sexuality, the chapter entitled "Nudism as a Therapeutic Community." The third major source of information comes from our three-year study of non-orgasmic women.[2] The last major source of information concerns the research and treatment of sexual dysfunction in married couples conducted at the Center for Marital and Sexual Studies, Long Beach, California.

From 1964 to 1968, approximately twenty five nudist parks were visited in an attempt to make a definitive, in-depth social-psychological study of social nudism. Our samples include 1,388 respondents to a simple one-page questionnaire in 1964 and 432 individuals who were studied more in depth through extensive questionnaire–interview–personality test procedures in a nudist setting during 1965–66. We also invited non-nudists to participate in social nudism so their personal reactions could be obtained precisely at the time of their first experience. Our sample of outsiders included 45 different individuals.

SOCIAL NUDISM

Participation in social nudism in America is more a male than a female motivated activity. This means that more men than women initiate participation in typical recreational activities without clothing. Specifically, males report that the desire is to view those forbidden parts of female anatomy culturally defined as sexual. These are the parts that our society specifically demands be covered, if only with a bikini. One way, then, that nudism enhances sexuality in our culture is that the basic curiosity about the sexual nature of humans is satisfied through a sex education experience of merely participating in social activities without clothing in groups involving members of both sexes.

While the females do not report this to be as significant an item for them, they do report that their sexuality is enhanced because they feel more like a substantial sexual being when comparing themselves with other females in social nudism. This finding was common among a group of females who were interviewed by us in a nudist park or camp during their initial experience with this phenomenon. The most specific comment made had to do with breast size; many were amazed to learn that their breasts were as large as most of the other females present.

The male counterpart of this phenomenon is the reaction to comparing penile size with other men. It was a surprising finding that male sexuality is more profoundly experienced in our culture while nude, but in the presence of both sexes. In other words, many male respondents called to our attention the fact that nudity experienced with same-sexed groups in YMCA's or other situations did not have the same impact as experiencing nudity in the presence of both sexes. In the latter instance, not only did the male compare penile size in terms of his feelings about his own sexuality, but the presence of women reaffirmed his feelings of masculinity and acceptance as a worthwhile person when seen in the presence of other nude males. This was a sexually validating aspect of one's self-concept, which was not possible outside a situation involving social nudism.

It should not be presumed or inferred that sexuality is an adult phenomenon alone. Freud suggested many years ago that sexuality in infancy and childhood is also important. Observing children in nudist parks suggests that not only was Freud correct in his theories of infantile sexuality, but that if enhancement of sexuality is to be regarded as a desirable goal in our society, the most probable beginning place would be with children.

During the course of the field research, several male and female professional psychologists, psychiatrists, and social workers asked to accompany us on field trips. On each occasion we asked that they make specific observations about the behavior of children in nudist parks where we were primarily involved in working with adults as research subjects. The material recorded by these outside non-nudist professional observers indicated that the children accepted and reacted to nudism very positively and wholesomely; in fact, it was difficult to determine whether the youngsters were even aware that they were experiencing nudism in a very emotional, clothed society where openness and honesty are not always possible.

The professionals' comments were to the effect that sexuality is a very important dimension of the human personality and that the children observed in nudist parks seemed better behaved, causing less problems for themselves and others, and more comfortable with themselves and their peers than children they had observed elsewhere. If we define sexuality, then, as comfort and acceptance of one's sexual assignment and roles, the observation of children in nudist parks would suggest that their sexuality is enhanced through their nudist experience.

We are saying that children learn to become comfortable with their sexuality from earliest infancy through experience in social nudism. By becoming comfortable with one's body and at the same time becoming comfortable with the bodies of one's peers, with all aspects of one's biological self as part of the basic interaction process, sexual curiosity is satisfied. The most effective way of enhancing sexuality appears to be in the informal socialization process while experiencing one's self in a situation involving social nudity. It suggests that the covert and overt concepts of sexuality may go hand in hand and be so closely interwoven as to preclude their meaningful separation.

On an adult level, however, they do not always appear to be so neatly interwoven. Some adults report extreme difficulty in experiencing themselves nude in a group. They expect the earth to stop moving around the sun the moment that they appear in such a condition. They become less insecure and uncomfortable with their ability to relate to others once they become comfortable with their own biological selves in a social situation.

This latter aspect deals with the more overt dimensions of human sexuality as reported by our respondents in the nudist research. Of 432 respondents, about 25 percent report being somewhat more interested in overt sexual expression with their spouses as a result of the experience with social nudism. They also report that, in general, there is no change in frequency of sexual intercourse (with only 11 percent indicating an increase and 3 percent a decrease). Some individuals indicate that the experience of social nudism is itself a substitute for sexual intercourse. One man explained that going to a nudist park was, for him, a similar experience to coitus but on a covert level. Even though frequency of sexual relations remains about the same for the majority of nudist respondents, a little more than one in three reported that their sexual happiness in life had increased to some extent. It would appear that, if sexual happiness increases as a result of nudist experience, then the nudism contributed something to the sexual dimension of the individuals experiencing it and that "sexual happiness" was not necessarily synonymous with increased frequency of coital activities.

There is some increase in desire for extramarital sex relations as a result of experience of nudism, although the largest single group of respondents report either no involvement or no change in desire for extramarital sex relations. It is difficult to determine from what frame of reference one would analyze whether sexuality is enhanced in terms of desire for extramarital sex. In our opinion, there are arguments that this could be interpreted as either beneficial or detrimental to the welfare of the individual and the welfare of our society as a whole. It might further be pointed out that, as a result of nudist practice, the respondents indicate that nudism per se contributed to more increase in extramarital sex than decrease. The respondents stated they felt that their desire for extramarital sex was a positive contribution to their sexuality. Conservative, moralistic groups in our society, however, would probably place a negative interpretation on this phenomenon.

The case history we reported in *Nudist Society* as having the most complete details about the therapeutic aspects of nudity was the psychiatric record of a 33-year-old, divorced, Caucasian male diagnosed by military psychiatrists as schizophrenic. He had a history of alcoholism and homosexuality, and a longstanding interest in nudity magazines.

Because of his emotional instability, he received an undesirable discharge from the service. While he was still an outpatient at an air force hospital, under sedation of 800 mgs. of Thorazine daily, this tense and uptight young man presented himself at a nudist park. He described his acceptance by the nudist participants present and explained how his general feelings of relaxation and relief from tension and anxiety were much more profound than those produced by extensive psychiatric therapy. For the first time in his life, he had meaningful heterosexual relationships, which were more significant than those in his previous marriage. His adequacy as a person was greatly enhanced by his acceptance in nudist circles and particularly by the realistic refutation of his feelings of inferiority because of supposed small penile size.

We had no way of determining whether this young man was accurate in attributing the changes in his sexuality to experience in social nudism, but neither did we have any realistic basis of denying that this was the major factor in producing change. We did have information later to the effect that not all of his mental and emotional problems were resolved, even though it was unrealistic to deprecate the evidence he submitted as to how social nudism had dramatically changed his behavior. His change from a fairly strong homosexual orientation to a heterosexual orientation certainly must be regarded as an important aspect of his overt sexual behavior.

Professionals in our society have described many individuals in the contemporary social scene as tense, apprehensive, nervous, depressed, and generally uptight. What does all this have to do with nudism and sexuality? In 1964 we asked 1,388 nudists to indicate their main reason or motivation for participation in social nudism. By far the number one item listed was "relaxation." We analyzed further data gathered in following years about motivating factors toward nudist experience and found that the two other items that were prominent after relaxation were rest and recreation. These, then, became for us the three R's of nudism, and these factors may be importantly related to sexuality.

If it is true that many people are uptight in our contemporary society, then probably any activity that provides for rest, recreation, and relaxation would logically relieve many of the tensions and pressures currently experienced. Individuals who are more stable from both a physical and a mental hygiene standpoint should logically be better able to function in all dimensions of their personality, including sexuality. Approximately two thousand people called the importance of these items to our attention during the period of our field research. While we do not possess the data to document a causal relationship between these factors in nudist settings and covert and overt aspects of sexual behavior, we are impressed with the possible significance of these items in the lives of so many practicing nudists.

NUDE MARATHONS

From July to October 1967, as part of our study of social nudism, we were leaders of the first three professionally conducted nude marathons. (A marathon is typically a weekend counseling session, extending from Friday night to Sunday night.) It was our desire to learn to what extent the use of nudity in a marathon situation would prove to be an effective therapeutic tool.

Nudist Society includes the results of these three nude marathons. In the chapter "Nudism as a Therapeutic Community," we report that in June 1967 two male and two female professionals assumed the responsibility for a weekend counseling session involving ten male and ten female adults who were seeking help with personal problems. Therapists referring participants felt that the nude dimension of this kind of encounter group might well provide greater movement toward resolution of personal problems than was typically to be found through the use of conventional modalities.

Both male and female participants seemed to benefit. One man, while discussing the fact that his feelings of inadequacy primarily had to do with his small penile size, burst into tears when several females spontaneously indicated that their encounter with him in the nude experience clearly demonstrated that his penis was very typical of the group in general. The women in the group indicated that the size of his penis was a relatively minor aspect of his personality rather than a major hook upon which he could attempt to hang all of his feelings of inferiority. As a result of the nude experience, this man dramatically reanalyzed his own sexuality and based his self-concept on a new and substantial foundation.

It would have been difficult, if not impossible, to achieve such a result through any more conventional method. Follow-up activities conducted six weeks later reaffirmed this therapeutic result. The same man and his wife participated some months later in another nude marathon, which they found to be very reaffirming in terms of their own feelings as sexual beings. Nudity emphasized certain aspects of their combined sexuality about which they had some feelings of inadequacy that were best dealt with therapeutically in a nude social situation.

Another dramatic illustration of how nudism may trigger emotional experience that may result in much more profoundly positive feelings about one's self as an individual and sexual being concerns a woman who had practiced nudism for years. In the first nude marathon, she experienced nudism very easily and comfortably, as would have been expected, yet the professionals responsible for the experience could not logically have expected the dramatic results which followed.

In a clothed encounter session following some nude sensitivity, body imagery, and movement under the direction of a dance instructor, several women in the group silenced the male leadership while the woman in question literally gave birth to her new self. She lay on the floor as the group watched in stunned silence, replicating all muscular and body movement typical of childbirth. Her fiancé and several women assisted as part of a real birth scene. This experience, while hard to visualize out of context, produced a new warm and responsive sexual being through a process of psychological and emotional rebirth triggered by directed therapy, which was utilizing social nudism as one of its tools. Even though the subject in this instance had previously experienced social nudism on a wide scale and was clothed at the time of the occurrence, still, according to her, the nudity proved to be an effective therapeutic tool to set the stage for a profound experience. She had had a number of previous group experiences that had not affected her in this way. She felt the structuring of the nudity in the therapeutic situation was an important difference for her from a traditional nudist situation, and after more than two and a half years she reports it to be as significant in her life as when she first experienced it.

In our first and third nude marathons, a young man who was referred by his therapist worked through both an authoritarian problem with his father and his fear of females. His sexual experience up to the time of the nude marathons had been only homosexual contacts. This did not come out in the first marathon but in the third marathon four months later. There he was accepted by the other individuals in the group, in which two men expressed their existing concern and fears of their own sexuality and feelings of negation for homosexuals and homosexual contacts. All three were able to work out their problems in the sexual area satisfactorily.

The young man who had had only homosexual contacts learned to interact with females and to be comfortable with them in holding hands, embracing, and talking to them, without the fear of having to perform sexually. Getting to know them as individuals, being accepted by them, and being reassured that they found him attractive gave him the self-confidence he needed. This recognition enabled him to accept his basic biologic self and then to reassess his own sexuality and redefine it in terms of maleness. In the follow-up six weeks later, he reported he had been able to date, felt very comfortable with females, was quite interested in a young lady in one of his ongoing therapy groups, had dropped another therapy group, had found a job, and all in all felt very positive about who he was as an individual.

The other two men in the marathon worked out their fears by

the holding of hands and embracing members of both the same and the opposite sex. They were readily able to perceive differences in how they felt in relation to males and females, and they expressed feelings of more comfort and relaxation. They found that they were much more sexually stimulated and turned on by the females than by the males that were present. The fact that one of the males had been involved with homosexual contacts added to their feeling of being able to accept other people and themselves for their own unique sexuality. They now defined themselves as being "male" and primarily interested in members of the opposite sex.

Another individual who came to the first and second nude marathons on referral from a therapist was having serious sexual problems with his wife, to such a degree that the therapist suggested that the wife move out of the home because of fear for her safety. In the nude situation, he was made comfortable with his own sexuality and nudity. He was exposed to females who made him feel more masculine, and who physically bounced his whole body up and down in the water by locking arms and lifting him up and down off the pool floor. He couldn't believe that something of this kind could ever happen to him. He defined it as the fulfillment of a fantasy. We were able to determine some of his sexual problems by using psychodramatic techniques and observing how he reacted when he took the role of himself and then of his wife. His own sexual tightness and tension became even more apparent when he informed us that this was exactly the way he felt and acted whenever he was around his wife or any other female. It was obvious to us that anybody so fearful of the opposite sex and of his own sexuality would certainly have difficulty in a marital situation. A considerable amount of work was done in the first marathon to help him overcome some of his problems. This included not only nudity but sensitivity, touch, eyeballing, body movement, and psychodrama. Some of the foregoing were done in a hot (100°) pool.

He returned after the second marathon for the six-week follow-up, and the therapist felt that he had been able to work through his sexual problems to the extent that his wife should now be able to come home. The last contact we had with him sometime later indicated that he was functioning well at home and that his marriage was intact.

One of the male participants, whose masculinity was profoundly influenced by the nude experience, was slightly over six feet tall and weighed something over two hundred pounds. He was a fine appearing man in his thirties who could easily be mistaken for an all-American linebacker. He was referred to the nude marathon because of his shy, retiring behavior and inability to express feelings and emotions either positive or negative. He seemed to have had little difficulty being sexually involved with women but had somewhat greater difficulty interacting with them meaningfully, particularly on a verbal level. In addition, he had trouble taking any aggressive part in relating to members of either sex. In a sentence, he didn't "feel like a man."

He attended a weekend session in which he participated in nude therapy with emphasis on touch and movement. In one particular scene he expressed so much physical hostility in giving vent to his new-found feelings that it required the combined strength of the male participants present to contain his movements. Once the hostility was openly expressed, he was no longer afraid of his feelings. This man reported in a follow-up session several months later that he was much more comfortable with his masculinity, was able to verbally stand up for himself, and his sexual involvements had taken a deeper, more mature meaning for him. He noted that in his interaction with both men and women he was much more desirous of being a willing and effective participant rather than remaining in his old shell. It was not only the nude dimension of the weekend but the professional help in his self-emergence that seemed to make him so much more comfortable with himself as a person.

Wholesome sexuality does not exist in shells and vacuums but rather in positive interaction. Nudity helped this man feel like a male and facilitated change toward greater comfort with, and expression of, his masculinity. It is entirely possible that he might have been helped in some more traditional method of therapy; however, the referring therapist, the man himself, and the professionals conducting the nude marathon, all felt that in all probability the progress made could not have resulted without the use of a profound catalyst, such as nudity and professional direction through many hours of therapy during the marathon. His therapist felt that nudity had been the major impetus for the dramatic movement that had not been accomplished previously with traditional methods.

A female participant in the nude marathon was brought by a

friend who learned that the sex ratio was not equal and that an additional female was needed. (The therapists considered it important for clients to learn how to relate not only to the same sex but opposite sex, and it was decided that this could best be facilitated with an equal sex ratio.) Her dating pattern had been one of insecurity; therefore, she only dated young men in their late teens, even though she was in her mid-thirties. She expressed feelings that anybody her own age would not find her sexually attractive, and that if a young individual rejected her, this was less of a blow to her age. While she did not attend the six-week follow-up, she did send word that there had been considerable change in her dating pattern; she was going out with men her own age, felt much more comfortable in their company, and was generally much more open and outgoing toward the opposite sex. People who knew her verified this.

Possibly her most profound experience over the weekend was when she stood nude in front of a full-length mirror while colored light patterns were projected onto her body. She had felt that she was ugly and unattractive, and would not previously permit herself to view her body while nude. The other participants were very supportive of her physical self and dimensions, which would be regarded as quite average statistically. As this young woman touched various parts of her body, as if to feel the material that was projected by the colored lights, she reported that she perceived herself to be not nearly so ugly and unattractive as she had felt for so many years. The fact that a number of other individuals, who had not known her previously and could have no ulterior motive for saying so, indicated that she certainly was average in physical attractiveness added to her self-acceptance. It was further suggested that if she would attempt to make herself as attractive personality-wise as she was physically, she might well get rid of many of her feelings of rejection and loneliness. Follow-up information about this young woman seemed clearly to document the fact that the counseling was essential to her, particularly the group reaffirmation of her own self-worth. The nude dimension itself acted as a catalyst and seemed to have more to do with her movement toward feeling worthwhile as a sexual being than any other modality utilized in the weekend counseling experience.

These cases reflect the significance not only of the use of nudity to enhance sexuality and feeling of worth as a person but also of professional guidance during nude therapy. The professional elicits and directs emergence of clients' feelings about their sexuality. It should be clear from this presentation that, with professional direction, nudity can be a very worthwhile therapeutic tool.

One weekend marathon was devoted specifically to married couples, although one male from a former marathon and a professional woman were allowed to join the group of four couples. It was our desire to see, when spouses spent a weekend together, to what extent nudity would be helpful in resolving problems that they presented as well as in enhancing their feelings of sexuality and self-worth.

We prepared a special five-page questionnaire including more than fifty specific items in an attempt to determine the effectiveness of this nude marathon with couples. While it is not possible to attach any statistical significance to the completed questionnaires because of the small sample size, it is possible to summarize the main benefits reported. The individuals reported a better self-image, more openness with others, a closer relationship to the spouse, greater acceptance of themselves as persons, greater degree of freedom in touching other people, greater ability to resolve conflicts between sexual and sensual feelings, and resolution of sexual curiosity. In the follow-up session, held as usual six weeks after the marathon, participants reported the same degree of maintenance of growth as in the first two nude marathons. One man specifically said it had made a profound difference in his marriage.

Where professionals choose to use nudity as a catalyst to facilitate changes in feelings of worth and value as an individual, these changes almost inevitably result in the client's being more comfortable with his or her own sexual self and more comfortable in relating to other individuals as sexual beings. It is difficult to separate therapeutic means in any area of the human personality without these, in turn, being related to improvement in this area labeled "sexuality." It seems probable that most therapists would regard any improvement in personality, wherein one becomes more comfortable with one's self and with others, to be synonomous with enhancement of one's own sexuality.

One of the other people responsible for the first two nude marathons was Paul Bindrim, a Los Angeles psychologist. He has conducted more nude sensitivity sessions and marathons than anyone else in America. In the first two and a half years after the first nude marathon in June 1967, Bindrim conducted approximately seventy separate group sessions with nudity as a major catalyst. In the same period approximately fifty other therapists have also used nudity as part of their professional work, specifically announcing in advance that nudity will be part of a particular program. Bindrim has published two articles dealing with his experience in conducting nude marathon and sensitivity groups, "A Report on a Nude Marathon: The Effect of Physical Nudity on the Practice of Interaction in Marathon Groups"[3] and "Nudity as a Quick Grab for Intimacy in Group Therapy."[4] In this last article, he wrote, "Frigid females, impotent males, and sexual exhibitionists have become at least temporarily symptom free [p. 28]." Certainly this would be a significant aspect of overt sexual functioning.

Bindrim estimates that between one third and one half of the participants have reported specific improvements in the overt aspects of their sexual functioning following his nude therapy groups. He also indicates that during the last several years as many as one thousand group leaders throughout the country have taken a more permissive attitude toward nudity occurring in their groups. Individuals and entire groups have experienced varying degrees of nudity, usually complete, with or without the group leader's specific consent. The inference here is that, in effective group functioning, where a great degree of cohesiveness and intimacy is achieved, nudity often becomes a very acceptable emergent type of behavior, although not previously scheduled or expected either by group leaders or participants. It appears that the more widespread use, by chance or design, of nudity in group therapy is not only on the upswing but, from limited knowledge currently available, is making significant contributions to positive therapeutic results in all aspects of human personality, including sexuality.

Persons interested in various aspects of nude group experiences may find a paper by Stephen B. Lawrence,[5] another therapist who has utilized nudity in his work, of interest.

NON-ORGASMIC WOMEN

A third major source of information about use of nudism in enhancing sexuality came from our three-year study of non-orgasmic women. The research included fifty-seven non-orgasmic women, about one-third of whom became orgasmic during the process of the research. We found, first, that it was most important how these individuals felt about themselves. Over and over again, the clue would come through loud and clear, "I'm such a worthless human being. I can't do anything good in life in any area, including sex." The research findings indicated that, until a woman had the feeling that she was worthwhile enough to be able to respond sexually, it was fruitless to attempt therapy designed to produce habitually orgastic behavior patterns. It was at this point that the use of nudity, with the individual touching and talking about each aspect of her anatomy, was a most effective way to improve her self-concept, sexuality, and finally sexual functioning.

It should not be inferred that hang-ups precluding positive feeling of sexuality always deal with sex organs per se. One woman who was seeking help in attempting to achieve habitual sexual climax was not at all inhibited to stand nude in front of a mirror but was reluctant when asked to remove her shoes. The symbolic meaning of the feet cannot be overemphasized. To have a strong, pleasant, and aesthetic foundation for one's personality and sexuality is important. While nudity was easily experienced, this particular young woman required several follow-up interviews before she was willing to remove her shoes and expose "the ugliest feet in existence." When her shoes were finally removed, and thus complete nudity achieved, she was somewhat at a loss to explain the details of the ugliness of her feet. They appeared no different than the feet of other women her age, but her feelings could not be changed until her feet were exposed, and she touched and expressed her feelings about her feet. This case clearly reflects the need for complete physical nudity without the inference that one's hang-up may necessarily be culturally determined to reflect conditioning about sex organs per se.

SEXUAL DYSFUNCTION

The fourth and final source of data refers to sexually dysfunctioning couples. It grew out of the study of non-orgasmic women, the study of social nudism, and the sexual research and counseling conducted at our research center. We found in research projects that individuals had great difficulty in perceiving themselves objectively, especially when clothed. This was particularly true with reference to sex organs. Unless mirrors were strategically used to give an objective nude view and to place realistic emphasis on the genitalia, it was extremely difficult for an individual to be fair with himself concerning the size of his or her genitalia and its possible comparison with others'.

Maslow was the first psychologist to suggest that simple nudity in the presence of others might be very therapeutic, particularly when a professionally trained person is present to bring feelings to the conscious level. It followed from this that greater transparency of one's emotional self might well be enhanced through the use of nudity. Maslow referred to the possible therapeutic value of nudism when he stated, "I still think that nudism, simply going naked before a lot of other people, is itself a kind of therapy, especially if we can be conscious of it, that is, if there is a skilled person around to direct what's going on, to bring things to consciousness."[6]

It has been previously noted that nudity need not necessarily refer just to exposure of the forbidden sexual parts of the human anatomy. We find it true in our culture that hangups usually have to do with the revelation to others of one's sexual parts; however, this is not always inevitably true. We find in working with sexually dysfunctioning couples that faces and feet, commonly exposed in our culture, often have symbolic meaning, that profoundly affects one's sexuality. To be a "faceless" creature is often to have such a feeling of inadequacy that it may cause problems of potency. In such a case, working with nudity but with emphasis on the face is often more significant than dealing with the genitalia per se. With one partially impotent male, this approach was particularly helpful.

The feet are likewise important in terms of providing a basic foundation for the human personality. We have noted that, when individuals are asked to "draw a person" involving a frontal nude view of themselves and their spouse, often there is no room left on the sheet of drawing paper for the feet. Often the sexuality is there but is floating around in the clouds, so to speak, and unless it can be tied down to a meaningful foundation, the individual is baseless.

In order to enhance feeling about the self, we evolved a system whereby we ask the individual to begin by placing the hands on his or her head and reporting what he or she feels about this experience. The client is then instructed to proceed down from the top of the head to the bottom of the feet, touching every aspect of his or her physical being and reporting the resultant feelings. This procedure is based on the idea attributed to Freud that the images one has about oneself come from the basic biological image. The importance of this being done nude cannot be overemphasized. With only a male and female therapist present, the individual is encouraged to be honest about the feelings elicited, not only visually but tactiley. They are encouraged not only to feel but to examine closely various parts of their own bodies so that they become comfortable, not only with looking, but with touching various parts.

A further way of enhancing sexuality in treating spouses for sexual dysfunction is to ask a husband or wife to touch that part of the anatomy of their spouse that he or she likes best. It is most significant that, with rather high frequency, the specific area of the anatomy that an individual feels negative about with reference to himself, is often, if not usually, the area of the body the spouse likes best. For example, a woman who expressed negative feelings about her small breasts was pleasantly surprised when her husband indicated preference for that part of her physical being. (At no time is the spouse informed about the mate's negative feelings. To divulge such information, which could be used as a possible club by a spouse, would definitely be contraindicated.)

A wife touched her husband's face as representing the most appealing aspect of his anatomy for her. He himself had expressed very negative feelings about his face and had drawn himself as faceless. The reassurance to his ego greatly affected his feeling of masculinity and was one factor in helping him to be able to function sexually.

Repeatedly, this phenomenon manifested itself while we were working with sexually dysfunctioning couples. It is our experience that it is essential that this procedure be done nude. Profound changes in one's feelings about self, about one's own sexuality, about one's spouse, and about one's spouse's sexuality can result in the use of this technique with or by trained professional counselors or therapists. Our work has always been done with a male-female therapy team present together at all times.

This approach is further utilized by having each spouse give the other a facial massage, foot massage, or complete body massage. To enhance one's sexuality with reference to overt sexual functioning with the spouse is a very positive and desirable goal. To learn to communicate nonverbally, with positive, warm feelings and emotions flowing between spouses, is accomplished most simply by using oils and lotions and giving spouses proper directions about how to communicate with each other without any words being spoken. Comfort with both their nudity and with touching one another in giving and receiving affection without talking is important. Learning to be sensitive to the feedback one receives when giving the massage is a very effective way of learning to communicate nonverbally. This type of interaction as well as good verbal communication is essential to positive sexual functioning.

Several efforts are currently underway to determine the extent to which sexually dysfunctional couples can be helped in an intensive one-day effort. Results on the first attempt were inconclusive. Nudity, sensitivity, massage, and hypno-suggestion were used. Questionnaire data completed at the end of the session and six weeks later suggested that all aspects were experienced easily, including nudity, with no negation or traumatic incidents. Gains in the area of sexuality, however, suggested more on the covert level of feeling than the overt level of activity in the weeks following the all-day session. The inconclusive results suggest that intensive work with individual couples may be more beneficial than group therapy for specific sexual dysfunctioning.

SUMMARY

In conclusion, through the enhancement of human sexuality we seek to improve the quality of human interaction and, thus, produce something of more substantial quality in terms of what transpires on our human scene. It is noted that no negative experiences have ever been witnessed by, or reported to, the authors where the use of nudity to enhance sexuality was concerned. No experience of nudity resulted in traumatic instances or in psychotic or antisocial behavior. Responsible educators and therapists use potent catalysts and learning devices with proper caution. Professionals concerned with enhancing sexuality are properly interested in new tools to do a more effective job. In this context, nudity, properly used, may be one of the most potent currently available.

CHAPTER NOTES

1. William E. Hartman, Marilyn A. Fithian, and Donald Johnson, *Nudist Society* (New York: Crown Publishers, 1970).

2. William E. Hartman and Marilyn A. Fithian, "The Problem of Non-Orgasmic Woman in Man's Modern World," (Paper presented to the National Council on Family Relations, New Orleans, 1968).

3. Paul Bindrim, "A Report on a Nude Marathon: The Effect of Physical Nudity on the Practice of Interaction in Marathon Groups," *Psychotherapy Theory Research and Practice*, 5 (September, 1968) : 180–188.

4. Paul Bindrim, "Nudity as a Quick Grab for Intimacy in Group Therapy," *Psychology Today* (June, 1969) : 24–28.

5. Stephen B. Lawrence, "Video Tape and Other Therapeutic Procedures with Nude Marathons," *American Psychologist*, 24 (April, 1969) : 476–479.

6. Abraham H. Maslow, *Eupsychian Management* (Homewood, Ill.: Irwin-Dorsey Press, 1965), p. 160. See also a discussion of emotional transparency in Sidney M. Jourard, *The Transparent Self* (Princeton, N.J.: D. Van Nostrand Co., 1964).

PART III

SEX AND LIFE-STYLE

Chapter 10

SEXUAL LIFE-STYLES
AND FULFILLMENTS

By John F. Cuber, Ph.D.

It seems reasonable to assume that there is some kind of linkage between one's life-style and the kinds and quality of the fulfillments that one experiences. Before discussing this linkage, we must first clarify the concepts "life-style" and "fulfillment."

A life-style is a reasonably objective phenomenon. It can be observed at least in part by the outsider and can usually be described in its more intimate dimensions by the participants in it. A life-style has many dimensions, and comes into existence and is perpetuated through the interaction of a number of factors or valences.

As the term sexual life-style is used here, it refers to a person's or pair's complex of attitudes, purposes, and overt actions, as well as to the satisfactions and frustrations that are intertwined. It seems reasonable to identify at least two major components of any sexual life-style: (1) The persons enacting a life-style have a certain identity, often called "personality," which is a product of their life history and is typically in process of becoming somewhat different as life unfolds. An important ingredient of this personality are sets of preferences (often called "values"), more or less established habits, and sets of skills and abilities. When the circumstances in which a personality is functioning permit the expression of the person's values, do not seriously confront his attitudes, and permit and encourage him to express his abilities, he feels fulfilled, happy, content. To the degree that any of these are thwarted, he is frustrated, unfulfilled. (2) The sexual personality functions in a context—a mate or lack of one; the mate's personality; conditions external to the pair, such as laws, degree of privacy, attitudes of peers, responsibilities to others such as children and parents, and the requirements of careers. Any of these or some combination may make it easy or difficult for a personality to express or inhibit itself.

In the light of the foregoing model it should be clear that a life-style, sexual or any other kind, is likely to be something of a compromise for all participants. Certain components may either set limits on or enhance the others. Thus, in simplistic terms, if a man's personality is aggrandizing and the wife's personality is ascetic where sexual matters are concerned, the actual life-style of the pair should not be expected to be a reflection of either's personality alone.

Important influences external to the pair may also be highly influential. In one instance a highly erotic man is married to highly erotic woman, and one would expect a very aggrandizing sex life. Actually, a very inhibited, frustrated, and atrophied sexual life-style emerged—and lasted for twenty-five years. The wife's widowed, semi-invalid, and totally dependent mother became the central figure in the household. The couple could afford only a small apartment and nothing that anyone did was private. The older woman, moreover, was very moralistic and negative where sex was concerned. The actual life-style, then, was one of infrequent, silent, and frustrating sexual expression. In other instances, the demands of a job—time demands, energy drainage, prolonged separation—preclude the kind of sexual patterns that one would logically expect, given the personalities of the mates.

External circumstances, of course, may be facilitative quite as much as restrictive. The right mate, rewarding employment, sufficient affluence, and satisfying interpersonal relationships may be very helpful to achievement of sexual life-styles that are compatible with personality needs.

SEXUALLY EXPRESSIVE LIFE-STYLES

Probably the central component of any sexually expressive life-style is a positive attitude toward sex and its expression. Sexually expressive people value sex intrinsically, and sexual expression is considered to be an important life goal. Such persons desire not merely a high frequency but also a high quality of sexual expression. Two quite different subtypes are omnipresent—monogamous and polygamous. Some sexual expressives are adequately fulfilled in a monogamous context, whether married or unmarried. These persons are able to find sexual fulfillment over long periods, possibly even a lifetime, with a single individual. To illustrate: a man of thirty established a satisfying sexual relationship with a woman of twenty-five, first clandestine but later ending in marriage. At ages sixty and fifty-five, the hours they spend in bed together still constitute the ultimate of life experience for both of them. Sex is still exciting, mysterious, and each is on the alert for something new that will add to the ecstasy. Their fulfillments are difficult to miss. According to their own testimony, they are spared the conventional uncertainties and ambivalence about sex. They aren't concerned about whether it is wrong to enjoy sex so much, or whether some newly discovered position is genteel. The physiological aspects of sex are unqualifiedly anticipated, enjoyed, and remembered. They are not impressed that by this age many of their friends find sex dull or don't find it at all. There is also fulfillment, sometimes very deep, in the fact that this is not their first intimate relationship, and so comparisons with the less fortunate days are more than a little comforting.

Polygamous patterns are also prominent in the expressive life-styles. It is difficult from the evidence available to determine whether sexually expressive life-styles are more likely to be polygamous or monogamous patterns. Anyone aware of current realities in the man-woman world is aware that what have traditionally been considered aberrations are widely known and practiced—for example, the pick-up, mate-swapping, affairs of various types and durations, group sex parties, and communal sex arrangements. The evidence seems clear that there exists in American society a solid core of persons who rationally accept such forms of sexual expression, follow one or another of them for substantial periods of their lives, and recommend them to others.

There is an appreciable number of married couples in their middle years who openly acknowledge that they have not found sexual fulfillment in the monogamous pattern. They join the ranks of unmarrieds or no longer marrieds in various expressive sexual patterns. There is a growing literature both popular and at least quasi-scientific that documents their efforts to find fulfillment through new social forms; mate-swapping, "swinging," and bi-sexuality are widely discussed. The typical pattern here is for a married couple, by agreement with one another, to participate in parties whose purpose is to provide sexual opportunities that they feel are more fulfilling. This may involve a shuffling of mates for the evening, either for completed intercourse or merely for erotic behavior short of completed intercourse. These activities may take place in groups, with heterosexual, homosexual, or bisexual behavior, as opportunities and impulses permit. From the information available about them, it appears that they are quite varied as to which rules of the game are observed, how well the rules are enforced, and how permanent or transitory the participating groups are. What all have in common, however, is an effort on the part of couples, who are not satisfied with their monogamous opportunities, to embellish the erotic fulfillments while remaining married. These patterns, while not entirely new, appear to be more frequent and more open. The underground newspapers, for example, regularly carry advertisements announcing the availability of persons, couples, or groups for such activities. No one knows, of course, how general these activities are. Estimates vary enormously but no one can deny that the motivations and the patterns are widespread. Even less is known reliably about how much and which kind of fulfillments these activities provide for the participants. It is reported that some persons and couples become disillusioned and cease participation, although the clear tendency is to continue the pattern once inducted into it. Whether the participants actually find the fulfillments they seek is not wholly known either, although the presumption is that patterns that continue and grow are in some way satisfying to the participants.

Ingenuity in the invention of life-styles that are deviant from majority practice and from legal and ecclesiastical proscriptions results in a number of minority sexual life-styles. For example, there are the campus live-ins, student couples living in *de facto* marriage but not legally married. In large cities this is apparently not a difficult arrangement to work out, and one unpublished study indicates that at least half of such students are known by their parents to be so living. The majority do not intend to get married; the relationships were entered into and maintained for a variety of reasons varying from deep love to such practical considerations as having steady sexual companionship and a reduced cost of living. At a somewhat older age level are the monogamous non-marrieds—the modern mistress and her man. A number of these relationships, without enforcement by law or public opinion, remain monogamous simply because they are fulfilling to the participants. Among singles there is the essentially drifting life-style —pairings for short periods, sometimes only for a night. Sometimes persons so living form lasting attachments and possibly marry, but others develop this as a permanent way of life.

SEXUALLY NON-EXPRESSIVE LIFE-STYLES

In clear and consistent juxtaposition to the expressive life-styles is one that, for lack of a better term, we shall call "non-expressive." Almost everything about the non-expressive is the antithesis of the expressive. The common element is that sex is defined negatively. This negative orientation is not necessarily explicit or expressed in any dramatic or overt terms. But nonetheless sexually non-expressive people, in one way or another, reject the sexual component as an important phase of life, if only by stressing something else. Sexually non-expressive life-styles are evolved by at least two separable types of people. The first is simply low in sexual affect. He is not non-expressive because he actively rejects sex; he is not actively negative; he is merely apathetic to sex. In one illustrative case the man is vigorous, healthy, athletic, and clearly the "outdoor type." He has from late adolescence had a great interest in children and devoted a great deal of his time and resources to enterprises designed to be helpful to children who have been deprived of natural opportunities. His first engagement was terminated because his fiancé became apprehensive about his lack of erotic interest. In a subsequent marriage to a slightly older woman, a strongly maternal type, he established a very satisfying life-style based primarily upon mutual recreational interests, children, and a high career accent. As he says, "I don't get all this preoccupation about sex. Of course, it's natural, like eating or sleeping or all the other biological functions—but why all the big attention?"

In another case a sexually apathetic personality seems to have been the outcome of disillusionment. The woman appeared in her teens and early twenties to be a "normal" woman where erotic matters were concerned. In her mid-twenties, she went through a period of sexual experimentation but her intention was to find, through her experimentation, a monogamous mate. She failed in this. Her "real love" married another woman. Then, after a number of liaisons, she felt she was being exploited. Another serious affair was terminated because the man refused to be monogamous. Now, in her early forties, she is oriented to an essentially asexual world. Even though still very attractive, she rarely dates, and when she does go out, she does not show any interest in sexual activity.

The second type of non-expressive is more extreme—it consists of those whose life-style is actively repressive and suppressive, rather than merely ascetic or apathetic. These persons, for whatever reason, turn their backs on the sexual side of life, sometimes with a vengeance.

An instructive case is that of a woman who, although very attractive, had shown no erotic interest whatsoever in any man. She was the only daughter of a highly moralistic, fundamentalist-religious father and a totally ineffectual mother. The father was completely satisfied that sex was the root of evil for young people and was deeply proud that his daughter had rejected it—even to the extent of dating rarely. Ultimately this woman married a fundamentalist minister who shared her negative and repressive attitudes about sex. She said that her attraction to him was based upon the fact that he made the least insistent sexual demands of any man she had ever known. Both are actively engaged in suppression of sex education materials and in any open discussion of sex or artistic expression of it. They do not view transgressors of the traditional moral code with any measure of tolerance.

Psychiatrists, clinical psychologists, and others who are familiar with sexual pathology typically emphasize that among the sexually repressives are people who are seriously psychologically ill. They can illustrate with abundant cases that sexually repressive people are the products of parental mismanagement and/or traumatic life experience. From the evidence at hand it is clear that such outcomes are by no means uncommon. But from the total evidence it should be stressed that in addition to these instances there are many, many others whose etiology is not so clearly neurotic. They are simply personalities that develop without visible parental mismanagement or traumatic experience in ways that depreciate the sexual component. Whether the products of more or less typical life disillusionment, physiologically low sex affect, failure to be awakened, or some other reason, they simply couldn't care less about sex.

It should not be assumed, however, from this description of sexually non-expressive life-styles, that frequency of sexual expression is always low for these people. Even for the sexually non-expressive, sexually provocative situations arise from time to time—and subconsciously they may even induce them. Drinking or exposure to certain conventional social customs such as dancing may result in accidentally stimulating situations and, in spite of conscious intention, in sexual encounters. But even then the experience tends to be negative—especially so in retrospect. So the experience is not savored, the satisfaction is not deliberately sought again, and the memory is not a positive one. In short, the sexual life-style is essentially non-expressive, even if the repression is not always sufficiently strong to achieve total suppression of sexual feelings and actions.

SEXUALLY AMBIVALENT LIFE-STYLES

If there is any cogency to the view that persons are products of their society, then it should be anticipated that sexually ambivalent persons should be exceedingly common—almost to be regarded as "normal." Using the concept "ambivalent" to mean that opposite ideas and incongruous actions are manifest characteristics of a person or a pair, this construction best describes the sexual life-style of a great portion of contemporary Americans —quite possibly the majority. Despite clear differences among them, there is one pervasive and inescapable condition that identifies them: an almost frantic effort to embrace ideas and actions that simply do not fit together. The contemporary individual in American society is exposed to a kaleidoscope of contradicting sexual models, images, rationales, and forms of expression. Controversy about sexual expression is rife. It engulfs almost everyone. Evaluations of the couple next door, the activities of the state legislature torn in some conflict over legislation regarding sex, or the latest scandal—all contribute to an unending dialogue in which the agonies and the ecstasies associated with sex are vividly portrayed. Meanwhile, the gaps widen not only between generations but also between the ideologies and practices of age and class peers. Almost everyone is aware that laws and moral dicta are violated with impunity, and no punishments (or very token and rare ones) follow for the violators. There is little agreement as to what the standards are or ought to be. In any community one finds people for whom sex means an ever diligent effort to achieve repression and, at the other extreme, persons for whom sex means one or another kind of ultimate human achievement. Moreover, some people regard sex as a primarily private experience, of concern solely to the consenting partners, while other people are preoccupied with ways and means of repressing or regulating every aspect of the sexual expression of others.

Ideally the clearly expressives solve the societal problem by closing out one set of influences, the clearly non-expressives by closing out the other set. But a majority cannot, or at least do not, find it possible to consistently solve the problem in this way. For some the orientation to sex is intellectually and sociologically explainable. Some represent subcultural traditions which de-emphasize sex as a recreational activity. Both the traditional Catholic and Protestant faiths, under the strong impact of Paulistic thinking, embrace this ideology. The ascetic stance is simply and clearly the good life, and the rationale has the sanction of a long and respected cultural heritage. One does not deny that he has a carnal nature; he merely restrains it in order to achieve a superior personal achievement. For many, satisfaction comes from control and inhibition of action, feeling, or communication regarding sex. The positive goals of life lie somewhere else, and for these people the top priorities are focused on activities other than sex. Sex education is an exercise in the inculcation of essentially negative and inhibitive control in the personalities of children. And, given the premises, this is logical. If sex is a manifestation of the baser nature of man, then when one yields to such impulses, he does so with reluctance and certainly derives little fulfillment from embellishing or aggrandizing the sensations that occur.

Another substantial segment of the American public prides itself on being open-minded, unwilling to close out either view totally. The sensitive individual can't close out either part of the dialogue—the conversation is too dramatic, too pervasive, and one is aware that he lives in a pelvically conscious world and a manifestly hedonistic one. Yet idealism and a sense of propriety based upon tradition are by no means dead, so the typical individual is caught in a quite understandable effort to integrate two opposite traditions, both of which have a seductive quality about them. When it comes to implementation, failures are often overwhelming. Here are a few typical configurations:

One couple had been married for three years and had found that sex had begun to dull. Friends invited them into a swinging group that they at first found very satisfying. Their sex activity within the marriage, they reported, also improved. After a time, however, guilt, shame, and fear lest the children later find out began to gnaw away at the relationship. Quarrels became more general, and ultimately there was a divorce. They somehow couldn't carry off the consequences of the emancipation of which they were at first so proud.

Another couple, very intellectual, serious-minded, and religious, were well mated along essentially non-expressive lines. Their lives were dominated by interests other than sex, and their children were reared humanely but repressively. When the children came in contact with the outside world, however, they became essentially strangers to their parents, rebellious, completely unsympathetic to their parents' intentions. In cases like these, parents seldom get a second chance.

A third couple had been sexually expressive from high school on. Both had had a wide variety of sexual experiences in high school and college, and prided themselves on their sexual sophistication and the fact that they had been fortunate enough to find each other. After marriage it seemed only natural to continue the emancipated way. Monogamy seemed no more appropriate then than it did earlier. "We had no hang-ups; we were honest with each other and with others; no one got hurt." Through an unfortunate exposure (the police broke up a mate-trading party where marijuana was suspected), newspaper publicity severely threatened the man's career, brought the children embarrassment and a probably lasting alienation from their parents.

A fourth couple had an essentially traditional upbringing but felt considerable misgivings about its adequacy for their children's generation. "They need to have more freedom—they're living in a more emancipated world." The children were provided with that freedom. Few restrictions were imposed, and before the parents quite knew what had happened, their children exceeded even liberal limits. The daughter became a campus "push-over." Moreover, she flaunted her emancipation by talking about it and boasting that her parents didn't care. The son, a freshman in college, began living with an older woman who had a reputation in the community as a prostitute. Obviously, this was not what the parents meant by "more freedom." They simply underestimated the linkage of op-

portunities and the "liberal" ideas about sex that they tried to pass
on to their children. Their attempt to be more "modern"—quite
possibly because it was not genuine to them—brought fulfillment
to no one.

Ironic outcomes such as these are by no means unusual. What
they all have in common is the inability of people to integrate the
paradoxes presented by a Janus-like society. Put tersely, and hopefully not too simply, the conditions of the sexually ambivalent are
the result of two conditions which are very difficult to avoid:
(1) more, and more open exposure to, justification of both the
expressives and the repressives, both of whom make a strong case
for their life styles, and (2) the forces of social change that con-
tinuously introduce new and sometimes unmanageable factors
into the life equation—the pill, the *"Playboy* philosophy," wider
mobility, secularization, to name only a few.

FULFILLMENTS

The linkage between fulfillment, attitude, and behavior has
proven hard to discover. Persons with high sexual appetites and
frequencies, who value sex as a prime life goal, are sometimes
deeply fulfilled, healthy, creative, and sociable. In other instances
their quest for proper partners and environments for expressing
such a preoccupation results in manifest frustration, if not trag-
edy. Thus, given a sexual profile, one cannot predict with any
confidence whether the individual will find fulfillment or unful-
fillment. At least part of the reason for this inability to prognosti-
cate accurately is, of course, that one does not fully know the
circumstances—personal, communal, occupational, and so on—
within which a sexual syndrome must express itself.

It is obvious, of course, that sexual needs are frequently frustrated by the circumstances of a particular mating. Merely because
a life-style exists and is tacitly accepted by the participants in it
cannot be accepted as *prima facie* evidence that it is fulfilling. To
illustrate, a couple in the middle years with five children have a
sexual life-style of an essentially non-expressive type. Intercourse
occurs typically once a week at a specified time. It is brief, minimally satisfying to the husband, as to the wife. The husband,
however, is of a more sexually expressive personality type. He
would like more gaity, more spontaneity, more prolongation of sex.
He is not really fulfilled by the assignment of sex to the half-hour

compartment of every week, but he tries to be reasonable and says that sexual excitement really belongs to kids, or at least to the younger marrieds. The wife's personality is not really fulfilled either. She, too, tries to be reasonable, by which she means that a man's sexual appetites ought to be satisfied; that if she denies him, he might seek expression elsewhere. The experience is not really offensive to her but she "could live about as well without it." Here is a life-style of a decade or more duration that is likely to continue but that is sexually satisfying to neither party and expresses neither's personality.

Attention must be given to total fulfillment as well as to strictly sexual fulfillment. People vary enormously as to how much of the total life fulfillment can properly be considered sexual. The non-expressive of any subtype does not expect or get much sexual fulfillment, whatever his overt life style. And even, as in the case of some of the expressives, when some are forced to settle for less emphasis on sex than they would like, they find it quite easy to rationalize their sexual deprivations as necessary to the achievement of other life fulfillments—the demands of career, responsibilities to children, civic duties, recreational and companionship satisfactions.

Superficially, it would seem that if one follows a pattern that he is free to change, then that path is fulfilling. Yet it may not be. As in the case above, the wife who submits to sex more often or in ways that she does not prefer may over long periods simply suffer through an habitual pattern of indignities, presumably because she can see no other way to manage her life. She wishes to hold her husband, keep the family intact, and she is willing to pay this sexual price. Even in cases of a very different nature, for instance in some cases of the swingers, the participants may have fallen into the habit of following this recreational pattern as people do other patterns, not really quite knowing or caring to know how they might find something better. Students of recreational patterns have frequently pointed out that many people continue a robot-like practice of an activity, once established, almost unconsciously. They don't even think about fulfillments or opportunities—it's just the thing to do.

Fulfillments when? A sexual life-style—any life-style—can be deeply fulfilling for a period of time and then cease to be. This is notoriously true of marriages but is also true of non-married life-styles. Not all those, for example, whose life-styles are currently non-expressive have always been so. Some quite rationally reassess the patterns, readjust themselves, and seek a life-style that is more compatible with reality as it has unfolded for them. Said one, "I don't say this to complain ... it's just that there's a cycle to life. ... I'll admit that I do sometimes yern for the old days when sex was a big thing. ... But then you get the children and other responsibilities ... you just have to adjust to these things." Thus, any realistic assessment of fulfillments must take into account the longitudinal dimension, not only how fulfilling but for how long.

Moreover, sexual fulfillments for the direct participants are frequently unequal. Exploitation is far more prevalent than is generally realized, whether or not anyone so intends it. Some persons are deeply offended when they become aware that they are the subject or object of exploitation; others seem not much concerned. There is widespread evidence, however, that both men and women use sex in a variety of ways to achieve other purposes—in marriage and out. Is this fulfillment? For whom? And compared to whom?

Finally, one irrefutable fact needs to be emphasized. Lasting, deep sexual fulfillment is rare in present American society regardless of the particular life-style. The inability of married couples to find sexual fulfillment in their marriages has been so widely publicized that little comment need be added. What is less widely recognized is that the gay, naughty, seemingly exciting kinds of life-styles frequently involve the same kinds of nonfulfillment and dull routine as occur in many marriages, and persons have almost the same inability to work themselves out of their felt predicaments. Disillusionment and cynicism about sex are exceedingly common and sometimes these very attitudes stand in the way. They prejudice the person—man or woman—against realizing the potentials that may exist. "Sex," says one, "is a practical joke on the human race." So general is this attitude that it is not uncommon to find intelligent, educated adults who flatly deny that it is possible to find deep and recurring sexual fulfillment in the middle years. That there are persons and couples for whom this is manifestly untrue is simply not recognized. It is not too difficult to understand, however, why sexual fulfillment is as rare as it is, given the conditions within which sex must be expressed. It would be reassuring to many, no doubt, if one could present an authoritative set of conditions or criteria that, if met, could give a reasonable assurance of high sexual fulfillment. To our knowledge, no such set of specifications can authoritatively be given.

Chapter 11

SEX AND MARITAL ENRICHMENT

By David R. Mace, Ph.D.

*Sex has a creative worth to accomplish ... in form-
ing the union between man and woman which is the
crown of wedded love.*

E. D. HUTCHINSON[1]

The widespread use today of the term "marriage enrichment" reflects the abandonment of the static concept of marriage in favor
of a dynamic concept. The aim is no longer just to keep marriage
intact, but to promote the growth of the relationship, together with
corresponding fulfillment and personal growth in the partners.
These new and higher levels of expectation are causing much discontent in marriage and many divorces; but at the same time they
are motivating many husbands and wives to strive together for a
broadening and deepening of their marital interaction, in a quest
for what I like to call "relationship-in-depth."

The concept of marriage enrichment is therefore tending to
replace the former concept of stabilizing or "saving" marriages.
The two are not, of course, mutually exclusive or antithetical. The
view is being increasingly taken that the best way, and in many
instances the *only* way, to marital stability is through marriage
enrichment. In other words, in our freer world of today marriages
are less and less likely to be held together by external coercion and
must therefore be cemented by internal cohesion.

The question before us in this chapter is, therefore, how far and in what specific ways can the sexual component in marriage contribute to the enrichment of the entire relationship between husband and wife?

THE SEXUAL REVOLUTION

We are emerging today from a long, dark era of negative thinking about our sexual nature. For something approaching fifteen hundred years our Western Christian culture saw sex mainly as a dangerous force in human nature—a force that, if not actually evil, could easily become an occasion of sin. We are speaking here not of sex *outside* marriage but of sex *in* marriage.

At the beginning of our present scientific era, the official teaching of the Christian church about sex in marriage was something like this: Sexual intercourse was a regrettable necessity, and the desire that prompted it was the vehicle by which original sin was transferred from one generation to the next. It could not therefore be pleasing to God. However, since it was the means by which children were brought into the world, and that *was* pleasing to God, the married couple might legitimately use it for the purpose of procreation. This they should do, however, in a cold and mechanical manner, with a minimum of passion. There was no other manner in which sexual intercourse in marriage could be prevented from being sinful. There was, however, an escape clause. If husband and wife were spiritually so weak that they were unable to control their sinful sexual desires, they might relieve them by having intercourse, if otherwise they knew that they were in danger of using sex in even more sinful ways. In this manner the sin of marital sex could be a remedy for a greater sin. It was still sinful, of course, in this context, but the sin was venial, not mortal; or as Luther expressed it, God was merciful and winked at it! However, this was no excuse for indulging in passion. The moment a husband and wife began to *enjoy* the sex relationship, they were being really wicked.

Our deliverance from that kind of thinking has been the result of what we call the "Sexual Revolution." This term is used often, and I think erroneously, to describe apparent changes in sexual behavior in our contemporary society. Although these changes may be its consequences, the Sexual Revolution itself, like all true cultural mutations, represents a radical change in the way in which we *think* about sex—a change from negative to positive, from repressive to acceptive. And the true beneficiaries of the Sexual Revolution are the twelve million married couples[2] in the United States who, every twenty-four hours through the year, come together in sexual union, free from the shadow of fear and guilt, together with the millions of others like them in other regions of our Western world.

This Sexual Revolution has been achieved for us by the studies of scholars and scientists who have brought us new knowledge and by the courageous men and women who, in the light of that knowledge, have challenged the negative attitudes and finally discredited them. To these pioneers we owe our freedom even to dare to speak of sex as a source of marital enrichment.

Some of these pioneers were theologians. One of them, Sherwin Bailey, challenged the traditional view of the church by saying that sex in marriage is not just intended for procreation.[3] It has also, in the teaching of the Bible, a *unitive* function, which is of equal importance; this latter is derived from the description of marriage as the "two becoming one flesh," while the procreative function is derived from the injunction to the marriage partners to "be fruitful and multiply."[4] Bailey's concepts have won support beyond Protestant circles. So, in these last stages of the Sexual Revolution, we find Catholic and Protestant scholars alike renouncing the false teaching of the past and uniting to testify that sex in marriage is a source of blessing to husband and wife—a view from which the Jewish faith has never departed.

The Sexual Revolution, therefore, is not something that is just happening now or will happen in the future. It *has* happened. It is over. The wheel has turned full circle. There was a time when many believed that sex, even in marriage, was evil. That time is past and is never likely to return. Now we nearly all believe that sex in marriage is good—or at least that it *should* be good and that it is our privilege to discover, express, and assert its goodness.

HOW IMPORTANT IS SEX TO MARITAL SUCCESS?

Answers to this question express a variety of opinions. There are those who suggest that sexual satisfaction is the only sure foundation on which marriage can rest. Frederic Loomis, a physician, says, "I do not mean that a satisfactory marital relationship is the most important thing in life. But I do believe, and with good reason, that it is essential to a happy married life and that to a considerable extent all else revolves around it. I believe that practically every divorce is a result, directly or indirectly, of either definite sexual unhappiness or the absence of positive sexual happiness. . . . Without the common ground of the mutual and intimate expression of love, the gradual separation of the paths of husband and wife, with or without divorce, is almost inevitable."[5] And William McDougall, a psychologist, declares, "The physical basis of marriage is all-important. . . . If it is all awry, the most fortunate constitutions, the most delicate sentiments, the strongest characters, the most generous and well-informed deliberations will hardly succeed in making the marriage a happy one; and it is much if they can prevent it from going to pieces on the rocks."[6]

Others take the view that the importance of sex as the basis of successful marriage has been overestimated. And Lewis Terman, a pioneer in the scientific study of marital happiness, reported, "Our data do not confirm the view so often heard that the key to happiness in marriage is nearly always to be found in sexual compatibility."[7]

The latter view has become widely accepted by those who have carefully examined what knowledge we have on this subject. Lederer and Jackson sum up the matter in the words, "Unsatisfactory sexual relations are a symptom of marital discord, not the cause of it."[8] They elaborate this point by saying, "Given adequate physiological and anatomical equipment (which Nature rarely fails to provide) and a modicum of knowledge of sexual techniques, the spouses will enjoy sexual union *when both are in a collaborative mood.*"[9]

The "collaborative mood" may, of course, occur fortuitously, but it is far more likely to occur when the atmosphere in which the marital partners are living together is happy and creative. We shall have more to say on this point later.

It is also true that the collaborative mood may exist within a wide gamut. The willingness to collaborate may be confined to collaboration in the act of intercourse and extend to nothing beyond that. "Sexual relations may keep some marriages going, providing virtually the only kind of contact that the spouses have. Psychiatrists and other professionals who treat marital problems are aware that some individuals have been able to establish successful sexual relations with each other although they cannot get together in any other context."[10]

The gamut also includes, however, the kind of sex relationship that expresses not simply an immediate agreement to have intercourse (though that is necessary) but an extensive intertwining of life patterns such as is established in a relationship-in-depth. It is with this kind of widely symbolic sexual interaction that we are here concerned—sex that expresses and reinforces a rich variety of aspects of the shared life of the married couple. Let us try to identify some of the many strands that can draw husband and wife, through their shared sexual experiences, into the full unity of a fulfilled conjugal relationship.

WAYS IN WHICH SEX ENRICHES MARRIAGE

Marital sex helps to establish, and then reinforces, the interdependence of husband and wife. Marriage is essentially a response to *needs*. Two people join forces on the basis of what they hope they can do for each other and give to each other. They believe that their individual lives will be enhanced by their union. So long as this proves to be true, they have no difficulty in staying together. Only when they become disenchanted about this do they begin to think of ending the association.

Many needs bring a man and woman together, but sexual attraction is, as a rule, what starts it all. This may be openly recognized by both, or it may be masked by romantic love, which is a state of diffused longing set up by unsatisfied sex desire. ("Love," said Freud, "is aim-inhibited sex.") It would be too great a diversion to discuss here the role of romantic love in marriage; but to use a contemporary analogy, it represents the power of the rocket that puts the capsule in orbit. Husband and wife come together because they are propelled toward each other by a force that is spent only when they are united sexually.

But the force renews itself. Sexual need, in normal men and women, dies down after intercourse; and then, after a period of time, it recurs. So long as other interpersonal factors do not create in the marriage a revulsion that overwhelms the sexual attraction, the couple will incorporate their recurring need for sexual release into a habit-pattern that is best fulfilled in a continuity of association. By staying together and being sexually accessible to one another, the partners both achieve what I have termed "biological peace." As Sofie Lazarsfeld has put it, "I have always observed that a mentally and spiritually successful intercourse awakens in the man as well as in the woman a profound feeling of real gratitude and a desire to continue with the relation. Whenever the man turns away quickly after the sex union, we may be sure that one of the two partners has failed."[11]

This contribution that sex makes to marriage could perhaps be called a sustaining rather than an enriching one; but it is appropriate to begin with it in order to provide a fairly complete and cumulative picture of the positive roles of marital sex. The importance of meeting recurring sexual need has, of course, been recognized in law and in religious teaching. Saint Paul, who was hardly an enthusiastic advocate of marriage, in addressing married couples nevertheless encouraged them not to "defraud one another" by sustained sexual abstinence.[12] And the church, aware of the wayward proclivities of the male, established the concept of the husband's "sexual rights," presumably as a contribution to the stability of marriage. The Jews had earlier established the right of a wife to sexual intercourse.

Marital sex provides the couple with a unifying experience of shared enjoyment. The cementing of the deepest and best human relationships seems often to be achieved through experiences in which ecstatic joy or profound sorrow are shared. The testimony of human experience is that sexual intercourse is one of the most supremely satisfying of all pleasures. It is for this reason, of course, that it is so eagerly sought.

The puritan mentality, which sourly rejects pleasure as ungodly, views this aspect of sex with profound suspicion. So the concept of sex as play, as an exhilarating game in which a man and woman can be engaged together and which will yield them transports of delight, is still strongly resisted in our culture. The tendency is to assume that such delirious enjoyment is found only in extramarital affairs—an impression widely held in medieval times and faithfully supported by our contemporary fiction writers. Marriage counselors and others who have access to the true facts find that this view needs correction. It is my distinct impression that not only most sexual intercourse, but also the best sexual intercourse, takes place in marriage. Perhaps in the past this was not so, but in my mind there is little doubt that it is so today. The Sexual Revolution has liberated the married couple to enjoy their sex life with an altogether new gusto; and to this pursuit, happily, much is contributed by the products of technology, such as warm and esthetically pleasant bedrooms, abundance of soap and hot water, and reliable contraception.

Eleanor Hamilton, in her delightful book *Parners in Love* (in my opinion the best of all the marriage manuals), has much to say about the new sensitivity we have developed toward the range of experiences that contribute to sexual pleasure. "Sometimes," she says, "we behave as if we had only one sense available for sexual stimulation, that of touch. We forget that sight, smell, hearing, and suggestive movement can play potent roles in heightening sexual pleasures. What are the sounds that thrill your mate—a crackling fire? Beethoven's Ninth? What are the smells that make him (or her) reach out for you, lungs expanded to drink in your fragrance—a pipe of tobacco? A certain type of perfume? Such psychological stimuli provide the environment for love that women, particularly, want and need. Men want them, too, though they are less dependent on atmosphere than on the primary stimulus, the loved one."[13]

The Romans had a dismal saying—*Post coitum omne animal triste* ("After sexual intercourse every creature is sad"). I have never heard a satisfactory explanation of this. The reference may have been to animals in the narrow sense and not to humans; or it may have been a disillusioned commentary on the sexual excesses said to have been widely practiced during the last days of the dying Empire. It is certainly not a valid comment on the sexual experience of married partners today. Husbands and wives do not often speak freely about such personal and private experiences, but when they do, they certainly do not speak of sadness. Frederic Loomis has given us a delightful firsthand description by one of his patients, which I confidently believe would be widely representative:

You know all that should come before?—the happiness of waiting; the loving words he says to me; the tender whispers which I save just for him; the so shaded light; the pretty nightdress which I am so lucky to have though we are all so poor; the kisses—all these we call the preludium, as if we were going to the symphony.

And after—ah, after, when he is even more tender to me, when I finally go to sleep with my head upon his shoulder, and our hearts are singing and our spirits are content—why, then we say it is the postludium, because we have indeed been to so sweet a symphony.[14]

The sharing of such joys in the intimate life of husband and wife brings renewal and enrichment to their entire relationship. And this perennial source of delight is readily available to all married couples who are inwardly free to receive it as a priceless gift. It has been said that the Indian peasant, living a life of privation and hardship, of much dreary toil with little fruit, and denied even the elementary satisfaction of a square meal, finds in his sex life with his wife a never-failing source of joy that is like a dazzling rainbow breaking out of a dark and clouded sky. Fortunately for him, Indian culture has cast no shadow of sin upon the sexual delights that the married couple may enjoy together. Indeed its sacred books teach the arts of sexual love.

Marital sex reenacts the courtship drama. Romance is highly prized in our Western culture, perhaps as a protest against the mechanized routines of a technological age. Certainly it was not always so; for there have been periods of human history in which it was held in low esteem and even in high suspicion.

The awakening of romance that leads to marriage, the wistful dreaming of young lovers, the wooing of the girl by the boy, the recognition of mutual love, and the final triumphant procession to the altar—these events are endowed by us with a rich aura of sentiment, appearing and reappearing in fairy tales we tell our children and in our cherished legends and sagas of love. Many of our noblest artistic productions—in poetry, painting, music, drama, and the dance—return again and again to these familiar themes of which we never tire, so that in our fervent imaginations every bride on her wedding day becomes a princess, and every groom a prince. In traditional Russian weddings they were actually crowned at the altar.

No tie binds two married people more closely together than the nostalgic memory of their courtship, when he was young and ardent, she sweet and demure. Alas, little of this may remain as the couple becomes submerged in the dreary routines of the passing years, when the struggle to bring up the children, balance the budget, and cope with the never-ending responsibilities and duties of family management rob them of their first wild, careless rapture. Yet there remains to them the sexual drama, when the world is shut out and the courtship courtesies are repeated as the husband woos his wife and asks for her love, and she responds. It is true that all this can be routinized and even brutalized. Yet it always must retain at least a semblance of the ceremonial; for he must ask, however churlishly; and she knows from his asking that she is still desired and still has the power to make him happy.

For married lovers with any sensitivity, sex therefore continues to be invitation and response; and this exchange can awaken the most tender memories and recapture the gaiety and the ecstasy of the days of carefree youth, when the world was fresh with the glory of spring, and the birds sang, and the sun shone out of a cloudless sky.

Marital sex symbolizes the shared life of the couple. The sexual episodes in marriage involve a withdrawal from others and a coming together in seclusion. This emphasizes the truth that, although both partners may be extensively involved in the wider world, they possess also a private and exclusive world of their own.

While the roots of romatic love lie in fantasy, the roots of conjugal love are nourished in the garden of "remembrance," as Felix Adler expresses it, "of many hours of ineffable felicity . . . of high aspirations pursued in common, of sorrows shared." It is this evolving pattern of shared experience that provides the sexual union of the married couple with its rich overtones and undertones. To quote Eleanor Hamilton again, "A sex relationship is a natural consequence of a relationship of total sharing. It is a mistake to try to reverse this sequence, to assume that, after sex, all else follows. It does not. You must touch a person's mind before you touch his body if you want participation of the whole person in the act of love. Without that participation, sex is ashes in your hand when the moment of pleasure is ended."[15]

Here we encounter the endlessly self-defeating quest of the Don Juan. Sex offers to all of us a choice between variety and exclusiveness. Both are attractive to us, but we have to choose. We may experiment a little with one and then move on to the other. But even this may not succeed, because the two patterns are really mutually exclusive. Those who choose variety surrender exclusiveness, those who choose exclusiveness surrender variety. There is without doubt an exhilaration in conquest, in a succession of new sexual experiences. For some this may prove to be an adequate way of life. But all too often breadth of experience ends in an empty superficiality. Rollo May has described the predicament of some of today's youthful advocates of "free love": "It is a strange fact in our society that what goes into building a relationship—the sharing of tastes, fantasies, dreams, hopes for the future, and cares from the past—seems to make people more shy and vulnerable than going to bed with one another. They are more wary of the tenderness that goes with psychological and spiritual nakedness than they are of the physical nakedness in sexual intimacy."[16]

"Tastes, fantasies, dreams, hopes, fears"—these represent the wide spectrum of shared experiences that are expressed, for the married couple, when they come together in sexual intimacy. In the medieval story of Abelard and Heloise, long years after their enforced separation, Heloise wrote to her husband, "Truly, those joys of love, which we experienced together, were so dear to my soul that I can never lose delight in them, nor can they vanish from the mirror of my remembrance. . . . Not only the deeds that were ours, thine and mine, but every place and every hour that saw them, have been printed with thine image, on my soul so deeply, that I live them again with thee, moment by moment. Nor does sleep bring respite, or oblivion. Often my body stirs and betrays my soul's desire."[17]

When such experiences and memories can no longer be shared, for sensitive people, sexual union grows empty and tenuous. "Sexual intercourse?" replied one wife to my question in a marriage counseling interview, "we don't do it any more." And then, wistfully, she added, "You see, there's nothing left for it to express."

The psychosexual difficulties that frustrate sexual performance represent, again and again, not any mechanical problem, but the inability of the person concerned to become involved in a shared life with the spouse. A wife suffering from vaginismus may well be saying to her husband, "I am afraid to let you come fully into my life, by opening myself freely and trustfully to you." The impotent husband may be saying, "I cannot come too close to you, because I don't trust you to accept me lovingly for what I am. This is as far as I can go." The unfaithful spouse may be saying, "When I try to enter fully into your life, I feel that I am only conditionally accepted, and I cannot meet your conditions; so I am turning to someone else for the experience of intimacy that I cannot find with you." The treatment of these problems, I am more and more convinced, is best undertaken in a relational rather than an individual context. They are not so much derangements of sexual functioning as derangements of the capacity to love.

Marital sex resolves episodes of alienation. All happily married people are aware of the healing and renewing power of sex. Following conflict and mutual misunderstanding, when acceptance and forgiveness have closed the frozen distance that separated them, the melting of feelings toward one another finds its completion most aptly in bodily union. One husband called this "making up and making out," and he may well have been one of those who consider the quarrel worth the exquisite delight of the final reconciliation!

We have long recognized that in marriage negative and positive emotions, though visibly at opposite poles, often are closely linked beneath the surface and indeed may phase into one another in a swift and unnerving metamorphosis. The solvent that transforms the one into the other is movement from distance to nearness, and the symbol of this is physical touch, culminating in physical union.

One great enabling agent, for the married couple, is the double bed. An English religious writer makes an interesting comment on this useful article of furniture: "The separate bed or bedroom habit must at all times support the wrong attitude to intercourse, making of it a separately considered, rather artificial act instead of simply one part of a life of love."[18] A couple of my acquaintance once told me how, on occasion, following a bitter quarrel, they would climb in cold silence into opposite sides of the bed. After a long time, one shyly exploring toe would make tentative contact with another; then foot to foot, hand to hand, mouth to mouth, body to body, the healing process of reconciliation and restoration would follow.

Marital sex ratifies gender identity. One of our most subtle developmental tasks in life is to establish clearly and comfortably our masculine or feminine identity and the roles that belong to it. A Belgian Catholic priest of my acquaintance some years ago wrote two books on preparation for marriage that have been widely read by young men and women in his country. This man (now dead) had a deep understanding of the aspirations of youth, and he called his books respectively *Pour Devenir Homme* and *Pour Devenir Femme,* because he sensed that the desire to become a man or a woman represented one of the most compelling goals in marriage.

We are well aware that nothing is more humiliating to any man than the suggestion that he may be failing to function as an adult male. We do not recognize so readily that the counterpart is equally true of the opposite sex. "To feel herself able to inspire passion," says Amber Blanco White, "is of very great significance to a woman."[19]

Ability to perform sexually, therefore, has always been a hallmark of manhood and womanhood. But this means much more than the mere accomplishment of coitus. Persuading a girl to accept him as a sexual partner may give a boy status in the "bull session," but unless he can follow through by learning the gallantries that make men pleasing to women, he is not far on his way. Likewise the girl may seem to make a start by being identified as "sexy," but this may lead only to her exploitation by the less mature males in her circle of acquaintance. The real test of effective manhood and womanhood is to be able to establish the kind of heterosexual interaction that will stand the test of marriage, for only in the total range of married living—and in its corollary, parenthood—are all the gender roles given their full and mature exercise.

It is true that the traditional rigidity in defining masculine and feminine roles is in our time giving way to the encouragement of more flexible and fluid forms of interaction. This is entirely desirable, not only because the changes in these role patterns are appropriate to our changing culture, but also because variations from the norm have always existed and are now being recognized as individual differences rather than abnormalities. We even go so far today as to speak in this connection of "role reversal," though it should be recognized that this is a rare phenomenon. It remains true for most of us, however, that the essence of masculine-feminine interaction does not significantly change, and that marriage provides the ideal situation in which we can discover in depth our true nature and function as man and woman. A Catholic writer, Emile Mersch, has thus expressed it, "Married love is the dynamic unity of human nature, working between two human beings under specially favorable conditions. Such favorable conditions are found nowhere in the order of nature, except between husband and wife, because two persons of different sex, who love each other, are more adapted for union without injury to their individual natures than persons in any other form of merely human association."[20]

Marital sex encourages relational maturity. Sexual intercourse is, according to Lederer and Jackson, "a highly satisfying male-female symbiosis, in that it requires a higher degree of collaborative communication than any other kind of behavior exchanged between the spouses. Sex is consequently precious, but also perilous. It is the only relationship act which must have mutual spontaneity for mutual satisfaction. It can only be a conjoint union, and it represents a common goal which is clear and understood by both."[21]

In other words, the challenge of sexual need is that in order to satisfy it you must find a partner, and in order to satisfy your partner in addition to yourself, you must recognize his or her identity as a person and seek to understand his or her individual needs, preferences, and moods. This is in itself a challenge to a higher degree of maturity than many of us possess and, therefore, creates a serious problem for the immature. One of the major functions of the prostitute has been to provide for the inept male, incapable of initiating or developing a relationally-oriented sexual experience with a woman, a convenient shortcut enabling him to purchase the temporary use of her body without the need to be involved with her as a person.

This predicament of the immature is graphically illustrated by the G.I.'s definition of an ideal girl friend: a beautiful, blond, deaf and dumb nymphomaniac who has no relatives and who owns a liquor store. Note carefully the way in which the interaction is limited. This girl must be beautiful and blond—characteristics that tend to inflate the masculine ego. She must be incapable of verbal communication, so that the G.I.'s very limited capacities in this direction shall not be exposed. The fact that she is a nymphomaniac relieves her partner of all responsibility for arousing sexual response in her—a role for which he would be poorly equipped. The absence of relatives delivers him from the danger of any social implications connected with the relationship, with which he would be unable to cope. And finally, just in case after all these safeguards he should fail to function, a ready escape is available in the plentiful supplies of liquor in which he can forget his humiliation in blissful intoxication.

It is an interesting fact that in the Old Testament the word "know" is used as a synonym for sexual intercourse. And it is a fact well-known to marriage counselors that the relationally inept are often also the sexually inept. Again and again, in dealing with sexual maladjustment, we find that the core of the problem lies in deficiencies in communication, in mutual understanding, and in cooperation. "We now know," says marriage counselor Tom McGinnis, "that good sexual adjustment usually reflects a reasonably good adjustment in all other areas, and that if a couple say they do not have a satisfactory sex life, their difficulty often is rooted in their inability to work through conflicts in their other relationships."[22]

Marital sex engenders spiritual exaltation. The Old Testament likens a bridegroom emerging from his chamber to the blazing glory of the sun in the heavens.[23] But as long as the Christian church was dominated by the dismal view of sex which we have already discussed, no Christian theologian was free to indulge in such imagery.

By a strange irony, therefore, it was through secular voices that our contemporary culture first recalled us to an awareness of the spiritual experiences we undergo in sexual union. Havelock Ellis, for example, described the married couple in their sex relationship as "moving amongst the highest human activities, alike of the body and of the soul. They are passing to each other the sacramental chalice of that wine which imparts the deepest joy that men and women can know. They are subtly weaving the invisible cords that bind husband and wife together more truly and more firmly than the priest of any church."[24]

Challenged by such bold utterances as these, religious writers began to look to their laurels and soon were trying to speak in similar terms. The trumpet at first had an uncertain sound. E. C. Messenger, an English Catholic writer, published in 1949 a trilogy entitled *Two in One Flesh*, which carried the official imprimatur of the Church. Aware that he was breaking new ground, he tried to suggest that he was putting forward aspects of Catholic teaching that by some unfortunate oversight had not hitherto been given sufficient attention. He declared that he was offering "a true Catholic solution, favored by the Church's best theologians, if not actually taught by ecclesiastical authority. Some features in this are not so well known as would seem to be desirable. They would indeed seem to be absent from the view of sex which some excellent Catholics hold."[25] Later he explains that "to assert that the sex act has a religious character will doubtless seem strange to those who have hitherto looked upon it merely as an animal act."[26] In order to establish the religious character of sexual intercourse, he quotes from the *Encyclical on Christian Marriage* of Pope Pius XI; but the quotation unfortunately refers only to the duty of Christian parents "to give children to the Church," with no reference whatsoever to sexual intercourse undertaken for any other purpose. No doubt this was the best quotation from any papal declaration he could find at that time. He struggles on, however, and ends his chapter on "The Religious Character of the Sex Act" with the statement, "Thus, the performance of the sex act in the right way and for the right intention becomes an exercise of the virtue of religion itself, and therefore a religious act." But honesty compels him to add, "One will look in vain, however, in the works of modern moral theologians for any such doctrine."[27]

Today both Protestant and Catholic writers are able to speak with greater confidence, and their pronouncements on this subject now match those of the secular pioneers of the Sexual Revolution. It is not necessary to quote them, because their statements have arrived so late that what they are saying is already accepted by all modern husbands and wives who have any kind of religious faith or perception of the spiritual dimensions of life and have freed themselves from the negative thinking of the past. Such married people are well aware that satisfying sexual intercourse is experienced as reinforcing and heightening spiritual awareness.

Marital sex provides husband and wife with their only true experience of union. The concept of marriage as a union of two persons has often been featured in love poetry and has in the past found expression in some of our legal codes. Outside of poetry and the courts, however, this is obviously an unattainable goal. A union of two persons is a complete impossibility, because they dwell in separate bodies and have separate individual identities.

Nevertheless, it is the nature of love to strive for closeness as an expression of unity, if not of union—even if the goal can never be attained. And in the sexual experience, when two bodies reach the highest possible degree of closeness, and at least symbolically "become one flesh," that striving for unity is partially fulfilled. In that sense, the experience of sexual union is unique to the two persons concerned, and it is precisely this that creates in them the desire that it shall be exclusive. "For two persons who love each other and therefore find life's meaning heightened and focused in that love," says Peter Bertocci, "there can hardly be conceived a more expressive symbol of the yearning for unity than a mutual harmonious orgasm."[28] This is reinforced by the fact that at the peak of the sexual climax there is a momentary loss of consciousness, and of the awareness of individual identity, which gives the sense of the one personality being merged with the other. The word "ecstasy," fittingly used to describe this experience, means literally to stand outside one's self; and the French, with their highly developed sensitivity to appropriate language, call the sexual orgasm *le petit mort* ("the little death"). That this is the supreme experience of marriage enrichment is not likely to be questioned. Other experiences that husband and wife share dramatize their love and the unity through which they strive to express it. But no other experience is like this one in its symbolic nature, its appropriateness, its expressiveness, and its intensity. Carl Jung says of it, "This condition is described as one of complete harmony, and is extolled as a great happiness ('one heart and one soul'). . . . It is indeed a true and undeniable experience of divinity, the transcending power of which blots out and consumes everything individual."[29] Van De Velde, whose book *Ideal Marriage* has probably been more widely read than any other on this subject, finds this theme of the mystical symbolic union of husband and wife in sexual intercourse to be the only fitting conclusion of his discourse, "What husband and wife who love one another seek to achieve in their most intimate bodily communion and, whether consciously or unconsciously, recognize as the purpose of such communion is a means of expression that makes them one. And this means of expression is the only perfect one that nature puts at their command."[30]

CONCLUSION

We have considered the part that sexual union plays in the nurture and growth of a marriage, at least for those who have set as their goal the attainment of relationship-in-depth. We have recognized with gratitude our deliverance from the unworthy and demeaning notions about sex that have confused and frustrated our culture in the past. We have discussed at least some of the many meanings that their sex life can have for husband and wife, and how those meanings can enhance other aspects of their comradeship.

It has been necessary to assume that the sexual experiences of which we were speaking represented the best and most mutually satisfying of which the partners were capable. It has not been our task to consider how in practice such experiences could be attained. Yet I hope that by presenting the great benefits of good sexual intercourse, I may have awakened in the reader the incentive to pursue this rewarding goal. The task proves to be easy for some, difficult for others.

It has seemed appropriate, in developing such a theme, to call upon many witnesses to contribute their testimony. Perhaps we may finally heed an injunction from El Ktab, an Arabic treatise on the art of love:

> When ye unite one with another, do so with deep consciousness of the greatness, of the dignity of that which ye do! Give yourselves to this work of love; with your souls and with your minds, even as with your flesh![31]

CHAPTER NOTES

1. E. D. Hutchinson, *Creative Sex* (London: George Allen and Unwin, 1936), p. 75.
2. There are about forty-two million families in the United States with husband and wife living together, and the average frequency of sexual intercourse in marriage is twice weekly.
3. See Derrick Sherwin Bailey, *The Mystery of Love and Marriage* (New York: Harper, 1950).
4. Gen. 1:28 and 2:24.
5. Frederic Loomis, *The Consulting Room* (London: J. M. Dent, 1939), p. 82.
6. William McDougall, *Character and the Conduct of Life* (London: Methuen, 1927), p. 225.
7. Lewis M. Terman, *Psychological Factors in Marital Happiness* (New York: McGraw-Hill, 1958), p. 376.
8. William J. Lederer and Don D. Jackson, *The Mirages of Marriage* (New York: W. W. Norton, 1968), p. 116.
9. Ibid., p. 114.
10. Ibid., p. 117.
11. Sofie Lazarsfeld, *Rhythm of Life* (London: Routledge, 1934), p. 301.
12. 1 Cor. 7:5.
13. Eleanor Hamilton, *Partners in Love* (New York: Ziff-Davis, 1961), p. 107.
14. Quoted by Frederic Loomis, *The Consulting Room*, p. 86.
15. Eleanor Hamilton, *Partners in Love*, p. 107.
16. Rollo May, *Love and Will* (New York: Norton, 1967), p. 45.

17. *Letters of Heloise to Abelard,* trans. C. K. Scott Moncrieff (London: Guy Chapman, 1925), p. 65.

18. A. G. Pite, *Christian Marriage and Modern Practice* (London: S. C. M. Press, 1931), p. 103.

19. Amber Blanco White, *Worry in Women* (London: Gollancz, 1941), p. 164.

20. Emile Mersch, *Love, Marriage and Chastity* (London: Sheed and Ward, 1939), p. 14.

21. Lederer and Jackson, *The Mirages of Marriage,* pp. 117–118.

22. Tom McGinnis, *Your First Year of Marriage* (New York: Doubleday, 1967), p. 107.

23. Ps. 19:5.

24. Havelock Ellis, *Little Essays of Love and Virtue* (New York: George E. Doran, 1922), pp. 132–133.

25. E. C. Messenger, *Two in One Flesh,* 3 vols. (London: Sands, 1948), 1:vii.

26. Ibid., 3:31.

27. Ibid., p. 33.

28. Peter Bertocci, *The Human Venture in Sex, Love, and Marriage* (New York: Association Press, 1951), p. 63.

29. Carl G. Jung, *Contributions to Analytical Psychology* (New York: Harcort, Brace, 1928), pp. 192–193.

30. Van De Velde, *Ideal Marriage,* p. 321.

31. Khodja Omar Haleby, Abou Othman, *El Ktab des Lois Secretes de L'Amour,* trans. de Paul de Regla (Paris: George Carre, 1893), p. 194.

Chapter 12

POSITIVE VALUES OF THE AFFAIR

By O. Spurgeon English, M.D.

The marriage relationship is a social contract designed for definite and clear purposes, for serving the ends of a more efficient social order, and is thus far the only accepted institution for the early rearing of the young. There are millions who have accepted it blindly as not only the best institution for this purpose, but one which they hold in reverence and will rush to defend if anything is said to dissect its shortcomings or suggest that it might be improved. Whether it is in truth actually the best institution which can be conceived by man for the purpose of rearing the young is debatable.

It must be admitted that an institution for the rearing of young human beings, which after centuries of effort can do no better than produce so many, who are bent upon war, riot, and even murder for the solution of human problems and who will succumb to alcoholism, insanity, a life of drug-taking, inertia, apathy, pessimism, and massive unconcern for their fellow man, certainly needs a long look and an analysis of its effectiveness. Over and above this, we need to consider whether it cannot undergo some improvement within its own ranks or abdicate participation in it for a different organization or arrangement for the important work of rearing a better earth inhabitant. Engineering minds, which can encircle the moon with a rocket and have it return to earth with the uncannny accuracy recently demonstrated, should prod social thinkers to come up with some better means of rearing human beings than the one with the present record, which marriage has achieved. It is possible that our pressing race these days to outer space may be partially motivated by the desire (or possibly need) to find a planet doing a better job along these lines. We may be looking for a method of producing a less aggressive, less selfish, and more peaceful, loving, and creative person able to enjoy this planet and what it provides for us. Certainly the formula seems to elude us. We are lagging sadly behind Apollo 8. If engineers could not do better than we have done in the individual or mass production of people, we wouldn't have a rocket leave the launching pad, and if it did, it wouldn't get farther than a hundred or two hundred feet in the air and would fall back a disappointing dud. Marriage (and the family, which usually follows with marriage) with its implicit license for two people who cannot make a harmonious relationship themselves to enter into the production of human beings, surely gives us a demonstration of the most unskilled labor being put to work on important construction.

As to whether a search for anything better in the field of emotional and personal relationships constitutes any motivating force in the race to the moon is highly speculative, we admit, but there is no ceiling on the possibilities of what motivates the human mind to do the unique things it does and the manner in which it does them. And, we should have learned that to set up an institution such as marriage, empower it to produce and shape the character and personality of people, and worship the institution as one containing love and perfection, indicates we have a tremendous blind spot somewhere in our evaluation of what we are doing. Millions of people yearly are constantly seeking to enter this institution and start the same activity over again, even though the home they have come from and were reared in was little above the limited freedom, the authoritarianism, and sometimes even the cruelty of a prison. It must be that they hope they can do better, or they are following blindly in the habit footsteps of those before them and cannot improve upon their record. This is just one demonstration of the power of ancestor worship, and the worship of tradition as well as the terror of losing the security of departing in any way from the original capsule from which they arrived on this earth and got their first lessons in living.

Any effort to suggest any modification of this inadequate model called marriage and its function of child rearing runs head on into the rigid thinking that has been a part of the human mind in the past. Anyone challenging the effectiveness of marriage and the two people within it in any direct and outspoken way invites resentment of tremendous proportions. He risks being branded an iconoclast if not a wrecker of the best and most sacred institution in the world. He is thus to be considered a profaner of a sacred institution, one that, for some reason he cannot explain, is inviolate to criticism and unassailable. In short, he puts himself in the same position as the neighbor who attempts to take sides in a family quarrel only to have both parties turn on him and send him home a bruised Samaritan.

However, if the product of one thousand of the best families in the world were pooled, it seems unlikely, on the basis of our knowledge of human behavior, that wisdom contained in these one thousand families would not make it possible to rear a family of six children whose performance in even a majority of the things supposedly expected from a normal and mature human being would approach even to a small degree the predictability of a machine manufactured on the assembly line in Detroit.

We know the human being is capable of producing happiness in his offspring, and the offspring can add to the original amount later in his life after leaving home. He can also produce a peaceful and nonaggressive attitude in his offspring that is stable and dependable, and the child by way of experience with life not only can add to this, but can extend its application to other people and affairs. He can also create sustained love and a balance of productivity with a sense of well-being and good will to go with it. Yet, society has yet to produce by design all these things well integrated within the same person so that these personality traits can function simultaneously within the period of a given day or week, much less endure for a lifetime. Nor does he have the slightest inkling of what these personality traits, formed in family life by two more or less well-intentioned people called parents, should *do* or *be* in order to reproduce in one or more offspring these very qualities described. After centuries of human effort to improve, we present a social contract such as the marriage contract (an imperfect instrument in itself) to two individuals, far from perfect themselves, as the partners who are to implement the responsibilities of marriage assigned to them. We assume this combination will produce love, a phenomenon of which we know all too little, and we know even less about how to bring it into being where and when needed. But, we do not need a priority committee to decide where and when love is needed; it is needed everywhere.

In addition, we expect these two phenomena, i.e., the institution of marriage and the two people in it, to be able to produce love and the inhabitants of a better world. This kind of expectation handed to a group of trained engineers would arouse their ridicule or their pity surely for the brashness, if not the insanity, of the task. And, this would not be because the engineers didn't have ability as engineers. It would be because the ones who handed them the problem of design had not done their simple arithmetic regarding the fundamentals, let alone their geometry or history. Furthermore, they know next to nothing about the fundamental rules of psychology operating all the time in the people around them, but whom they are ignoring as completely as possible. Yet, ignorance of the basic nature of human beings will never succeed in producing more intelligent and peaceful and mature offspring, able to do all of the loving and creative order-making that religion, philosophy, and psychology have been attempting to define for centuries.

THE AFFAIR AND ITS POSITIVE POTENTIALITIES

It so happens that a widespread individual effort in attempting some alleviation of this over-burdened institution called marriage has been going on practically since Adam and Eve left the Garden. Moreover, it increases in frequency daily. This individual effort, arising spontaneously and usually without consultation with anyone, is called an affair. The word *affair* has more than one meaning according to Webster. He states that an affair means (*a*) a thing to do, (*b*) business, (*c*) any matter, occurrence, or thing, (*d*) an amorous relationship or episode between two people not married to each other. The affair in the sense of the last definition has been in existence as long as the others listed. Furthermore, centuries of effort have shown, without room for equivocation, the incapacity of one man and one woman to make marriage the congenial and mutually growth-promoting arrangement wherein they can grow simultaneously as personalities. They furthermore fail as they grow older or to increase their love, good will, and enjoyment of each other, as well as to become of greater interest to each other. Directly in line with this, they fail to become more in the way of individuals functioning as a source of pleasure and interest to their children as well as to their friends and fellow workers.

So, in this widespread individual effort on the part of many married people of both sexes to bring some added vivacity, inspiration, and personal fulfillment to themselves and to the other, they have, in addition to taking up bridge, golf, and riding, become involved in this phenomenon called the affair. The affair, incidentally, has been greatly on the increase in young people before marriage and greatly increased among younger married women in proportion to the number of men. However, since the men already have had such a long head start on the wives in this matter, it will be some time yet before the women catch up to the men, either in numbers or frequency of involvement in an affair.

At any rate, this attraction and the frequency with which so many people of both sexes seek out and either enjoy or suffer through an affair, in spite of its complexity and its risk of denouncement by one or more persons if discovered, must indicate that it offers a highly rewarding combination of delights and elevation of moods as well as a necessary and welcome enhancement to that which the partner in marriage can supply. This is not stated as criticism of the partner in marriage, even though all too many will insist on interpreting the statement that way. Either or both of two marital partners may in themselves be remarkable people, but still unable to fulfill the role placed upon them by the rules of the institution of marriage that are little less rigid than those of a concentration camp. Incidentally, community criticism can sting harder than any metal contraption yet invented, not to mention that it is charged with the current of envy, jealousy, prudery, and fear of the wish to copy those involved in an affair. The values of an affair are such as cannot be substituted by anything else. The late comedian, W. C. Fields, made a statement concerning sex, which is an acceptable and uncriticizable one yet truthful, when he said, "There may be some things better than sex, and some things may be worse. But, there is nothing exactly like it."

The sexual relation far from being a devastating, destructive, dangerous, humiliating, degrading one for those who engage in it, stands as man's (and woman's) greatest source of emotional and mental well-being. It is man's greatest single act, which symbolizes his total social and personal meaning and significance to another person and hence extends itself by way of a long-sustained emotional reverberation through his whole life awareness; it brings that sense of satisfaction, which accumulates as we grow older and always reminds us that life has had meaning.

It has been said that we are formed by people, deformed by peo-

ple, and reformed by people. However, while an excellent statement as far as it goes, it still does not say that we are or can be
more than "formed" by people or reformed by them. Why does
someone not say we can also be transformed by people? Also, no
one has yet attempted to say much about those things that raise
us above the repetitive activities of a plodding personality, responsible, yet doomed to a lifetime of unrelieved, routine duty. And, it
remains to be said in many different ways and by many people
from all walks of life that the sexual experience is one of the few
in life that will achieve this goal. Few if any activities we engage
in in our whole lifetime can approach it in its capacity for bringing
the fullest sense of how much we are and how much is the value of
another to a human being. It can and should be considered our most
mature activity, not our most neurotic, immature, or in any sense
inferior.

Certainly, sexual experience may serve neurotic ends for some
people temporarily, and occasionally permanently. Nevertheless,
all who utilize it and engage in it and involve themselves fully in it,
seeking earnestly its positive returns, should not be categorized
with the few who misuse it. One of the greatest and most dependable bulwarks against sadness, discontent, mental depression, or a
sense of futility about life approaching the stage of apathy, or a
too frequent and continuous sense of personal worthlessness
accompanied by the usual pessimism of spirit, is a vivacious sexual experience shared by two people of affinity for even as short
a time as three days, three weeks, or three months.

THE ORIGIN OF LOVE AND ITS MAINTENANCE

One of the greatest boons of childhood is a sense of having been
significant to one other person in the beginning phases of life, and,
of having this widen out with time to being accepted to a sufficiently high degree to maintain a sense of personal worth to others.
When more experience in life with an ever-increasing meaning
expands the enjoyment of life to a person, he grows in wisdom
as long as he lives. Memories of those personal interactions, which
bring to him a sense of his value, are all registered and remain
forever in the form of what we call personality, spirit, or essence.
Memory of a sad, neutral, or unappreciated childhood or adolescence may not be vividly recalled in any detail. Yet, those people

who have experienced it often enter marriage under the great disadvantage of never knowing happiness or knowing how to contribute enjoyment to another person. They unwarrantedly assume they will find happiness and an elevated sense of well-being in marriage and all of its shared activities including the sexual relation. However, if they are unenjoyable people, they are certain to become part of an unenjoyable marriage, and no matter how vivacious the partner may be, there is certain to be a tug of war, whether intended or not, which ends in the sad and depressed, the gloomy and pessimistic one pulling down the liveliness and effervescence of the other, never the other way around. Depression, pessimism, and the slow attrition of the low mood and bitter cynicism of the disillusioned one seems always to destroy the lightheartedness, humor, and happier spirit of the mate. The sad and moody one will maintain that he wants happiness and expects happiness, and yet in his own subtle way he will destroy it or diminish it every time it appears in his presence or crosses his path. Never having been acquainted with it previously, he does not trust it, is suspicious of it, and unconsciously will destroy it and try to bring the other one down to his level so that he is more comfortable with his familiarity with grimness of environment and discouragement of frivolity. The fact that both parties have legalized and sanctified this relationship, which is supposed to contain a happier existence for each, does nothing whatever to raise the level of enjoyment, which these two people can bring about between them in their daily lives. And, it is useless for them to blame marriage for this sad state of affairs. The blame rests on their own responsibility for contributing a joy to the home.

The many good experiences of life, particularly the highest, are being called these days "peak experiences." And, the sexual experience is one of the few of the so-called peak experiences, and one of the most important. Of course, there are dozens or perhaps thousands of experiences in living, which occur and can be enjoyed prior to and in addition to entering into the sexual experience and its intimate union of bodies and minds. But, this is not to say that the sexual experience never needs to have its time and place in life. (The sexual experience is the finest of all human activities,) and not only contains the mystery of our self-perpetuation as human beings, but it is also a source of the greatest tenderness, the greatest versatility in creating pleasure, the widest and greatest opportunity for self-expression known. It is never the same twice, even when participated in by the same two people. It is ennobling at all times and never degrading or denigrating. It always contains a gain for one party at least, and if the other does not succeed in obtaining the same gain, he certainly is entitled to inquire into the reasons why. And, if either should suffer any loss from sexual activity, this loss we must confront, understand, acknowledge, describe accurately and adequately, and do everything in our power to eliminate it.

Out of the feelings, emotions, and ideas generated through the sexual relation arises the best that mankind has produced and not only within or by way of the sexual act itself, but also by elevating the woman of the experience, without whom it would never come into being, to a place of importance due her. She should be given a far higher place in the importance of the relationship to the man and a creative place of higher worth in the total life experience of the male. The female already is and will become in the future what man sees her to be and wants her to become, nothing more, nothing less. While woman slowly takes an ever-increasing hand in her own fate, she can never be allowed to reach the plain of value and usefulness and creative effect upon man she merits unless he raises his esteem of her and gives her an appropriate place beside him. Man should cease restricting her self-expression as he has done over the centuries because of what he felt originally to be important concerns for himself. He now can eliminate these if he will help to educate her in preventing unwanted pregnancies, which is a social matter, and thereby dissociate this social aspect of her importance from that one having to do with his love life shared with her, his entertainment by her, and inspiration through her. He has complained so bitterly about her deficiencies in the home and acted secretly, selfishly, and often cruelly to seek outside those things the woman did not provide him, rather than exert himself and seek her cooperation in creating them within the home.

Man's inhumanity to man has not been limited to war, slavery, and penal incarceration. His inhumanity has placed a heavy hand upon his natural mate, the female. Now, that he has the means within his control to inculcate her in measures to prevent conception, he should make her as free as he would like himself to be, and thereby have greater opportunity to be a more complete person, rather than a frightened, limited, housekeeping drudge. This would in no way prevent the institution of marriage from being successful, even more successful than it has been to date. Both men and women want very much the comforts of a home, and if they want children, they must know they must conduct themselves as models of concern for the education of children, in order to make of them more mature, self-directing, buoyant, altruistically functioning citizens.

People are capable of learning a better, more democratic, and more emotionally expanded way of living. This would mean merely extending themselves in the lives of a few people to a greater extent, so that the response they obtained would give them a sense of worth and a sense of well-being and stimulate them to an ever-expanded altruistic self-expression. This is a definition of "the essence of living" about which we hear so much today, and this formulation of it would at least give people a point of departure. If they did not have the imagination to see how this formula or definition could be implemented, they could at least ask some more imaginative friend or counselor. What people want, people get, and to date, they apparently have not wanted very much in the way of love.

Rather than overlook the full meaning of what our modern writers have to say about the sexual experience (and this becomes more descriptive every year), the prudish or embarrassed reader should reflect that people have said that no prose or poetry has yet been adequate to truly describe what the full meaning of a good sex relation can be. Prior to it, both parties are wondering if it will occur at all, and when it does, the act and the accompanying feeling are too transient to obtain any description. Nevertheless, the modern movie and novel must make it clear that much that is inherent in lovemaking between people goes on at the mind level while bodies serve to unite minds so that feeling and thinking about the relationship, which occurs, can be brought about and continue to have some meaning in the time intervals between. Hence, the cautious and uneasy reader of romantic novels of today, including the descriptions of the sexual experience, should not only become better acquainted with some of the best in the spectrum of life's experiences, but also enlarge his knowledge of the whole meaning of why we are here at all.

If we attempt to trace the history of our slow gains in releasing the sexual experience from such strict taboos, it would have to be said that religious and secular authority, with the aid of state law, grudgingly permitted sexual activity within marriage primarily for the propagation of children. Only within the last fifty years, these same authorities began cautiously to be explicit about the possibility that sex might have the additional potential of enriching and strengthening the marriage relationship in a more definite support of the personal enjoyment of sex available to the partners in it and cause them to look more kindly upon each other as a recurring source of mutual joy, pleasure, inspiration, and recreation as well. This still left the perplexing problem of an overabundance of children, but it at least lifted them above the level of the animal husbandry, and for this concession they were appropriately grateful. Crude and uncertain methods of contraception appeared sporadically and were known and practiced by those eager to separate the child-producing function of sex relations from the enjoyable and the recreational. All the same, due to their unreliability, legal abortion was often resorted to in order to limit offspring, and it still is all too prevalent; some of its occurrence is due to the fact that few people can openly admit they intend to participate in sexual relations, even when they know they will doubtless do so. However, to make a demonstration of lack of interest as well as intention, they refuse to take appropriate means of contraception at the appropriate time. By the time the twentieth century had advanced very far, more contraceptive devices came into existence, and when adopted and used carefully, conscientiously, and intelligently, they would in most instances prevent undesired pregnancy. As contraception has come to be relied upon, even though it is not used as intelligently as it should be as yet, the amount of premarital and extramarital intercourse has increased considerably during each decade of this century. And, if we take the recent figure increase seriously, the trend will be further upward.

It should be clear to all of us that young, unmarried people have seized for themselves the right and privilege of sexual experience prior to marriage so that there are few left who marry without having had experience in sexual intercourse. While approval for this behavior is not universally extended by the parents or any other authorities, the custom nevertheless prevails. Whether the older generation has been more permissive in rearing the young or whether the young have been more demanding and insistent upon gratification of their sexual needs and impulses, the freedom of sexual expression, nevertheless, is existent and is affecting other age levels of the population also. Rarely does the influence of the older generation not hold sway over the young, but this is one instance in which the young seem to have strongly influenced the older generation.

The next segment of the population that has been influenced

by the freer and more permissive attitudes taken by the young has been those young women between thirty and forty-five who feel a strong discontent and dissatisfaction with their existence, and feel they have been cheated of an enlightening and growth-promoting experience in their early lives. Consequently, they wonder if a love affair outside the established family pattern would not give their lives more excitement, more vivacity, more knowledge of authentic human, emotional reactions, and hence bring to them more of the elevated sense of living and well-being that has been said to come from a wider emotional involvement such as is known to arise (or is reputed to arise) from sex relations with more than the one person they marry.

ATTITUDES IN MALE AND FEMALE ON INFIDELITY

The reasons for such a long delay in thinking through a more accepting and benign attitude regarding greater sexual freedom at all levels of our society is a complex matter to analyze, and there is little agreement on the most basic reasons. In the first place, more freedom for the single woman and the male's wish to have her before marriage is forcing him to be more consistent and fair-minded when he chooses a wife. If he is a true believer in equality, he must extend to her the same freedom to express herself sexually with another man that he heretofore has reserved for himself with other women. He still likes to think that tradition would support him in such a privileged liaison, should he feel the need for it or the occasion for it arises. Fairness to the opposite sex and the presence of safe contraception practically demand that he permit the woman to regard an occasional departure from absolute fidelity in the same manner as he has taken for himself in the past. Many men say or strongly imply a woman couldn't be trusted to utilize contraception safely. However, why should he regard her as so undisciplined in this matter when he apparently has trusted her for nineteen centuries to abstain completely from any extramarital sex relation whatever? If she could do this for him in previous centuries, she should be able to adopt a safe contraceptive pattern and use it conscientiously, if he first would allow her a sexual affair, but at the same time make clear he has not yet advanced to the point of wishing or even cheerfully accepting responsibility for the care and education of a child conceived with another man. This may sound far too open as an invitation for wives to be what man is so ready to call "promiscuous." But, never having thought much about women or paid much attention to what women say and do, the average man has little idea of what women would do. He doesn't even know how their minds work. So far he has only done some guessing, and in this he tends to swing between extremes of having them oversexed or undersexed. And, he is usually wrong in both instances. It is not easy for him to think his wife as intelligent or as dependable as he. On the other hand, would she be more careless, less considerate, and permit herself to become pregnant by another man and with untroubled conscience present the child to him as his? Certainly we have no evidence to support any assumption that a woman would more readily deceive her husband, than he would deceive her, in matters each knew to be important to the other. Even if he has since time began arrogated to himself the privilege of deceiving her in his extramarital sexual life, this does not give him the right to regard her as possessing less moral fiber or ability to deal with truth and reality than he.

Moreover, in considering the reality of sexual affairs, the man is prone to say, "Yes, but women are different. Women are more emotional than we men and couldn't cope with an affair as dispassionately and detachedly or as resolutely or decisively as we men." To this assumption it could be said, "Little do you know, my friend, how coolly, and detachedly, and dispassionately women can manage affairs or the sexual experience with a man." If there were any study made of the differences, it would be most likely the women would excel the men in their ability to love and leave or participate in sex and afterward go home calmly to their obligations without remaining as emotionally involved or in as much need, or carry strong guilt, or compare the high capacities of the lover with those of her husband to the latter's disadvantage as he sometimes has done. The one in the marital duo who has ranted, raved, threatened, punished, divorced, and even killed his mate or her lover, or both, following the discovery of infidelity has been in the majority of cases the male, the dispassionate and controlled one with his emotions. The woman has been reproachful and sometimes revengeful, but never to the high degree of indignation and violence as the man when marital infidelity was an issue between them.

The woman has all her life been more closely attuned to the meaning as well as the necessity of close human bodily contact.

She has seen its value at work with her children in many forms, and she is more in tune with sensual emotional need as natural for her to give, while the man has done little or no giving of this kind. He has always been the one pursuing the gifts of pleasure and comfort the female possesses for him. When a man finds a woman who gives more than his wife by way of her body or personal emotional interest, or both, he has found something new and highly satisfying, and he tends to want to retain it. When the woman finds the same, it may be important to her, but it is not as frequently the entirely new or the unique addiction it can be for the man, at least temporarily.

A woman who enters into an affair is usually looking for a higher appreciation of herself as a woman, a human being with a personality she wants recognized and appreciated. If her husband has been unable to see the woman she is, or even if at the beginning of their marriage he has been able to see the woman she was, yet he is not able to address himself and to acknowledge the woman she is and act accordingly with her, she may finally conclude she must have something better suited to her deeper inner emotional needs. People whose emotional needs are too long ignored become social problems in some varying degree of severity, either in terms of psychosomatic illness or unconventional behavior. Hopefully she and her husband will never grow so completely far apart they become unable to find the way back to each other when dissatisfaction becomes high enough to threaten dissolution of the marriage. Ten years of denial of the real self in marriage by either or both partners can lead to great estrangement, and in addition the pride of each may be of such a nature, they can no longer communicate their needs or dissatisfactions.

Just as untreated grief will take its toll on the personality and spirit, so will unrequited love. Both phenomena are deficiencies of the spiritual, emotional part of the self and are to be understood as being analogous to oxygen, vitamin, or water deficiency, the distress of which has far-reaching effects of no small magnitude. It is said that "ignorance of the law of the state or local community excuses no one," and this dictum applies no less and perhaps even more to grief, loss of friendship, or a love deficiency. These all too often are, through lack of understanding, treated cavalierly by man or woman. People who fail to understand another, be it parent and child or spouse, employee, employer or anyone else, should realize when they fail to understand, they should not compound their original obtuseness and indifference with the defensive position of pretending once more not to understand why the neglected one is hurt or withdrawn. The person who "didn't mean to" or is "sorry" should realize he has been deaf, dumb, and blind too many times when the hurt one was doing his best to make his need or needs and his state of mind clear. Thousands of people are still too unaware of the fact that there *are* states of mind in other people beside themselves, and some person or some set of circumstances bring these negative moods about, and they should be given attention, inquiry, and the needed care and treatment whenever possible. And, the fact that so many people fail to realize that there exist states of mind, i.e. a multiplicity of ideas, emotions, and attitudes surrounding the sexual experience alone, is why it remains in the realm of the most mysterious and poorly comprehended areas of human behavior, and the one most unacknowledged and neglected. Man can make a machine of infinite complexity and power and accuracy that will put him far into outer space, yet he cannot make a design for love or even one aspect of its expression, i.e. the sexual one.

To accomplish this understanding however, education in the positive values of sexual relations would have to be taken more out of the control of the fearfully minded, the ungenerous, the caterers to traditional values and placed with those realizing the inevitability of change, as well as the need for change, when change is safe, sane, and possible. The close-minded followers of the old, because of a fixed idea that age-old custom must perforce be the best custom, are the ones who are helping to keep sex in its former long-held reputation of being a sordid, dangerous, and wicked expression of man's most necessary emotional needs.

The male is prone to take the position that the woman owes it to him to be at the time of marriage and thereafter a higher symbol of purity, beauty, and fidelity and to exist for him permanently as such throughout a marriage of whatever length. Why should this be demanded of her any more than of him? His dealings with her outside the bedroom would not confirm this high regard, self-discipline, and otherwise sterling character. He tends to go into a tantrum of furious condemnation at the thought of her receiving, by way of anyone else, the joy and pleasure he ever was able to give her or obtain from her sexually. Even if he has never been able to give this to her or obtain it from her, he is all too prone to assume she and the other man could and would unquestionably reach greater heights of delight and pleasure than with him. What he should realistically know as the truth of the matter, is that if she were to enter into a sexual adventure with another man, the other could be a *different* experience than she has had with him, but would not be very different, and certainly unlikely to be any better. It is only his sense of inferiority that causes him to see his rival as achieving or receiving so much more with her. If he thought twice about the matter sanely, he would realize that "differentness" contains no guarantee of "betterness." In reviewing his own experience he probably cannot recall encountering any such remarkable variations in a woman's abilities to elevate him to any higher level of intense pleasure so exceeding any other. Nor has he been able to produce such great variations in a woman's response to him. How many women has he ever known who found such rapture in a sexual relation with him, she could never do other than reminisce upon the ecstasy of it daily, and as a result be unable to function normally in her current environment? A few may sometimes be highly preoccupied emotionally with a man for days or weeks, but when this is the case it is not his sexual technique alone that serves to keep him in her mind. It is due to his many other personality characteristics, characteristics that intrigued her prior to any sexual relation with him and to which the sexual relation may or may not have added anything one way or the other.

THE HISTORY OF SEXUALITY'S RISE IN REPUTATION

For over nineteen centuries religion branded all who wanted, needed, and sought more of the inner soul of his fellow man (50 percent or more of whom happen to be women) as sinners unless they contracted for a monogamous marriage. In the twentieth century, psychology came on the scene in greater force and branded the same person neurotic, or infantile, or immature, or unstable. This may have been a step forward, but nevertheless, the words sinner and neurotic are hardly complimentary names in the idiom of modern medicine and law.

There is a phenomenon often seen by any observant individual that reveals that vivacity is imparted to the unvivacious only by another person possessing the vivacious quality. Two over-serious or over-intellectual people do not activate a new species of man-kind, who develops and shapes his personality pattern in their presence. There is an infectious quality to the emotional integra-tion taking place within a personality of humor, gaiety, the ability to laugh, to enjoy nature, the arts, one's fellow man in his various costumes and posturings and the capacity to give his productions more than one interpretation. There are those whose training in early life makes them terrified of a new and unstructured situation into which they have not been indoctrinated with the learned pre-cision of a seventeenth century minuet. They go into panic if asked to function by the dictum recently propounded in psychotherapy that our only security is the versatility to deal adequately with the constantly unexpected event or personal interaction.

These people love the rules formulated so long ago regardless of how inapplicable they are to the current scene. Rules, dogma, and absolutes give them security and they try to get everyone else to follow their set plan. They call their plan the moral one, the only safe one, when in truth they are afraid they cannot keep up with or adapt themselves to any different plan.

To speak to the phenomenon of love for a moment (which should never be divorced from sex or sex from it, because both these phenomena are always mutually complementary to a varying degree), love demands that we enjoy the one we claim to love, and that we wish him well and direct our energies to help him in the way he needs, i.e. educationally, emotionally, economically, or assuage his discomfort if in need or distress. We defy anyone to say the factor of love in a sexual relationship is never there at all, be it ever so slight. And, in the best sexual relationships known to an individual and to any historical recounting of them by the most eloquent of writers, the amount of love present and generated in largest measure *by* the sexual aspect of the relationship has approached the sublime and carries with it the highest form of devotion and dedication and help to the very essence of the human being or personality history has on record. Hence, to brand sexual relationships outside of marriage as neurotic is to disavow the elements of courage, the defiance of tradition (a phenomenon often praised in other human activities), the rewarding and ful-filling enrichments to the participants, all of which have drawn forth the awe, admiration, praise, and as well furnished inspira-tion for millions of people, and is only a sign of mental retardation in embracing a valuable part of man's endowment.

There is a series of occurrences existent in our society daily that we should think about as we attempt to find some sane and constructive position for sex in our daily lives. The death toll on the highways in 1967 was 53,100 and the injured 1,900,000. If every parent could receive the same guarantee to safety on the highway for his child or children that he can obtain for safety from the reputed dangerous or evil results of sexual intercourse (if contraception were observed and the community would cease being hypocritical), most of them would doubtless choose it without argument. We don't worry too much about this staggering toll in human death and injury. Yet, parents will become rabidly critical at the possibility of a sexual experience by their child from age three to age sixty or more. So, the young person goes ahead anyway out of sight and sound of parental disapproval. This same parent knows he cannot control the young person's behavior by the volume of his denunciation of the act, but he doesn't know any other way of imparting some sexual education, so he grasps at this silly one. These same parents would raise more storm and strife over a known sexual escapade of their children than they would at their son's departure for the Vietnam War.

THE AFFAIR AS A SELF-CHOSEN MEANS TO A GREATER SENSE OF LIVING

There are many more or less controlled group efforts these days whose avowed use is to live more, love more, and feel more deeply. More people by far become involved in an affair than undertake psychotherapy first as a means of ascertaining how they might direct their energies toward greater personal happiness and fulfillment. People often enter into affairs without thought of consequences, or whether each is capable of living and taking care of much more than one person emotionally, i.e. of intending to give them sufficient tokens of their personal meaning and value to insure a continuity of the relationship. These considerations should be weighed so that an individual can form some estimate as to whether he is capable of making an affair of value, rather than a guilty piece of behavior, hectic and reproachful because one participant cannot be available when the other is free. Each should be able to appreciate the values in meeting together and take the experience for what it contains for them, an addition in one of life's adventures or a fortunate interlude handed them by fate, and into which they bring a side of themselves poorly or not at all understood or fulfilled at home. If replaced by the affair each should make himself a better mate or spouse at home, and people so often enough to invite the public to view the affair with less prejudice.

It is highly probable that most people who enter into an affair would have a difficult time living together as man and wife, were it possible to make an easy and uncomplicated change. Why? The answer to that question is simple and has long since been given by the one who first noted that man is basically not a monogamous animal and of course woman is not either. Woman is more educated to monogamy historically and woman has a greater investment of psychic energy in most instances in home and children. But, this still doesn't make her sexually monogamous by any means. She is only relatively more monogamous psychologically than the male and has used this comparative difference as a virtue in itself. Women have been known who lived monogamously and they do exist, but they weren't monogamous by nature according to their own admission. Those who were latently sexually vivacious were merely waiting for the appropriate man and the sufficiently romantic setting. Those less highly sexed admitted they would doubtless respond to chivalrous treatment and high need of them bespoken by a man on an occasion when they felt sufficiently needed or the implicit rewards were great enough. Any devotion to a husband that could never, never be breached has never been put forth as the reason for a monogamous existence on the part of a woman. Such single-hearted devotion may have a high level of importance in the earlier years of marriage, but decreases with greater experience and knowledge of the world through longer living, aided by some of the husband's failures to continue to make her feel that previous importance to him.

THE FORMER ETHIC AND THE AFFAIR

What of morals, what of ideals, what of Biblical and other ethical injunctions? As stated earlier it must be noted that we are moving rapidly away from a society in which religion alone controls man's behavior, or even influences it greatly. Yearly, for better or worse, he is taking responsibility for his behavior into his own hands and living by the results. These results, good or bad, are his own decision and it is high time he took over this responsiblity. He has been shunning it long enough with his prayers and incantations, rather than face up to a more honest appraisal of his own abilities and a better use of the assets given him long since by nature and mind power, and by God also for the believer.

Man thinks and experiments in all scientific areas and also in many areas of human behavior. He has shown himself far better at thinking and arranging the elements of technological progress than those in human progress, health, and welfare. He has been so reared that he holds his own self-esteem dearly and wards off any suggestion that would place him as other than a perfect person beloved and cared for by as many others as he can place at his control and disposal.

Hence, an affair is a venture that threatens to reduce in some measure the control man (or woman) holds upon those he committed himself to once upon a time. But, it has been shown in how many ways man errs and hurts himself, as well as others, by attempting to arrogate to himself so much control of others, and what is more, uses harsh means to maintain this control. A greater freedom for all has slowly been coming in the affairs of men, and the affair in marriage is but one of the many evidences of it. Therefore, rather than complain at mention of an affair, as if mention of it really exacerbated its practice, the reader is appealed to to give the affair, and at least these few comments in connection with it, consideration. Ignoring it will not cause it to disappear, and to give it higher meaning, prestige, and a place of usefulness and high purpose rather than one execrable conduct should lead to better human understanding and compassion for what has been found to be good for many.

HOW NEUROTIC IS THE AFFAIR?

It could be conceded that plenty of sexual relationships in and out of marriage are, and have been, neurotic. But, to label all of them neurotic is arrant nonsense. The number of neurotically-held together marriages would doubtless by far exceed the neurotic sexual affairs outside of marriage! It is often the affair outside of marriage that prevents the neurotic marriage from being made and neurotically maintained, and doubtless at times has

prevented mayhem or murder, divorce, or complete disillusionment and misery to the children of this despotically neurotic
enslavement to social form called "marital fidelity." And, likewise
it has been fear, not virtue nor maturity, that has prevented thousands of people from starting or maintaining a congenial sexual
liaison with another person outside their marriage. If they
believed they could manage it without discovery and censure, they
would begin it within the next forty-eight hours. The hypocrisy
in this field of potential action is collosal. We also have no data
whatever as yet to enable us to know how many marriages would
have existed without affairs, had the participants been knowledgeable about how more intimacy could be exchanged at the social
level without sexual relations. The beginning of an affair may be
the result of both parties feeling that intimate conversation and
personality exchange must be followed by an affair or each has
merely been "teasing," an unfortunate word connoting a challenge
that neither were courageous enough to pick up. Yet an affair
should have much better and more mature reasons for its inception. But, people will never come to know more about intimacy
and what to do with it as long as the human touch of a sexual
nature is so frowned upon and is held up as such inferior behavior.

Since so many centuries of marriage in its original form has
done so poorly at creating happy, even relatively satisfied and creative people, why not do some serious thinking about what a more
accepting utilization of the unused love and creative potential can
do, which is lying formant in all people? But, regrettably it often
will not, or cannot, be released to the spouse due to long-standing
resentments against a long series of people previously. Yet, it will
release itself for another, differently constituted and a differently
behaving person, and once this occurs it may then, and only then,
find its way back to the spouse.

If 1,968 years of monogamy have not brought people of the
world above the level of alcoholism, drug-taking, bribery, crime,
rioting war, and insanity, any gain, which might lie in an affair
as described, seems worth full discussion at least. The affair has
not been devoid of heartaches, pain, and discord, but neither is
any other human activity, even tennis, pinochle, skiing, or horti-
culture. Adultery is being practiced by large numbers of devotees.
Why not permit its reality and thereby give it an opportunity
to succeed or fail within more public scrutiny and a more open
knowledge of whether its results and effects are so very good or
so very bad!

Chapter 13

SEX AS FUN

By Harold Greenwald, Ph.D.

Enlightened parents now tell their children all about sex except its most important aspect—that it's fun.

Thus, I have heard parents explain in detail the function of the penis and the vulva, how entrance is effected, what the usual positions are, and how semen is deposited, but almost never do they explain that it is exquisitely pleasurable. Rather, they make it sound like some complicated physiological exercise that for some strange reason has to be sanctioned by a host of irrelevant factors. Once it was marriage; now the more liberal ones will admit that love is the requirement for this biological experiment. This is probably the foundation of the generation gap over which there is so much anguished wringing of hands.

Nor are parents the only ones who eliminate the fun element. The very organization of this symposium shows the existence of a new kind of puritanism, or perhaps more precisely, the continued existence of such puritanism in a new form. We are bidden to perceive sex as a holistic experience, as a form of communication, as regeneration, as anything but what it now usually is for civilized man—a form of play.

With the perfection of birth control techniques, sexual relations no longer have biological functions; instead they are a form of play. With the grim seriousness, characteristic of our profession —particularly in those of us engaged in the study of sexual behavior—play has been one of the most neglected human activities.

The essence of the puritanical approach is not necessarily antisexual, but it is definitely anti-pleasure. To accept sex as fun, as a relaxed form of joyous play, is to look at it as a form of that dreaded emotion, pleasure.

Much of the generational gap that exists now and in the past has been around the issue of pleasure. On one side are arrayed the forces that look on life as a grim business devoted to good works or earning money, and on the other is that strange, subversive group that considers the pursuit of pleasure an aim in itself. It might be argued that the heedless pursuit of immediate pleasurable gratification can be destructive to long-range hedonism. Anyone who has more than a theoretical knowledge of sex knows full well that it is a pleasure unmeasurably heightened by delay of gratification, particularly if that delay is enhanced by the exploratory behavior known as foreplay. Again that ubiquitous word—play—appears.

I am not alone in believing that many of the world's ills are the product of the pleasure-destroyers. Why, even in this permissive era, is there still so much anxiety about pleasure, particularly sexual pleasure? Every clinician, who is willing to look at the evidence, rather than make the evidence fit preconceived notions of his own, has to make sense of the apparent paradox that children raised in the post-Freud, post-Spock period still show evidence of severe impairment of their ability to enjoy sexual pleasure, despite parents who seemed to be enlightened and permissive. For example, one highly attractive young lady I saw, whose parents made no objection to her bringing her lovers home with her and permitting her to sleep with them in her bedroom, had a serious problem with frigidity and could achieve a rare orgasm only after the most Herculean labors on the part of both partners. The parental permissiveness was not even a recent occurrence but was characteristic of her entire upbringing. Even on the subject of masturbation, she remembered only understanding and a lack of punitiveness about her childhood self-explorations. However, that was what she remembered consciously. The problem, I feel reasonably certain, on the basis of material that came out while she was in hypnotic age-regression, was due to the preverbal injunctions against masturbation. It is my belief that the very early reactions of the mother when diapering her infant created much of the young woman's still-lingering anxiety about sex.

Some time ago, I had an opportunity to observe some films of mothers diapering their children. Again and again the good Gesell-indoctrinated mothers removed their infants' hands from their genitals when they eagerly reached for their centers of pleasurable sensation. Many mothers, no matter what their intellectual beliefs, still suffer from such anxieties and transmit these anxieties non-verbally, through muscular tension, to the children. The child then is conditioned against sexual pleasure at a pre-verbal stage, thus making it difficult to remove the inhibition through purely verbal interventions.

So strong is the taboo against masturbation that it was not until the best-seller *Portnoy's Complaint* that the subject had even been treated in literature.

For five years I lectured weekly on psychology at a large resort hotel. During these years I spoke about prostitution, group sex, premarital sex, perversions, and adultery, and there were no complaints. Once I was asked, "Will masturbation drive you crazy?" I answered with a simple "no," and there were five complaints to the management that I had advocated masturbation. A call girl who had spent almost two years discussing in great detail and with considerable calm, some of the more aberrant requirements of some of her clients finally broke down when associating to a dream and said, "Now you will know why I'm crazy; yes, I play with myself."

On another occasion, when I asked a 25-year-old married woman of considerable sexual experience how frequently she masturbated, she leaped off the couch with crimson cheeks and said, "Does your wife know how you talk? I left my last analyst for talking to me that way."

I have been so impressed with the powerful taboos still operative on the subject of masturbation, or "self-abuse," as many dictionaries still define it, that I have frequently contemplated writing a treatise on the "Art and Pleasure of Playing with Yourself." Now Philip Roth has saved me the trouble. However, I wonder if Roth didn't underestimate the role that the taboo against masturbation played in the etiology of that formidable syndrome known as Portnoy's Complaint. After all, the protagonist spends most of his time masturbating both literally and verbally.

Another taboo that still exists and is perpetuated by many of the most enlightened pundits of sex is that against casual sex—sex for fun. Recently I was on the beach at Fire Island, speaking to a charming young writer of pornography whom I know, and I commented on the physical attractiveness of two bouncy bikini-enhanced young ladies. My writer friend stared at me, shocked, and said, "I'm surprised at you, a psychologist talking that way. My shrink says that it is an expression of hostility to be interested in other women."

Apparently his doctor was enforcing the puritan dictate against sex-for-fun by defining it as hostility. Of course, sex may be used that way, and often is by passive-aggressives who openly flaunt their interest in others before the eyes of a loved one. However, I cannot understand how a discreet expression of admiration for a female other than my wife is an expression of anything but an esthetic appreciation.

Other hidebound therapists define the human tendency to stray occasionally in equally censorious terms. It must be realized that an interpretation of a patient's behavior may not be the statement of an immutable truth but an effort to devise an aversive stimulus that becomes self-administrating when it is accepted by the patient. Thus, telling this friendly, warm young man that passing interest in a woman other than his wife was a form of hostility aroused a self-administering aversive stimulus whenever he began to experience such interest and would, if reinforced enough (sometimes the process of such reinforcement is referred to as "working through"), result in the extinction of the pleasurable response to other females.

A skilled therapist will intuitively choose the interpretation best designed to eliminate or enhance certain kinds of behavior. The proper administration of such interpretations can be infinitely more effective and pervasive for humans than such minor stimuli as mild electric shocks or hard candies. Among the aversive stimuli utilized by therapists interested in controlling their own and their patients' tendency to casual sexual encounters are: "It shows a lack of commitment"; "You are orally fixated, looking for another breast all the time"; "It is a defense against feelings of sexual inadequacy"; "It is a reaction formation against deep-seated fears of homosexuality." When you reach the proper age, it becomes: "You are a dirty old man!"

If you wish to maintain your interest in sex-for-pleasure, it is necessary to take effective measures against such statements and turn them into compliments. For example, since I have been apprised of my dirty-old-man-hood on more than one occasion, I have convinced myself that it is merely a testimonial to my continued potency and virility. Similarly, what in the world is wrong

with looking for another breast? Art-collecting is an honored and esteemed hobby, and what *objets d'art* compare in beauty and function with a well-formed or uniquely proportioned breast? The ability to respond to external stimuli is a characteristic of living organisms; the more ready the organism is to respond, the greater the intelligence.

If I wanted to use interpretations on the other side—that is, in favor of casual, non-monogamous sex—I could point out that it is a characteristic of highly successful individuals in all fields of endeavor, from artists to actors to senators. Having reread portions of Freud's *Three Contributions to the Theory of Sex,* I must sound a warning against some of his characterization of sexual activity, though of course he was aware of the pleasure-giving qualities of sexual play. In discussing my observation of the non-monogamous character of most highly successful men with my former teacher, Theodor Reik, who had been Freud's protegé, I asked him if he knew any such men who were monogamous. He answered simply and directly, "No, not one."

"How about Freud?" I inquired.

"Well," he said, "Freud was not really monogamous. He had many involvements with women other than his wife, but never at a sexual level. You see," he added, "Freud had some very funny ideas about sex."

Chapter 14

THE NEW SEXUALITY AND THE HOMOSEXUAL

By Del Martin and Phyllis Lyon

At the end of the 1940s the paradoxical and hypocritical sexual attitudes and mores of the American people were nakedly contrasted with actual sexual behavior by the Kinsey reports.[1] The double image in the mirror revealed a puritanical, repressive sexual moral code on the one hand and an active, expressive sexual behavior on the other. The degree of sexual inhibition of an individual appeared to be dependent upon his or her ability to cope with, or rationalize, the fear and guilt imposed by society's codes in relationship to one's personal development of self-knowledge and sexual identity.

It was in this atmosphere at mid-century, with the awakening of intelligent inquiry and a healthy skepticism of a sexual morality based upon medieval superstitions, that the homophile movement came into being. (Homophile is a word coined or put into usage by the Mattachine Society during the 1950s. Whereas homosexual denotes sex with same, homophile connotes love of same. Too often people think of homosexuality solely in terms of specific sexual acts and do not regard the homosexual's sexual behavior in context, as a single facet or characteristic of the whole person.) Certainly the knowledge that an estimated one-third of the male population of the United States had experienced overt homosexual activity during their lifetime exerted some influence on those who started the Mattachine Foundation in Los Angeles in 1950. The foundation began with a series of secret discussion groups meeting

regularly "to pool what we know, to explore what we feel is wrong, and to remind ourselves that we are mutually dependent members of one of the world's largest minorities."[2]

Prior to this time homosexuals had been successfully isolated— isolated from society, from each other, and from the realization of their human potential. The knowledge that "I am not alone" had a terrific impact on homosexuals across the country. They began to seek each other out to organize for mutual protection and to promote public education and research. During the fifties there were three major national organizations: the Mattachine Society, headquartered in San Francisco; One, Inc., in Los Angeles (both offshoots of the Mattachine Foundation); and the Daughters of Bilitis, founded independently in San Francisco as a women's organization dealing with problems of the Lesbian, in particular, and homosexuality in general. The movement expanded and accelerated in the sixties and by 1970 there were at least one hundred organizations throughout the country, many of them on college campuses, and more forming every day. They run the gamut from radical to conservative, from purely social clubs to those both social and educational and/or political action groups. In addition, there are "tavern guilds" (associations of bars and restaurants catering to homosexuals) and councils on religion and the homosexual, involving clergy and laity of various religious denominations.

Because of these organizations homosexuals need no longer feel completely isolated or alienated. With the support of their peers they have learned to accept themselves and have gained a sense of identity and dignity as human beings. Through the security of the group, they have attained a sense of community in which they can deal with and overcome society-imposed guilt and fear. And they are able to view themselves in terms of the *whole* person of which homosexuality is but a single facet.

As they organized into a movement and became more vocal, homosexuals inevitably turned their attention to social reform— homosexual law reform, realistic sex education, elimination of job discrimination, and changing sexual attitudes and mores. They found that it is impossible to discuss homosexuality without dealing with human sexuality in general. The Judaic-Christian tradition is clearly anti-sexual, not just anti-homosexual. Arbitrary, culturally-conditioned sexual roles and life patterns are just as ill-defined, just as ill-fitting, to heterosexuals as to homosexuals. Society's definitions of masculinity and femininity have little to do with the realities of basic human feelings and potentialities. The lines of division between previously conceived polarities of heterosexuality and homosexuality are not so clearly delineated. It is not so much a matter of different sexual behavior as of self-identity, gender of sex or love partner, and the arbitrary decision that one style is better than the other beacuse of the "nature" of procreation.

The Rev. Dr. Robert L. Treese, professor at Boston University's School of Theology, participating in a 1966 Consultation on Theology and the Homosexual sponsored by Glide Urban Center and the Council on Religion and the Homosexual in San Francisco, had this to say:

> In the realm of human sexuality, I, as a churchman, feel moved to confess that a great deal of the blame for preserving, if not indeed creating, the fears and guilt of sex which permeate our culture, lies at our feet. The failure to see sexual relationship in any other light but the functional one of reproduction has resulted in the limitation of sex to the purely physical with no concept at all of the depth of significant interpersonal trust, empathy, and love of which sexual intercourse, at best, is the expression.[3]

The proscription against heterosexual physical expression that interferes with the normal function of procreation, and against homosexuality in particular, dates back to the Old Testament at a time when it was incumbent upon the Jewish people to increase and multiply for survival of the race. The story of Sodom and Gomorrah has been traditionally interpreted as a condemnation of all homosexuality.[4] However, Dr. D. S. Bailey, an Anglo-Catholic theologian in England, has built a convincing case that this was due to a Jewish reinterpretation or mistranslation of the passage and that "nowhere does it identify that sin explicitly with the practice of homosexuality."[5] Helmut Thielicke, distinguished German theologian, agrees that "it is uncertain whether the passages concerning 'sodomy,' which have been traditionally authoritative, actually refer to homosexual acts at all."[6]

Thielicke, however, points out, "In the New Testament homosexuality is again listed in catalogue fashion with other forms of disobedience, such as idolatry, fornication, adultery, greed, drunkenness, and thievery. Accordingly, there can be no doubt that Paul regards homosexuality as a sin and a perversion of the order of human existence willed by God, even though within this catalogue of vices it is not accented as being *especially* horrible, as many moral theologies would make it appear. The listing of homosexuality with heterosexual offenses like adultery and fornication would rather suggest the problem of whether, along with the total rejection of homosexuality we must not also consider the question to what extent this refers to the libido-conditioned disregard for one's neighbor, in other words, a particular *way* of homosexual behavior (possibly analogous with adultery, polygamy, etc.)."[7]

But this examination of theology with reference to homosexuality is very recent. From Thomas Aquinas' thirteenth-century designation of homosexual practices as *peccatum contra naturum* to the mid-twentieth century there was no reexamination of the nature and meaning of this phenomenon.

In the meantime, the Judaic-Christian tradition of regarding homosexual practices as sinful also became a matter of law. The "buggery" felony statute was enacted by Parliament during the reign of Henry VIII in 1533, thus removing prosecution from the ecclesiastical courts to the criminal courts.[8] With the exception of the penalties of death and forfeiture of property, for which life imprisonment was substituted in 1861, the act remained on the statute books until 1967. At that time the recommendations of the Wolfenden Committee[9] were adopted by Parliament (after ten years of debate), thus legalizing homosexual acts between consenting adults in private. Although the laws on the books of the United States of America are, for the most part, an inheritance from English common law, only two of the fifty states (Illinois and Connecticut) have to date followed England's example. The United States remains the last bulwark of resistance to homosexual law reform—but apparently not without conscience.

For, while law enforcement agencies, which by practice have become the guardians of God's law and society's moral code, cling tenaciously to their authority and control over homosexuals, churchmen have been all too willing to refute the status of homosexuality as a sin or crime per se and to accord the phenomenon a psychopathological label, as claimed by a few vocal psychoanalysts. What the worthy clergy fail to consider is that the symptoms of this so-called mental disorder are in truth the *effects* of repression by society. The consequences of "cure" (change to heterosexuality) as dependent upon reconditioning of behavioral response (as with Pavlov's dogs) is overlooked. The broad dimensions of the homosexual's personhood are violated and sacrificed to the goal of heterosexuality—the standard set by heterosexuals for all citizens.

Meanwhile, in their attempts to articulate the sameness of the human experience, which they share with heterosexuals, homosexuals found themselves victimized by the stereotypes perpetuated by the rhetoric of sin and crime and sickness, as exemplified by the sensation-hunters of the communications media. When they attempted to clarify the actualities of homosexuality as opposed to the purported theories of the academicians, they were accused of being defensive, apologist, or injustice-collectors. In a patriarchal society that idealizes the authority and objectivity of the scientific method, subjectivity had no validity. The consequence of this attitude was research based on preconceived theory and methodological selectivity of subjects into objects to gather a body of data to maintain the status quo. For the study of sexuality, if it is to be complete, cannot be limited to mere observation of actions or behavior. It must deal with the *whole personality*—the intangibles, the subjectivity of feelings, attitudes, emotions, and spiritual consciousness—in terms of itself, not the heterosexual "norm." Sexual energy, the creative force of one's being, cannot be measured in the same way as nuclear energy— even the latter is proving chancy these days. Abstract interrelationships between people must be taken into account, and until the phenomena of mental telepathy and empathy are more highly developed in the human species, this experience remains subjective.

Sociologists Simon and Gagnon point out, "The homosexual, like most significantly labeled persons (whether the label be positive or negative), has *all* of his acts interpreted through the framework of his homosexuality."[10] They go on to say, "What we are suggesting is that we have allowed the homosexual's sexual object choice to dominate and control our imagery of him and have let this aspect of his total life experience appear to determine all his products, concerns, and activities. This prepossessing concern on the part of non-homosexuals with the purely sexual aspect of the homosexual's life is something we would not allow to occur if we were interested in the heterosexual."[11]

The situational factors directing *human* sexual activities, according to Dr. Paul H. Gebhard, director of the Institute for Sex

Research, include the physiological state of the body (age, health, degree of fatigue, nutritional state, intake of alcohol or other drugs, thermal environment, recency of drive fulfillment), cultural factors, and specific, immediate situation stimulus.[12] These situational factors would, of course, apply to homosexual and heterosexual alike.

In a statement issued during the North American Conference of Homophile Organizations in San Francisco in August, 1966, by Dr. Joel Fort, public health specialist and sociologist-criminologist; Dr. Evelyn Hooker, research psychologist at the University of California at Los Angeles, and Dr. Joe K. Adams, psychologist and former Santa Clara County mental health officer, argument is made against too simplistic an approach to homosexuality:

"Some homosexuals, like some heterosexuals, are ill; some homosexuals, like some heterosexuals, are preoccupied with sex as a way of life. But probably for a majority of adults their sexual orientation constitutes only one component of a much more complicated life-style."[13]

Simon and Gagnon outline current standards of mental health and point out that when the heterosexual meets these minimal definitions, he is given a clean bill of health. On the other hand, in practically all cases, the mere presence of homosexuality is seen as *prima facie* evidence of major psychopathology no matter how well the individual may be adjusted in nonsexual areas of life.[14]

The Sexual Revolution which gained momentum in the 1960s raised the very same questions among heterosexuals that had already been posed in the homophile movement during the fifties. Emerging sexual life-styles indicate definite trends toward acceptance of ambosexuality, or regard for personhood rather than fixed masculine and feminine roles, of morality in reference to sexuality only in terms of personal harm to parties involved, of openness to a varied sexual experience to circumvent the guilt-fear-anxiety syndrome, which separates people, of the reaffirmation of love and the regenerative force of its sexual expression, of the validity of the subjective experience upon which personal growth is dependent, of concern for the dehumanizing effect of institutional precepts that are inapplicable to the human experience.

Though many may protest otherwise, it is impossible to consider the homosexual movement without dealing at the same time with Women's Liberation. For both movements are protesting against a sexist society characterized by rigid sex roles and dominated by male supremacy. Both are decrying their dehumanized condition and redefining their identity in human terms rather than by the physiological evidences of one's genitalia.

Lesbian-baiting, a favorite ploy of male antagonists in deprecating the women's movement, has not been as divisive as it once may have been. If anything, it has done more to bind the two movements together into a true sexual revolution. At first, many women fell into the age-old trap, it is true. But women's liberationists in their small rap groups, devoted to raising of consciousness of what it means to be a woman, are coming to realize that their immediate response has been male-defined. In this sexist society, for a woman to be independent means that she *can't be* a woman—her beingness is valid only as she relates to a man or men. That her "femininity" depends solely upon male approval is also made apparent in the various media interviews with women who have claimed some measure of accomplishment or success in the business or political world, when the inevitable questions of loss of femininity and family management are asked.

Yet the alliance between the homophile and women's movements produces its share of paradoxes. While women are protesting being used as sex objects and are seeking alternatives to marriage and the nuclear family, male homosexuals of Gay Liberation are regarding sexual objectification as a focus in their quest for freedom, and others, both male and female, are demanding that marriages between members of the same sex be recognized and legalized.

Carl Wittman, in *Refugees from America: A Gay Manifesto*, says, "For us, sexual objectification is a focus of our quest for freedom. It is precisely that which we are not supposed to share with each other. Learning how to be open and good with each other sexually is part of our liberation. And one obvious distinction: objectification of sex for us is something we choose to do among ourselves, while for women it is imposed by their oppressors."[15]

While the expression of her sexuality and her life-style may tie her to the homophile movement, economically and family-wise the Lesbian is very much bound to the women's movement. As the male homosexual perceives the overall plight or dilemma of his Lesbian sister and examines his own male chauvinism (although one doubts that much of this perception or examination is actually going on), he begins to see that the women's movement is a protest against a male-dominated heterosexual system, which pervades all of the American institutions (political, religious, educational, etc,) and is just as oppressive to *him* as a human being.

Wittman says, "All men are infected with male chauvinism— we are brought up that way. It means we assume that women play subordinate roles and are less human than ourselves."[16] Even the outcast male homosexual feels superior to women, just as the Black male, the Latin male, and the Asian male, while fighting for ethnic or racial equality, still maintain superiority over *all* women.

"Male chauvinism, however, is not central to us," Wittman says of male homosexuals. "We can junk it much more easily than straight men can. We have largely opted out of a system which oppresses women daily—our egos are not built on putting women down and having them build us up. Also, living mostly in a male world, we have become used to playing different roles, doing our own shit work. And finally, we have a common enemy: the big male chauvinists are also the big anti-gays."[17] It should be pointed out that Wittman's comments and attitudes are more common among the younger, radical male homosexuals than among those who consider themselves more middle class or establishment oriented.

Kate Millett, in *Sexual Politics*, observes, "Divorced from their usual justification in an assumed biological congruity, masculine and feminine stand out as terms of praise and blame, authority and servitude, high and low, master and slave."[18] Male heterosexuals scorn male homosexuals and regard them as "effeminate" because they have rejected competition in the conquest of women.

At the Daughters of Bilitis convention in New York in July, 1970, a panel was held on "The Lesbian's Role in the Women's Movement." Minda Bickman of the New York Radical Feminists contended, "Women as a class cannot be divided into Lesbians and non-Lesbians."[19] She said that women are becoming increasingly sensitive to Lesbianism as a political statement, since "the institution of sexual intercourse is another way of oppressing women."[20]

Caroline Bird, author of *Born Female*,[21] at the same conference put it this way: "Due to the population explosion the prestige connected with human reproduction is losing its stranglehold on our culture. Once women are liberated from childbearing there will be a need for a change in cultural values and a need for a choice of alternate life-styles. One of these choices is the same-sex marriage."[22]

"Laws requiring marriage partners to be of different sexes are unconstitutional,"[23] declared Rita E. Hauser, United States representative to the United Nations Human Rights Commission, during a "Women's Liberation and the Constitution" panel discussion at the 1970 national meeting of the American Bar Association.

"Legal distinction on the basis of sex is no longer reasonable, and I am willing to apply that view to any and all sets of circumstances the mind may conceive," the New York attorney said. State laws that require marriage partners to be of opposite sexes "predicate reproduction as the legal consideration of marriage, and that view, I submit, is no longer consistent with fact." If limiting reproduction has become the social goal, "I know of no better way of accomplishing that than marriages between the same sexes."

"I am not urging this as a social policy," she added, "rather I am arguing that the right to marry, a right guaranteed by law, cannot be premised on sex distinctions which serve to deny equal protection of the law to all persons."

The fact that both Lesbian and male homosexual couples have indeed filed applications for marriage licenses and have requested and received religious rites consecrated by a few concerned and courageous clergymen, marks a trend apparently taken seriously enough to warrant a protest from the Vatican.

Two Lesbians filed suit July 10, 1970, to force county authorities in Louisville, Kentucky, to grant them a marriage license. They contended there was nothing in Kentucky law that prohibited marriage between parties of the same sex. However, County Attorney J. Bruce Miller took the position that while the law did not specifically forbid the marriage of homosexuals, there were laws against homosexual acts.

On conclusion of a two-part series of articles on the prospects for same sex marriages, the San Francisco *Chronicle* editorialized:

Marriage is the public announcement of a civil contract between two people showing binding intent to share their lives. It is also a personal contract, showing intent to share their mental and

emotional "resources." Members of the heterosexual
derive great security, pride, and social acceptance from t
dering public" of an honest, social commitment in the eye
and man." It would seem only in keeping with the times that consideration be given to allowing the homosexual minority the same
rights to this sense of fulfillment.[24]

A homosexual is a person whose primary psychological, emotional, and erotic interests are directed toward a member of the
same sex, whether or not this is ever expressed overtly(For homosexuals are like other people. They are capable of deep and abiding
love.)They may suffer from personal rejection and unrequited
love. Or they may form lasting relationships, obviously bound by
mutual commitment—there being no laws or religious rites or
community support to keep the couple together. Homosexuals may
also be celibate, males may suffer from impotence, and Lesbians
may be frigid. For homosexuals, despite popular conceptions, may
suffer from sexual hang-ups the same as do heterosexuals in this
puritan anti-sexual culture. Homosexuals, however, seldom, if
ever, obtain the benefit of marriage counseling or even of very
knowledgeable personal counseling.

Traditionally, the social, legal, and religious sanctions and
pressures have conspired against the formation of homophile
"marriages" and against their continuation once established.
Partners in lasting relationships have had to reject the butch-
femme, dominant-submissive, aggressive-dependent roles, which
mimic the only marriage they know—that of Mom and Dad. Homosexuals in love embark upon a mutual adventure in growth, and
amid much pain and good humor, they modify preconceived concepts, shift, and redefine roles in order to build their own pattern
of marriage.

Robert W. Anderson, in an address on "Gay Marriage" at a
Symposium on the Life-Style of the Homosexual, sponsored by
the Council on Religion and the Homosexual in San Francisco on
April 25, 1969, said he felt "companionship, equality, and mutuality play a bigger part in the gay marriage than in the straight.
While developing from rather spontaneous origins, the relationship endures and has longevity only so long as mutual goals continue to be fulfilled."[25]

"In the gay marriage," such as the one Mr. Anderson has
"happily and gaily" been an integral part for over thirteen years,

"there is opportunity to test each additional step toward complete involvement. At the very outset, the guys have made it a few times and have already discovered certain special ways in which they are important to each other. They may decide that they wish to share an apartment together. They are very careful to share expenses equally, they don't combine their bank accounts immediately, and possessions like cars and furniture can still be split up into 'yours and mine.' Somewhere along the way they discover that 'my family' means my lover and me and not my parents' family and that 'my home' has become our apartment on Pine Street, and not the house where I grew up in Davenport, Iowa. They make such daring moves as naming each other as beneficiaries on their group life insurance policies. Ultimately, all your plans are your mutual plans, and you find your life completely involved with that guy you love and see every day and who means more to you than anyone else in the world."[26]

While it is generally believed that Lesbians form more lasting relationships and that the male homosexual is more promiscuous, many males do form long-term partnerships. However, they are less apt to require sexual fidelity as a prime requisite in their mutual compact. Conversely, many Lesbians are promiscuous, both heterosexually and homosexually, during that period in their lives when they are trying to determine their sexual identity. But, as in heterosexuality, there are varying values and behavior patterns among homosexuals.

The literature describing homosexuality has been primarily devoted to the male—a fascination with the enigma causing a man to abdicate, whether consciously or unconsciously, his role of supremacy in this patriarchal society. The Lesbian, being secondary—a woman—is generally disregarded, or mentioned in passing, and is further alienated.

This is best explained in the treatise, "The Woman-Identified WOMAN," by the Radicalesbians of New York: "A Lesbian is the rage of all women condensed to the point of explosion. She is the woman who, often beginning at an extremely early age, acts in accordance with her inner compulsion to be a more complete and freer human being than her society—perhaps then, but certainly later—cares to allow her. These needs and actions, over a period of years, bring her into painful conflict with people, situations, the accepted ways of thinking, feeling, and behaving until she is in a state of continual war with everything around her, and usually with herself. She may not be fully conscious of the political implications of what for her began as personal necessity, but on some level she has not been able to accept the limitations and oppression laid on her by the most basic role of her society—the female role. The turmoil she experiences tends to induce guilt proportional to the degree to which she feels she is not meeting social expectations, and/or eventually drives her to question and analyze what the rest of her society more or less accepts. She is forced to evolve her own life pattern, often living much of her life alone, learning usually much earlier than her 'straight' (heterosexual) sisters about the essential aloneness of life (which the myth of marriage obscures) and about the reality of illusions. To the extent that she cannot expel the heavy socialization that goes with being female, she can never truly find peace with herself. For she is caught somewhere between accepting society's view of her—in which case she cannot accept herself—and coming to understand what this sexist society has done to her and why it is functional and necessary for it to do so. Those of us who work that through find ourselves on the other side of a tortuous journey through a night that may have been decades long. The perspective gained from that journey, the liberation of self and of all women, is something to be shared with all women. . . ."[27]

Inability to identify with inherited sex roles is but one part of the problem male and female homosexuals face. Alienation from the mainstream of society and sanctions against a state of being have forced most homosexuals into a dual life based on lies and hypocrisy as a matter of self-survival in protecting their careers and families. Aside from the obvious vulnerability to blackmail, maintaining a two-faced existence causes much anguish, fear, and guilt, with inevitable debilitating effects on the personality. For it is only at that point where the homosexual can truly say, "The hell with what 'they' think—*I* know who I am," that he or she can come to terms with inner being and attain self-acceptance. Stability, sanity, spiritual growth can only emerge when there is self-acceptance—recognition of the worth and dignity and validity of the essence of one's being, one's spirit, regardless of his or her homosexuality. From that point on, the homosexual is able to function in, and contribute to, society, but still with certain calculated risks because others do not recognize this holistic view he has of himself.

Homosexual youth today, unlike their predecessors, are not satisfied with this rationale for living. Inspired by the black people and their freedom movement, learning from the hippie revolution to trade the ugliness of pretension for the beauty of openness and love between people, they reject the homosexual ghetto of self-protection. Gay Liberation groups have surfaced on the streets of American cities to proclaim, "I'm Gay and I'm Proud!" The largest such demonstration was the march in New York City—fifteen to twenty thousand strong, according to the *New York Times*—on June 28, 1970, as a celebration of the first anniversary of the Christopher Street riots, the first time homosexuals ever rose up together in rebellion against police abuse.

"Homosexuality is *not* a lot of things. It is not a makeshift in the absence of the opposite sex; it is not hatred or rejection of the opposite sex; it is not genetic; it is not the result of broken homes, except inasmuch as we could see the sham of American marriage. *Homosexuality is the capacity to love someone of the same sex*," the Gay Manifesto declares.[28]

And inherent in Gay Liberation is openness and honesty about one's sexuality. "Come Out," the youth are demanding of their elders, who have been closeted for too long. "Gay Is Good," they proclaim.

While some are opting for legalizing gay marriage, others are seeking a number of social relationships and living situations. "Things we want to get away from are: (1) exclusiveness, properties attitudes toward each other, a mutual pact against the rest of the world; (2) promises about the future, which we have no right to make and which prevent us from, or make us feel guilty about, growing; (3) inflexible roles, roles which do not reflect us at the moment but are inherited through mimicry and inability to define equalitarian relationships.

"We have to define for ourselves a new pluralistic, role-free social structure for ourselves. It must contain both the freedom and physical space for people to live alone, live together for a while, live together for a long time, either as couples or in larger numbers; and the ability to flow easily from one of these states to another as our needs change," declared Wittman.[29]

The new sexuality, if it can be defined and if indeed it is to come about, must be a freeing experience allowing human beings to respond to one another freely and reciprocally without rigid role definition. It must take into consideration man's ambosexual nature, as exemplified by the Kinsey scale of human behavior. It must be viewed nonjudgmentally, sexuality in and of itself being neither moral nor immoral. It must provide an element of choice, unrestricted alternatives in sexual life-styles. It must encompass the trans-physical qualities of love, empathy, and concern for one another's personhood.

In this context the new homosexual will emerge—a whole person whose unlimited creative potential can be realized to society's benefit.

CHAPTER NOTES

1. Alfred Kinsey et al., *Sexual Behavior in the Human Male* (Philadelphia, Pa.: Saunders, 1948), and Kinsey et al., *Sexual Behavior in the Human Female* (Philadelphia, Pa.: Saunders, 1953).
2. Marvin Cutler, ed., *Homosexuals Today* (Los Angeles; One, Inc.: 1956), p. 9.
3. Robert L. Treese, *Homosexuality: A Contemporary View of the Biblical Perspective* (San Francisco: Glide Urban Center, 1966), p. 2.
4. Gen. 19:1-28.
5. Derrick Sherwin Bailey, *Homosexuality and the Western Christian Tradition* (New York: Longmans, Green, 1955), p. 9.
6. Helmut Thielicke, "The Problem of Homosexuality," in *The Ethics of Sex* Trans. J. Doberstein (New York: Harper and Row, 1964), pp. 277–287.
7. Ibid.
8. Montgomery H. Hyde, *The Love That Dared Not Speak Its Name* (Boston: Little, Brown, 1970), pp. 37–39.
9. *The Wolfenden Report.* Report of the Committee on Homosexual Offenses and Prostitution, England (New York: Lancer Books, 1964).
10. William Simon and John H. Gagnon, "Homosexuality: The Formulation of a Sociological Perspective," *Journal of Health and Social Behavior* 8, no. 3 (September 1967): 177.
11. Ibid., p. 179.
12. Paul H. Gebhard, "Situational Factors Affecting Human Sexual Behavior," in *Sex and Behavior*, ed. Frank Beach (New York: John Wiley, 1965), pp. 484–488.
13. Authors' notes.
14. Simon and Gagnon, "Homosexuality," p. 180.
15. Carl Wittman, *Refugees from America: A Gay Manifesto* (San Francisco: Council on Religion and the Homosexual, 1970), p. 6.
16. Ibid., p. 2.
17. Ibid.
18. Kate Millett, *Sexual Politics* (Garden City, New York: Doubleday, 1970), p. 343.
19. Authors' notes.
20. Ibid.
21. Caroline Bird, *Born Female* (New York: McKay, 1968).

18. Kate Millett, *Sexual Politics* (Garden City, New York: Doubleday, 1970), p. 343.

19. Authors' notes.

20. Ibid.

21. Caroline Bird, *Born Female* (New York: McKay, 1968).

22. Authors' notes.

23. Rita E. Hauser, *San Francisco Chronicle*, 11 August 1970.

24. *San Francisco Chronicle*, 16 July 1970.

25. Robert W. Anderson, "Gay Marriage." Unpublished paper presented at a symposium on the Life-style of the Homosexual sponsored by The Council on Religion and the Homosexual, San Francisco, April 25, 1969, pp. 2–3.

26. Ibid., pp. 4–5.

27. Radicalesbians, "The Woman-Identified WOMAN," *RAT*, 22 May–4 June, 1970, p. 18.

28. Wittman, *Refugees from America, p.* 2.

29. Ibid., pp. 3–4.

PART IV

SEX
AND SOCIETY

Chapter 15

SEX AND HEALTH

By Joel Fort, M.D.

Although sex is not a four-letter word, it is often treated as such, being omitted from most conversation, locked in the bedroom or back seat, and blended in our thinking with the concepts of unhealthy, dirty, wrong, unclean, evil, sinful, illegal, and Communist. The latter day outcry of the Sons of Birch that sex education is a Communist plot (along with gun control, fluoridation, mental health, and social change) has not only increased the well-known generation gap but led some young people to take a far greater interest in Communism. Totalitarian movements, whether right, left, or ambidextrous, have always been highly moralistic and puritanical. This certainly includes such early church fathers as St. Paul, who although advocating celibacy, thought it much better to marry than to burn; and St. Augustine, who after a rather full sex life, retired to proclaim that a woman's thighs are the gates of hell.

We really have no well-defined and agreed-upon definition of sexual health or healthy sex, but generally depend upon subjective and arbitrary standards of normality (= health) promulgated by the various moral entrepreneurs of the society: politicians, ministers, and journalists. We routinely shift from statistical to biological to moral to legal to social standards, or a mixture. Frequently we cop out, as we do with "mental health," by considering as sexually healthy anything that isn't a "disease" (undefined, but most of the time meaning perversion, crime against nature, or illegal act).

Leaving aside the symbolic biblical concept that the thought
of sex with your neighbor's wife is the same as adultery or the
possibility that everything good in life is either illegal or unhealthy, probably the only form of sexual behavior generally
accepted in the United States as healthy or normal is heterosexual
intercourse within marriage. Some would qualify this by requiring
that the coitus be solely for purposes of procreation. The criminal
law—local, state, or national—collectively bars all but penile-
vaginal intercourse between a man and a woman legally married
to each other, where both have consented to this specific act
without duress and where it takes place in private, and with the
man on top of the woman in the so-called "missionary" position.

Among the diversity of sexual phenomena considered unhealthy
by different people are: using words such as *fuck* or *cunt*, telling
dirty jokes, screwing during menstruation or late pregnancy, not
having an orgasm or failing to reach a climax together, nakedness,
the use of force, practicing birth control, involving children or
someone roughly ten years older or younger than yourself, doing
it with a member of another race or someone physically deformed,
and so on.

Closely connected to this concept of "unhealthy," and really
interchangeable with it, is the idea of deviance or perversion (the
unnatural, abnormal, immoral), which broadly refers to everything not directly connected with reproduction. This includes
masturbation; foreplay; open-mouth or tongue-to-tongue kissing;
fondling of breast, penis, or vagina ("necking"); homosexuality;
premarital or extramarital relations; interest in pornography;
exhibitionism; group sex or marriage; voyeurism; bisexuality;
transvestism, mouth-genital contacts; coitus interruptus; and
pleasure itself, particularly for women. Statistically, often biologically, and socially, many of these "perversions" are natural
and extensively, if hypocritically, engaged in by most Americans
over eighteen.

Two jokes illustrate well this hypocrisy—and the generation gap.
A young boy regularly attending Sunday school was one day asked
by his teacher: "Are you troubled by evil thoughts?" His answer
was: "No, I enjoy them!"

A little girl was told by her mother that if she didn't stop
masturbating, she would become blind, at which point the daughter
asked whether she could just continue until she needed glasses.

Celibacy or continence is presumed healthy for priests and nuns, the unmarried, children, the elderly, those institutionalized, and members of the armed forces away from home, but it is considered unhealthy for married adults.

More specific "diseases," i.e., unhealthy sexual adjustments, are impotency, frigidity, premature ejaculation, infertility or sterility, dysmenorrhea, gonorrhea or syphilis, sado-masochism, and trans-sexualism.

With sexual behavior as with various patterns of drug use, ranging from alcohol and tobacco to amphetamines and heroin, we have institutionalized a pathological rather than a normative frame of reference, especially in the medical-psychiatric profession—a one-dimensional, viewing with alarm, out-of-context, sensationalistic, polarized approach fostered by politicians, advertising and public relations executives, and the mass media. This kind of morally corrupt exploitation of sex or other phenomena is well rewarded in a superficial sense by our society. It sells products and stimulates the economy, gets mediocrities elected to office, and makes headlines. It does not provide knowledge, perspective, understanding, or solutions.

I am reminded of a debate I had with an American Medical Association psychiatrist who received national attention from *Time, Newsweek,* the wire services, and other gossip disseminators for his statement that "all the homosexuals in my practice are seriously disturbed people." Among other things this appealed to the predominant professional and public attitude that homosexuals are "sick." When I then pointed out that all the heterosexuals in his, and other psychiatrists' practices were also seriously disturbed people (since these are the ones who go to a psychiatrist), his statement became meaningless. But the damage had already been done.

The simplest and fairest way of reacting to minority, unpopular, or disliked sexual behaviors would be to take the approach of an American tourist who visited London for the first time and observed the traffic on the left side of the road: he simply referred to the English as driving on the *other* side, not the *wrong* side, of the road. There are many sexual roads, not just one.

If we were to use physiology as our frame of reference for sexual health, the proper responses as determined by Masters and Johnson of the male penis, muscles, skin, testes, and vital signs (breathing rate, heart rate, blood pressure), and the proper responses of the female vagina, clitoris, nipples, labia, skin, muscles, and vital signs during the phases of excitement, plateau, orgasm, and resolution would define health or sickness in connection with intercourse.[1]

Unfortunately, social or psychological health and other types of sexual interaction are not so easily delineated. General health, as well as sexual health, is not adequately described by the circuitous referral to an absence of disease, and sex is more than a simple physical merging of a conscienceless erect penis with a moist, receptive vagina. Really involved are the totality of one's attitudes and behavior as a woman or man, the fuller interpersonal relationships, social and mental health rather than just erotic and physical factors.

Our laws against sex and other private behaviors by consenting adults show most clearly our societal view of sex as unhealthy and evil. The modern barbarians who make and enforce these proscriptions, which make most American adults sex criminals and sex offenders, are of course without sin themselves. As "honorable men" they never patronize prostitutes or have other extramarital heterosexual or homosexual relationships, never view dirty movies, and never violate other criminal or civil statutes. These crusaders for a puritanism which probably never existed sometimes contend that sex is un-American, although our Declaration of Independence guarantees us life, liberty, and the pursuit of happiness. The most insightful comment ever made on Puritanism was by H. L. Mencken, who defined it as "the hauting fear that someone, somewhere, may be happy."

Our sex laws are minutely detailed, ancient, rarely amended or repealed, highly variable from state to state; call for harsh penalties; and fortunately have a low ration of enforcement to violations. They brand as criminals tens of millions of otherwise generally law-abiding people, foster the growth and power of sex or vice police whose practices, including spying (surveillance), the use of informers, entrapment, bribery, and blackmail, are more characteristic of totalitarianism than a free society and whose results, including arrest records and imprisonment, are more destructive than the original "evil." The hypocrisy, the stigmatization, the disrespect for law and for police that is engendered, and the diversion of our limited enforcement resources from real crimes such as rape and child molesting are other high prices we are paying in a neglected cost-benefit analysis.

Not only are the widely practiced fornication, seduction, adultery, prostitution, exhibitionism, voyeurism, and obscenity-pornography listed as criminal sex offenses, but also such exotic behaviors as the mating of animals within a certain number of yards of schools, churches, and *taverns*. Presumably, it would be the owner or custodian of the animal, and not the dog or cat, that would receive the benefits of six months in jail. In one southern state the penalty for oral-genital relations even between wife and husband is life at hard labor, while intercourse with an animal gets only five years in prison. This must reflect the rural control of the legislature.

Our gross inconsistencies, paradoxes, and injustices are particularly well demonstrated by exhibitionism (indecent exposure) and voyeurism (Peeping Tom) statutes. Almost the entire women's clothing industry, the huckstering of products from toothpaste to deodorant to alcohol to automobiles, and the development of the adolescent males' interest in girls is dependent on various stages of socially approved and encouraged exhibitionism (exposure, or skin-tight accentuation, of breasts, buttocks, thighs, and legs) by *women*. Even mild degrees of such behavior by men, however, except at beaches or on the stage, is frowned upon and criminalized. Conversely, some types of voyeurism by men, particularly girl-watching (ass men, leg men, and tit men) is fostered by Madison Avenue and accepted as totally healthy and desirable by our brainwashed society.

Possibly the most confusing of all is our concept of obscenity, a term for what others call erotica, explicit sexual material, beavers, porns, or simply dirty books and films. We do not think of violence, mendacity, or injustice as obscene, but much of sex is thus categorized when it is something engaged in by other people. One Supreme Court Justice has stated that he couldn't define it, but he knew it when he saw it. Some of the definitions given by my students at the University of California in courses dealing with human sexuality were: visual representations of sexual intercourse, sado-masochism, anything arousing prurient interest, anything manipulative of human beings, unnatural or grotesque portrayals of sex (as in the Kama Sutra), anything arousing sinful thoughts, anything leading to the commission of a criminal sexual act, one's personal bias, graphic portrayal of any illegal sexual act, things which glamorize and promote acts detrimental to social and psychological development, depiction of women as playthings of men, something you would be ashamed of with your own wife or children. The legal definition as determined by a long series of U.S. Supreme Court decisions, some with such prurient titles as "Memoirs of a Woman of Pleasure versus the Commonwealth of Massachusetts," says that to the *average person, applying contemporary standards,* the *predominant appeal* of the matter, *taken as a whole,* is to *prurient interest,* i.e., a shameful or morbid interest in nudity, sex, or excretion, which *goes substantially beyond customary limits* of candor in description or representation of such matters and is matter which is *utterly without redeeming social importance.* Therefore there are some seven operative factors, which expert witnesses, juries, and judges must decide in each situation. To a significant extent each of these concepts is subjective not objective and ultimately obscenity exists in the eye, ear, or mind of the beholder. As Lenny Bruce, a pioneer in sexual libertarianism (but not a libertine) was fond of saying, "If you have trouble declining the verb 'to come,' you probably can't come."

Even the most innocent material such as Mother Goose rhymes can be translated into something appealing to prurient interest just by inserting a blank and making it ambiguous: "Jack and Jill went up to _____." Or, "Peter, Peter, pumpkin eater, had a wife and couldn't _____ her; he put her in a pumpkin shell, and there he _____ her very well."

The 1970 report of the Commission on Obscenity and Pornography found that established patterns of sexual behavior were very stable and not substantially altered by exposure to erotica.[2] Their empirical research found no evidence that exposure to explicit sexual materials plays a significant role in causing criminal behavior in youth or adults. The commission's studies showed that erotic stimuli temporarily increased the frequency and variety of coitus among sexually experienced persons with established and available sex partners, married or otherwise. More open and agreeable marital communication was also reported following such exposure. Such responses I consider healthy and desirable.

As always, the context in which something is used or done, and moderation as opposed to excess, have to be considered. The sociologist William Simon has aptly written of the exaggeration inherent in pornography (and in advertising commercials) where self-comparisons by the viewer by duration of intercourse, penis size, breast dimensions, and so on, may lead to feelings of inadequacy. Also, the commission found that boredom, indifference, and diminished sexual responsiveness, sometimes lasting two months followed heavy exposure to erotica.[3]

Looking now at homosexuality, and later at promiscuity-prostitution, in terms of sex and health, we have a sexual adaptation involving somewhere between six and ten million males and females, depending on whether you include bisexuals and those (37 percent of males in the Kinsey study) who have had at least one homosexual experience.[4] Often called "gay," though frequently sad because of society's rejection, a homosexual is best defined as one who regularly feels sexual desire toward, and sexual responsiveness to, someone of the same sex; when he seeks gratification of this desire, he does so with his own sex.

The cause of homosexuality is not known, although numerous psychiatric theories have been put forward. The complexities of explaining why someone is homosexual are as great as explaining heterosexuality. There is no scientific basis for defining it as a sickness or illness instead of simply another type of sexual orientation .We do not look around a room and speak of "that heterosexual over there" as we do in speaking about the homosexual, as if his life was dominated by sex to the exclusion of everything else. Homosexuals cannot be identified by appearance in most instances, they are in all occupations and socio-economic levels, and many are involved in a heterosexual marriage, and sometimes have children.

Most do not want to change their sexual identity, and their major health problems are the psychological reactions of alienation, anxiety, or guilt, produced by society's rejection, and venereal disease brought about, as with heterosexuality, mainly through promiscuity. Differing patterns of sexual interaction occur, ranging from continence to oral copulation to anal intercourse, and again as with the heterosexual, this may be a casual pickup in a steambath or a long-term, full interpersonal relationship ("marriage"). As with other minority groups they have reacted to oppression and labeling by forming their own institutions, such as San Francisco's Society for Individual Rights, the Daughters of Bilitis, the Council on Religion and the Homosexual, gay bars, and so on.

Although they are no more infectious than masturbators, commit fewer acts of child molesting or assault than heterosexuals, and contribute to our social health by reducing population pressures and adding variety, they are punished under sodomy laws that are global statutes, making no distinction between heterosexual and homosexual, married or unmarried, voluntary or coerced, child or adult, and lump together fellatio, cunnilingus, animal intercourse, and anal intercourse.

Their health and that of American society would be greatly improved by taking out of the criminal law (as did the English with the Wolfenden reforms) private sexual behavior between consenting adults, homosexual or heterosexual. We have nothing to be afraid of. Heterosexuality is quite capable of competing in privacy and in the marketplace with homosexuality. Homosexuals, like heterosexuals, should be treated as individual human beings, not as a special group. Some homosexuals, like some heterosexuals, are ill; some homosexuals, like some heterosexuals, are preoccupied with sex as a way of life. But for a majority of adults their sexual orientation constitutes only one component of a much more complicated life-style.

With prostitution we have another phenomenon that isn't as clearcut as we generally presume. It is a continuum involving prostitute and client ("John"), often a madam or pimp, sex policemen, and others. There are, in addition to the full-time female heterosexual whore that we think of as the prostitute, male heterosexual and female and male homosexual prostitutes; part-time hustlers; streetwalkers; and call-girls. The indiscriminate or public offer of the body for sexual purposes—a definition of prostitution—blends with any use of sex for material reward, by the married or unmarried, and with promiscuity. Benjamin's studies found that prostitutes constituted 5 to 10 percent of the total sex outlet for American males or some twenty million contacts per week.[5] This is probably decreasing as "free love"—premarital and extramarital—increases, but it still represents a significant segment of the economy.

Among the reasons for clients using prostitutes, including several that objectively can be considered healthy, are: quick availability of a sex outlet, no emotional involvement, variety, emotional or physical handicaps, semi-impotency or frigidity, desire to avoid pregnancy, interest in sexual practices that are, or are felt to be, not available, as oral-genital or sado-masochistic ones.

For most girls in the trade, the economic return is
vation although psychological and chance factors
Both client and prostitute may suffer the unhealth
of venereal disease, disturbed family relationships
image, and impaired ability to have a total sex-lo
with mutual satisfaction.

Certainly arresting the woman (while ignoring the man) constitutes a destructive and wasteful revolving-door approach.
Changing the sexual mores of the society rather than criminaliza-
tion or legalization (where most would not register) offers the
most hope. Ultimately, it must remain a woman's own business
whether she sells it or gives it away.

Sex and health, like other complex human behaviors, can only
be understood in the context of American society and culture.
Among the aspects of the society that most specifically affect sexual health are: the rapid social change, including technology and
urbanization; simple, effective, and readily-available contraception; increased leisure time through affluence, underemployment,
or unemployment; the increasingly sex-ridden nature of our
advertising, books, magazines, films, and plays; the automobile
and the motel; increasing influence of youth and a cult of youth-
fulness; increasing education and secularization; growing disrespect for age, seniority, and conventional "wisdom"; consumerism
with its stress on instant gratification; egalitarianism and the
emphasis on individual rights; mass television; and the social
problems of the nuclear bomb, the Indochina war, pollution, pov-
erty, racism, and so on.

A positive concept of sex is needed. Something we could call
healthy sex means much more than the absence of physical or
psychological diseases. It means a good feeling about your maleness or femaleness and about your sexual responses; an ability to
respond and relate with full body and mind contact on sexual and
other levels; kindness and understanding, openness, variety, and
imagination with equality and mutual understanding; and free
consent without exploitation. The major purpose would be to give
and obtain physical and psychological pleasure and love, and only
sometimes and secondarily to procreate. This sexual health or
healthy sex is one important aspect of self-maximization or self-
development, of joy, happiness, and altruism. Sex, then, is one
component of the individual's life-style and of total interpersonal
relationships. It involves healthy exercise and relaxation, and

creative use of leisure. Unhealthy sex would include the use of force and violence, blackmail or bribery, transmitting infection, seduction of children, compulsive "affairs," and unfounded guilt, fear, anxiety, or impulsivity. Healthy sex, by contrast, stresses long-term gratification, quality rather than quantity, and acceptance of individual differences in masturbation, pornography, oral-genital contacts, and so on. After all, it is a matter of taste. No girl was ever ruined by a book, although many have been bored by them, whether it was formal pornography or the legal pornography of the scissors and paste marriage manual with a clever title. I think it was W. C. Fields who said that sex isn't the best thing in the world and isn't the worst, but there is nothing quite like it.

Heterosexuality may or may not be the healthiest form of sexual interaction, depending on the aspects of health which you most emphasize, but it is certainly the most natural in terms of anatomy, physiology,and social attitudes; and it is fully able to compete with other patterns in terms of pleasure. This does not mean that a heterosexual is better than a homosexual. We must go beyond sexocentric and ethnocentric views which, from a woman's perspective, might call the penis a large clitoris dirtied by urine, or from a heterosexual view might call a homosexual a queer or pervert. If anything, we should move toward considering reproduction as perverted and deviant if we are to save the human race from extinction. Polarized generalities—everyone should have premarital relations and no one should have them; everyone should masturbate and no one should masturbate—have no place in healthy sex. We are dealing with a biological and social continuum, with ambiguity and complexity, and with vast differences in attitudes and preferences, all in what is supposed to be a pluralistic, free, and civilized society. Just as the risks (side effects) of pregnancy are greater than the significant risks of the pill, so are the risks of intolerance, oppression, conformity, and hatred greater than the risks of healthy sex as defined above. All orientations, positions, orifices, techniques that are voluntarily consented to, and pleasurable to mature people should be considered healthy, or at least not necessarily sexually unhealthy.

It seems appropriate to conclude with quotes from two English citizens of the twentieth century, since the English common law, the Victorians, and the Puritans (along with Judeo-Christian traditions) have strongly influenced American sexuality. Mrs.

Patrick Campbell, actress and friend of George Bernard Shaw, once said: "I don't care what people do as long as they don't do it in the streets and scare the horses." And the Beatles tell us: "All you need is love."

CHAPTER NOTES

1 William H. Masters and Virginia E. Johnson, *Human Sexual Response* (Boston: Little, Brown & Co., 1966).

2. Commission on Obscenity and Pornography, *Report of the Commission on Obscenity and Pornography* (New York: Bantam, 1970).

3. Ibid.

4. A. C. Kinsey, W. B. Pomeroy, and C. E. Martin, *Sexual Behavior in the Human Male* (Philadelphia, Pa.: W. B. Saunders, 1948).

5. H. Benjamin and R. Masters, *Prostitution and Morality* (New York: Julian, 1963).

FURTHER REFERENCES

Ellis, Albert. *Sex and the Single Man.* New York: Dell, 1963.

Kinsey, A. C., Pomeroy, W. B., Martin, C. E., and Gebhard, P. H. *Sexual Behavior in the Human Female.* Philadelphia, Pa.: W. B. Saunders, 1953.

Masters, William H., and Johnson, Virginia E. *Human Sexual Inadequacy.* Boston: Little, Brown & Co., 1970.

Schoenfeld, Eugene, M.D. *Dear Doctor Hip-Pocrates.* New York: Grove Press, 1968.

Sexology: Educational Facts for Adults.

SIECUS. *Sexuality and Man.* New York: Scribner, 1970.

Society for the Scientific Study of Sex. *Journal of Sex Research.* New York.

Ullerstam, Lars, M.D. *A Sexual Bill of Rights for the Erotic Minorities.* New York: Grove Press, 1966.

Wells, John Warren. *Tricks of the Trade.* New York: New American Library, 1970.

Young, Wayland. *Eros Denied: Sex in Western Society.* New York: Grove Press, 1964.

Chapter 16

SEXUALITY: REWARDS AND RESPONSIBILITIES

By Ethel M. Nash, M.A.

Preamble: Coitus is such a simple act. Yet almost since the beginning of their sojourn on earth, human beings have surrounded it with rules. Most of the regulations were concerned with ensuring that sufficient progeny were born and enabled to grow to maturity, since on this human survival depended. Now human survival depends on limiting the number of births. It can be done as, for the first time in history, effective means of separating procreation from coitus are available. Will these be used or will the *I* be permitted, for the first time since civilization began, to take precedence over the *We*? Maybe the requirement of a license to marry is obsolete when the root concern is no longer protection of the female and her progeny but the limitation of births. If parenthood rather than marriage were licensed, we could prevent the extinction of the human race through the fertilization of too many ova and leave ourselves freer to discover how to merge sexuality and loving.

A Symbiotic Relationship

"Painting done, with love, husband-wife team." Having found this advertisement in the "Services Available" column of our local paper, I was immediately curious about "painting done with love." As our home was in need of a coat or two, I contacted the advertising team and invited them to discuss the matter. They proved to be as interesting as their ad. This young couple, nineteen and twenty, met in Africa—each searching for his "own thing," and since their marriage several months prior to my meeting them, they had found even the shortest separation unbearable. They were not attending college because class time separation was too frustrating. Separate jobs were unthinkable, so they turned to house painting—a vocation they could manage with togetherness.

While discussing colors, times, and costs, this inseparable pair overlooked no opportunity to express their love. Every sentence uttered by one brought a gesture of affection—on the hair, on the ear, on the nose, on the knee—from the other. For this couple loving and the expression of sexuality in loving is the warp and woof of their life—time apart is time lost. After contracting with them for the painting, I wondered if they could manage to wield separate brushes. They do, but they take every opportunity to express their love by touch or gesture. They even stand on either side of the same stepladder so they can kiss as they paint. Privacy is no concern of theirs, and to be around them is a little wearing. On the other hand, our home is often lightened by their current happiness as they listen to jazz, discuss Bach and Beethoven, and, to our surprise, break into singing such hymns as "O God, Our Help in Ages Past" and "Breathe on Me, Breath of God." They definitely do paint, as advertised, with love. And the loving greatly handicaps their speed.

As symbiotic as two adults can be, this pair revel in the close bond that is filling some of the void left by unmet needs in infancy and childhood—needs for closeness, tenderness, and warmth. But this total love commitment will also face, in the future, the inevitable pain of separation and loss. This highly vulnerable pair— vulnerable economically and emotionally—will have to come to terms with the world of those who live and work outside of their love bond. Further, since no one is consistently a perfect partner, disagreements will crop up. Nor is their emotional development likely to be simultaneous. One or the other will, almost certainly, outgrow the neurotic need for perpetual togetherness. Or, since such immature personalities are seldom given to planning ahead, a pregnancy will result. Then the twosome has to accommodate to include a baby—a demanding, even if much loved, third party. Scheduling, earning, and a greater degree of separation then have to be accepted. Whatever the outcome of this marriage, I am sure that these loving partners will agree with the poet who wrote:

If love should count you worthy, and should deign
One day to seek your door and be your guest,
Pause! ere you draw the bolt and bid him rest,
If in your old content you would remain.
For not alone he enters; in his train
Are angels of the mists, the lonely quest,
Dreams of the unfulfilled and unpossessed.
And sorrow and life's immemorial pain.
He wakes desires you never may forget.
He shows you stars you never saw before,
He makes you share with him, forevermore,
The burden of the world's divine regret.
How wise you were to open not! and yet,
How poor if you should turn him from the door.[1]

A Triangle

I shared this same poem with a counselee who, unmarried at thirty-four, experienced her first sexual awakening. I met her when the love affair was drawing to its close. It had begun the year before when, at a librarians' convention, her company was sought out by a successful member of her profession. They shared many meals and walked and talked, and then on the final evening they danced. She found that her body had lost its rigidity. The phrase "dancing with twinkling toes" flashed through her mind. Someone had said this about her when she was a three-year-old. That night her new friend became her lover. In this, her first experience of sexual intercourse, her whole being responded passionately. Much of her passivity and self-doubt left. For the next year her life revolved around the rare weekends they spent together. But always in the background were the wife and children waiting for him in another city. The day came when her lover decided to discontinue their trysts.

The pain of withdrawal and loss hit her in long, relentless waves. For a while she felt that life was unbearable. During this time she found that coitus with almost anyone afforded brief anaesthesia from pain. But the ersatz qualities of sexual expression without love made her feel even more alone, estranged even from herself. Yet, never at any time, has she wished that she had not loved and been loved. She knows that she will love again, when the opportunity comes.

For the sophisticated few who are able to manage the complexities of the social, emotional, and geographical meshing required and who have a "cooperating" spouse (i.e., one who acquiesces to a relationship which does not include fidelity), triangles may persist for years. Or there may be a series of brief encounters taken part in rather lightly but which do involve coitus and love. Generally, an unfaithful spouse feels guilty enough to break off voluntarily with the loved one. Or one of them sets up a situation in which discovery is inevitable and a choice has to be made.

Fidelity in Loving

"I take thee—for better, for worse; for richer, for poorer; in sickness and in health; and forsaking all others cleave only unto thee, so long as we both shall live."

One couple has been married thirty-five years—a span that seems to them short for all the laughing, loving, and suffering they have shared. Quite opposite to the inseparable house painters, this couple places great value on independence and separateness as well as on togetherness. Both have careers that take them circling the globe, often in different directions. When they meet after a long day's work, or in some city where they have managed to link up engagements, they know the joyous response of discussing ideas and plans, successes and failures; they know heartbreak and happiness—all in a sharing that includes sexual loving.

It is not that such a couple necessarily finds fidelity easy. They too experience almost magnetic pulls toward other love relationships. However, they believe that, for them, the rewards of fidelity outweigh the rewards of any other way of living together. And because they have sought to provide for each other an intellectual climate and emotional soil in which both can thrive, that enemy of monogamy—boredom—holds no threat to their relationship.

Such couples know the experience of which Irving Stone writes in his interpretation of the diary of Abigail Adams, the wife of President John Adams,

> She could not sleep for sheer happiness. She marveled at marriage which dissolves the accumulated strains and restraints, the sense of standing still while moving through vacant time. The fulfillment of their love had been more meaningful than she could have dreamed. It had had in it elements of the sublime, and had soared, a magnificent blending in which spiritual ecstasy had been born of

the marriage of the flesh. A man and a woman who loved totally
were multiplied by infinity. It was one of life's gifts, this tender
and profoundly stirring physical passion which each night swept
them far out to sea on the hurricane that engulfed them; and then,
the storm spent, allowed them to drift slowly, gently back to shore,
to the protected cove where they could lie quietly at anchor, falling
asleep in each other's arms.[2]

Later in the book, toward the end of this couple's life together,
following John's defeat in his try for a second term as president,
this conversation takes place:

> "The ingratitude kills my soul. All I wanted was one more term.
> A peaceful four years to prove our country can expand, grow pros-
> perous. To be part of this new capital city. Then I could have
> retired to Quincy in honor. I feel humiliated, dismissed."
> "We have wanted to serve, John. And we have served. There is
> now a capital called Washington City, of a nation called the United
> States; it is a long way from the injustices of the Stamp Act. Your
> courage, your vision, your dedication have brought us far from the
> Massachusetts Bay Colony. With His help you have been part of
> building the freest civilization the world has ever known. It's all
> there for the world to read: the documents, the reports, the consti-
> tutions, the treaties, the laws. All that King George's 'brace of
> Adamses' fought for and won. You are a historian, John. You know
> history will say that."
> "I will say that!" A sparkle came to his eyes, the corner of his
> lips twitched in a reluctant smile. "In that beautiful library you
> built for me. The Republicans are not the only ones who have ink.
> It will take several volumes . . ."
> "Would you like me to leave a little early, to prepare the house
> and your study against your arrival? I could have the ink in the
> inkpot, pens, and writing paper on your desk . . ."
> "Thank you, Miss Abigail, for the wonderful gifts of life you
> have brought me over the years."
> She replied softly, "Life is for those who love."[3]

Enjoyers and Endurers

Twenty-five percent of all marriages in the United States are
terminated by divorce. A great many more become conflict-
habituated or devitalized to the point of making staying married
an endurance feat. As a marriage counselor, my working life is
spent trying to help the endurers of bad marriages become the

enjoyers of good ones. Fortunately, most of the "endurers" are, at least consciously, trying to make a lasting partnership in love and sex.

One example is the twenty-seven-year-old parents of three children, the products of homes which provided only poor gender identification. The wife's mother is a carping, unloving woman with verbal diarrhea. She spues out dislikes and demands. Her husband is an effeminate male who detests his wife and is afraid to be fond of his daughter. This daughter is pretty and intelligent, and hates her mother whose visits are always disturbing. She consciously despised her father, but in therapy found that he was, thus far, her only love.

Her husband's family of orientation also is typical of those of many young couples who seek marital therapy. His father, although professionally very successful, would never confront his bitchy, domineering wife. When he found her impossible, he left the house. This left their son as her target. Now married, he is often his wife's target, so naturally he responds by avoidance, silence, or scowling appeasement—the only weapons he had available as a child.

Both want the status of being married. Both want to provide a warm two-parent home for their three children. Both want to love and be loved. Both want, consciously, to give and receive sexual gratification. But this husband, like many others, was a premature ejaculator and had experienced several periods of impotency. During intercourse he is worried about sustaining an erection and tends to concentrate on his own performance rather than making love. His wife is of little help. She says: "Candidly, sexual intercourse with Bill is such a dull idea. He's just my husband and will always be there. There's nothing exciting about sex with him. Besides he is so serious all the time. Even when he's happy, he's seriously happy. I'm not any better myself really. Whatever is laughable about sex is dirty to me. I like laughter. I'd like us to be silly in intercourse. I guess that if I'm really frank, I'd have to admit that I only really like coitus when I'm helping an older man enjoy it."

This couple, like many others, have not only suffered severe damage to their ability to love sexually, but are passing it on to their children. Wives, angry with husbands, leave the marital bed and sleep with a son, who, in adulthood, will pay a high price for his mother's self-indulgence. Fathers who want a son but get a

daughter concede later: "Mary is as good as a boy." Such daughters will have a hard time enjoying their femininity.

It's a mixed-up world. Husbands and wives, dissatisfied with
the present partner, find comfort with someone else's spouse. A
typical remark is: "He's not in love with his wife, and I'm not in
love with my husband, so we don't consider either of us married."
As a result the existing legal contract is dissolved. New partnerships are entered into, and it soon becomes clear, especially when
children are involved, that there are strains in this relationship,
too. This does not imply that second marriages may not prove
better than first ones. Research[4,5] indicates that they often do.
Those entering them are older. Besides few people want to be
marked as two-time losers. But the situation is often made difficult
by the fact that children have to accommodate to a new parent—
usually to a new father. The new father is often bitter about the
estrangement from his own children. It is not surprising that the
inability to fuse sexuality and heterosexual love is passed down
from generation to generation. The best predictor of enjoying
marriage is to have been reared by parents who enjoyed theirs.[6]

HOW YOUNG IS TOO YOUNG?

This chapter began with a description of three couples whose
route to love and expression of it are widely different, but all had
in common that, in terms of chronological age, they were at least
nearing adulthood. Each had undertaken responsibility for earning a living and for making decisions about the way their lives
would go. It is not unreasonable to expect that all, in their several
ways, will add to society's well-being, or at a minimum, not be
antithetical to it.

But our society encourages early, unchaperoned dating. As a
result, children in early adolescence are playing with sexuality,
often believing that this is love. Adolescents can become enthralled
with the idea of being in love while at the same time being afraid
of being emotionally close to a member of the opposite sex. Strange
though it may seem, many feel under social as well as emotional
pressure to alleviate their anxiety by coitus. The result for those
unlucky in the game of ovarian roulette is pregnancy. Of 337,700
out-of-wedlock births annually, 6,200 are to children under fifteen.
To become a parent so young is clearly, in our society, inimical to

the well-being of the mother, the father, and the baby. Eighty percent of all high school marriages begin with the bride pregnant. Fifty percent break up within five years. It is not surprising that premarital pregnancy, early-age marriage and divorce, are statistically associated.[7] The expression of sexuality in coitus is not "just one's own affair." Its results affect generations yet unborn.

THE CONCERN OF THE HUMAN RACE

Being in love may be one's own affair, but only if no baby results. Today babies are the world's affair. As Robert McNamara pointed out at, of all places, the University of Notre Dame, if our present rate of population growth should continue, "in six and a half centuries from now—the same insignificant period of time that separates us from the poet Dante—there would be one human being standing on every square foot of land on earth: a fantasy of horror that even the *Inferno* could not match."[8] The population disaster has been creeping upon us and has only now begun to be recognized, and then only by an international elite. The world has as many people as it can comfortably sustain. But with present standards of medical care and nutrition and early-age marriage, we are increasing at a fantastic rate. If a couple marrying in their early twenties have four children, and if these children each have four children, and so on, then the original couple will have *eighty* decendants (even allowing for mortality) by the time they are in their eighties. Sexuality in loving, for this generation, needs to be bounded by the recognition that love, elbow room, peace, and indeed survival are closely related.

Our society, whose mores presently encourage sexual freedom, has not yet accepted the need to see that babies are not robbed at birth of the conditions essential to emotional and physiological well-being. Central to any universally accepted standard for the expression of sexuality in loving should be insistence that it provide an optimum environment for the rearing of children. My experience as a counselor is that voluntary control of conception is insufficient. The two-child family has to become the norm, if the human race is to survive. Under these circumstances, it is scarcely conceivable that babies who are not wanted should be carried to term. Even when they are wanted, I doubt they should be permitted to be born under circumstances such as the following:

Betty is pregnant as a result of—to use her words—"grass and alcohol." She says "Jim is the father, but I'm not going to marry him. Our personalities clash. I'm not sorry I'm pregnant though. It has given me something to live for. I work harder in school. I get better grades. I've always dreamed about having a baby, and my three brothers and two sisters are all excited about my pregnancy. I know they will treat the baby like a doll. When my mother got over her shock, she was sort of pleased because she would have a grandchild. She tells me that my stepfather wasn't really shook about my being pregnant because his own daughter was pregnant at fifteen. She says he is sort of glad there will be another baby around." The attitudes of these family members toward the birth of this baby are not in any way unkind, but they are more suitable for bringing a puppy into the home.

Pregnancy for a Cause

In *Ebony,* the leader of New York's militant black Five Percenters is quoted as saying to a visitor, "See that sister there? She's having another baby for me. I need an army and that is how we are going to get it."[9] This, too, is an expression of sexuality in loving. The love is for a cause, and the baby is a "thing," an "object" to serve the cause. The incident calls to mind other wars—wars that one generation decides to wage and another generation has to fight. No love relationship on the part of one individual should cancel out the rights of another individual or individuals.

A Concluding Reverie

As true yet deceiving; as possessing all things yet having nothing; as living and behold we die. This reversal of St. Paul seems, in many ways, near the truth about the modern world as it journeys through today's sexual wilderness. As yet no promised land is in sight. Indeed, we have little concept of how sexuality and love can mesh in ways that will serve the well-being of individuals, couples, and families. Except for archconservatives, we do have a fair consensus that the current sexual frankness and freedom is preferable to the deceit and repression of the past. An old Spanish proverb says that "the way is in the going," and in the following mirages, oases will sometimes be found. Among all the myriad problems concerning sexuality and love that we seek to solve, only one as yet has an answer that would seem to stand as possible to affirm without qualification—wombs should be reserved for children who are wanted for themselves.

CHAPTER NOTES

1. Sydney Royse Lysaght, "The Penalty of Love," in *Poems of Today: Second Series* (London: Sidgwick and Jackson, Ltd., 1922), p. 113.

2. Irving Stone, *Those Who Love* (Garden City, New York: Doubleday & Co., Inc., 1965), p. 80.

3. Ibid., pp. 644–645.

4. Jessie Barnard, *Remarriage* (New York: The Dryden Press, 1956).

5. William Goode, *After Divorce* (Glencoe, Ill.: Free Press of Glencoe, 1956).

6. Gerald Albert, "Marriage Prediction Revisited," *Journal of the Long Island Consultation Center*, 5, no. 2, (Fall, 1967): 38–46.

7. Harold Christensen, "The Method of Linkage Applied to Family Data," *Marriage and Family Living*, 20, no. 1, (February, 1958): 38–43.

8. Robert S. McNamara, Address to the University of Notre Dame, Notre Dame, Indiana, May 1, 1969.

9. Mary Smith, "Birth Control and the Negro Woman," *Ebony*, 23, no. 5, (March, 1968): 29.

Chapter 17

CONTROL OF PROCREATION:
A NEW DIMENSION OF FREEDOM

By Walter R. Stokes, M.D.

Incredible as it may seem to us today, there was a long period in the early history of man when his sense of freedom about engaging in sex relations was untroubled by concern or fear over possible ensuing pregnancy for the simple reason that, like his mammalian relatives, he did not associate sexual intercourse with reproduction.[1] Indeed, it has been reliably reported that some isolated, very primitive bands of Australian natives are still unaware of this association, believing that pregnancy is the result of eating certain foods or of exposure to such natural phenomena as the light of the full moon.

When our ancestors did clearly perceive the relationship between the sex act and pregnancy, the result was a psychological disaster, particularly for the female who had to face the principal burdens of pregnancy, childbirth, and parenthood. The causes of the puritanical sex mores of Western civilization are many and are obscured by antiquity, but it is safe to speculate that the most powerful contributing element has been fear of pregnancy as a probable sequel to intercourse. Much of the mystique of the sexually frigid female virgin, to whom presumably sex will remain disgusting after marriage, represents in considerable part a defense against the hazard of undesired pregnancy.

During the present century two trends have been in motion that have tended insistently to break down our Victorian sex heritage.[2] The first is a growing challenge to the religious and legal authority behind Victorian sex repression. The second, which has served to implement this challenge, is the appearance of a relatively effective technology of contraceptive procedures that permit sex relations with little or no chance of pregnancy. The importance of our progress in this area of human welfare was significantly dramatized in a statement by Dwight L. Wilbur, then president of the American Medical Association, as quoted in the May 5, 1969, issue of the *American Medical Association News*. In an address at the University of Nebraska Medical Center, Dr. Wilbur said that we are on the threshold of "the control of human reproduction. Perhaps not the genetic aspects but those that influence the mind, the body, and family life." He went on to observe that this development "will completely change the psychological attitude of women . . . until now, women have lived in fear of becoming pregnant. I predict this will be the greatest revolution that mankind has ever experienced or will ever experience."

Except for the possibly greater revolutionary effect of some day learning to cope rationally with hostile human emotion, I readily agree with Dr. Wilbur's prediction. Incidentally, it seems appropriate to observe how powerfully interconnected are the great human problems of population density, sex repression, and hostile behavior.

It is especially gratifying that Dr. Wilbur's statement comes from the leadership of the AMA, which until recently has supported an extremely conservative attitude toward both birth control and sex education. As Dr. Wilbur's statement suggests, within recent years the AMA has drastically revised and liberalized its position. This is indeed fortunate because the medical profession can contribute so much when it is free to improve and apply contraceptive measures and to promote the progressixe sex education that is indispensable in directing the practical usefulness of our contraceptive technology.

Since the early 1920s I have been personally involved in the fields of both birth control and liberalization of concepts of sex behavior. In 1924, while a freshman medical student in Washington, D.C., I became active with the National Committee on Federal Legislation for Birth Control, which sought congressional legislation to liberalize the highly restrictive "Comstock Law," enacted in 1873. This law completely banned the use of contraceptives, with no exemption for the medical profession, and bracketed the subject with illegal abortion and hard-core pornography. Until

1934, when liberal federal court decisions provided relief from this onerous legislation, a group of dedicated liberals, under Margaret Sanger's leadership, assembled annually in Washington to testify before congressional committees in favor of new, liberal legislation concerning birth control.

Perhaps the most important contribution of these gatherings was that they brought together many of the persons who have since become stalwarts in the field of sex education and who generally liberalized appreciation of sex in human life. Among the participants were Drs. Abraham and Hannah Stone, Robert L. Dickinson, Lovett Dewees, Sophia Kleegman, Lombard Kelly, Alan Guttmacher, Robert Laidlaw, Lena Levine, Valeria Parker, Frances Shields, Stuart and Emily Mudd, Mary Calderone, Rev. Foster Wood, myself, and others not so much identified with sex education. Most of us moved along to deepening interest in sex reforms that could scarcely have been possible without reliable contraceptives. It would be difficult to overestimate the support and stimulation we provided to each other in those early days of organized rebellion against Victorian sex laws and mores.

During the 1920s and '30s, we were constrained by public and medical opinion to advocate the use of contraceptives only where there could be some show of a "medical indication," that is, some reason why the use of contraceptives was required to protect the health of a married women. This doctrine was construed to include adequate child spacing and reasonable limitation of family size. At that time it would have been considered immoral folly to advocate the use of contraceptives by the unmarried or by a married woman who might choose to have no children. Even today the prevailing legal view has not changed much in this regard. However, among the medical profession and the general public, there are many who sharply challenge the old restrictions about such limited use of contraceptives.

To a humanistic liberal such as myself, it seems altogeher probable that within a few decades the use of contraceptives will be freed from all restrictions and accepted as a basic human right, available without moral taint to all. Indeed, this view is likely to become part of a new morality founded upon the protection of individual dignity and the urgent necessity to maintain human population within essential bounds.

It may reasonably be predicted that in the rush of cultural changes now upon us, we shall soon be hearing the last of those irrational objections to birth control or the methods implementing it that are continuing to obstruct progress at this time. This is foreshadowed by the extraordinary relaxing of traditional moral and religious opposition that we have witnessed within the past few years.

While this discussion is concerned primarily with moral values and cultural change, it seems appropriate to introduce a casual survey of available and projected technical efficiency in our means for containing human reproduction. It is obvious that without efficient contraceptive procedures it becomes a mere academic exercise to examine the freedoms they might foster. As a clinician long concerned with contraceptive techniques, I shall offer some observations.

I have been a firsthand observer of the relative efficiency of the condom, vaginal diaphragms and chemical agents, intrauterine devices, hormone pills that inhibit ovulation, and surgical sterilization. Each has disadvantages and limitations, but it would be inappropriate to discuss them here. I venture the prediction that it will be a considerable time (if ever) before any one procedure will solve our entire birth control need. It seems probable that refinements of present methods for the biochemical suppression of ovulation can be expected. Also, it is quite possible that harmless biochemical means will be found for temporarily arresting fertility in the male. It seems likely that biochemical means will be found for interrupting an established pregnancy in its very early stages. The use of surgical sterilization (particularly in the male) is increasing rapidly and proving entirely satisfactory in wisely selected cases. Through improved surgical techniques, vasectomy may well become a dependably reversible procedure, thus extending its usefulness.

It appears to me a rational necessity to include induced abortion in our birth control armamentarium. Increasing numbers of physicians and others are accepting the view that it should be the right of any woman to decide for herself whether a pregnancy should be interrupted and that it is immoral not to support this right. It is inconceivable that abortion will ever be taken lightly or that it is likely to be other than a rare supplement to other ways of controlling reproduction. However, of necessity, it must have a dignified place in our total approach to the control of procreation.

It is interesting to observe that until quite recently our preoccupation with the control of human reproduction has been largely in negative terms: how to control the size of families; proper child spacing to protect maternal health; medical or psychiatric contraindications to pregnancy; wise conservation of family economic resources; and general reduction of population. These factors have not lost their importance, but now we are coming to feel a greater degree of open and lively concern for the positive ways in which effective birth control can contribute to sex freedom and enjoyment for women and enhancement of the sexual relationship for both sexes. This is a relatively new dimension of birth control and is what Dr. Wilbur had in mind when he referred to it as involving "the greatest revolution that mankind has ever experienced or will ever experience." As I reflect upon my lifetime of clinical observation of the emotional lives of people and families, what Dr. Wilbur says does not seem an unjustified or exaggerated prophecy.

At this point in the history of our culture, none can predict with accurracy the precise shape of all that the revolutionary new sex freedom will mean; yet I do not find it too difficult to imagine the general nature of things to come. Human sexuality is so profoundly culture-bound that prediction of its expression does not follow the rather simple patterns that prevail among our closest mammalian relatives,[3] whose behavior is uncomplicated by fears of conception or by irrational social-moral taboos. Because of these factors, human sexuality is just lately beginning to emerge from the morbid effects of a difficult era. Full emergence is certain to require the passage of many future generations because of the need for more reliable scientific knowledge and the difficulties inherent in discarding deeply rooted traditions, however erroneous and harmful their nature.

While attainment of the new sex freedom is profoundly related to secure control of fertility, it would be a ridiculous oversimplification to permit ourselves to believe this is the only element involved. The present century has produced considerable important animal and human research that invites our attention to other facors. I cite the clinical investigations and hypotheses of Freud and other psychiatrists and psychologists (with continuing improvement in research data and modification of hypotheses); many ongoing investigations of psychosexual development in infancy, childhood, and adolescence; new studies of total family interaction; insights provided by the studies of Kinsey and those of Masters and Johnson; the studies of John Money and others on establishment of gender identity during early childhood; and the social studies of John Cuber and Peggy Harroff, Winston Ehrmann, Lester Kirkendall, Clark Vincent, and Ira Reiss.[4] There are also many important animal studies, particularly those of Ford and Beach on mammalian sex behavior; Scott on imprinting and critical early learning periods; Harry Harlow and others on how maternal and social deprivation affects sexual behavior in the rhesus monkey; and the work of John B. Calhoun and others on the social and sexual behavior of rats, in both favorable environmental conditions and under excessive population density.[5]

All of these studies and similar ones to follow will have much to do with releasing and shaping our new sex freedom, and I do not wish to detract from their importance. Nevertheless, the utilization of such contributions must rest upon a foundation of our ability to control human procreation in a sure, practical, esthetically acceptable manner.

After observing the use of effective contraceptive procedures by married couples over a period of many years, I have a firm clinical impression that for most it has meant a more active sex life, intensification of marital affection, stabilization of the marital relationship, and a greatly lessened susceptibility to extramarital involvement. At the same time it has become easier for those with a poorly adjusted sex life to enter extramarital affairs. This has helped focus upon the quality of the emotional relationship existing within a marriage, as opposed to the bland traditional assumption that marriage as an institution is more important than the kind of interpersonal relationship found within it. It appears to me that in the days ahead we shall become increasingly less respectful of marriage as an institution and more concerned with the quality of the relationship. Our concern about this must involve adequate preparation of children and young people for marriage, deferment of children until marital compatibility has been reasonably demonstrated, suitable marriage counseling when needed, and new, realistic laws dealing with divorce. In the future we will not strive to hold deeply incompatible couples in marriage and will find wiser ways for handling the grave problems of child custody and welfare when they arise.[6]

The heretofore unchallenged right of parents to have all the children they may desire can no longer be accepted. If we do not have the wit to see this today, it will become painfully apparent to all by the time of the next doubling of world population some time near the end of this century. Birth control will then be accepted as a moral imperative (perhaps a legal one also).

I do not find it difficult to foretell these things about the future of birth control and marriage. Much more obscure, however, is the way in which birth control is to become involved in the lives of teenagers as they reach reproductive capacity. Here we encounter both irrational taboos and practical, commonsense problems. It is not easy to separate the two, particularly since we are at present so deficient in giving sympathetic support to the sex needs and aspirations of our young people and are so lacking in clear knowledge about what is wisest under circumstances of so much social and environmental change. Nonetheless, it is quite evident that young people are tending to force the hand of their elders by clamoring for new sex freedoms, perhaps at times blindly and unwisely. There is a desperate need at this time for rational dialogue between the generations. Young people need the benefit of our wisest adult thinking and personal support, while adults need improved assurances regarding their concern for their children and the oncoming generation.

Extreme hostility and refusal to undertake dialogue on the part of either generation is likely to have destructive results. On each side there are some who are so alienated from sound human values and relatedness as to be incapable of reasonable dialogue, and this minority is exceptionally vocal. On the one hand are those adults who see in youthful sex rebellion only a demand for criminal license, and on the other hand are those young people who are sure that all adults are unreachable authoritarian monsters who leave them no alternative but anarchy and a vague hope that something desirable will arise from the ashes of the Establishment. The members of each extremist group have a pathological defect in capacity for trusting human relatedness, and each is lacking in realistic perspective about the nature and rate of cultural and social change. Neither of these groups will be able to make a constructive contribution to the new sex freedom. The job must be done by others, despite the discouragement thrust upon them by the extremists, who had best be quietly dealt with as mentally ill segments of our society.

As I see it, the new sex freedom, of which birth control must be such an essential part, will not unfold at puberty. It will have its beginning from birth, in all the new and wiser ways we shall learn for recognizing, accepting, and managing the sex and other social needs of children. Human sexuality can not mature adequately without experiencing in early childhood what Ira Reiss has aptly called "nurturant socialization" of an essential kind.[7] As we acquire new skills in fostering this process, children will reach adolescence and the need for birth control measures in a state of preparation and readiness, which none of us is now clearly able to visualize. Accomplishment of this is to me the most critical aspect of the dawning Sexual Revolution. After we have mastered its tasks, I am confident that adjustment to the new sex freedoms of puberty and young adulthood, including the wise use of contraceptives, will be relatively simple. Without it, the difficulties could well be insuperable.

When we speak of sex freedom for teen-agers, it is well to make an effort at defining what is really meant. Is it simply the right of any mutually consenting pair to have intercourse, regardless of the nature and quality of the interpersonal relationship? I doubt that this alone is sufficient for a reasonably mature young human being. He or she is a complex person, with a great need for warm personal relatedness, colored by expectations that are partly individual and unique, and partly a reflection of the surrounding culture. Thus sexual intercourse becomes a great deal more than a mammalian act of copulation. To be abundantly gratifying (and therefore impart a sense of freedom), it must be both erotically spontaneous and achieved in an atmosphere of social and esthetic security and satisfaction, with a partner who is regarded with special trust and affection. Attainment of such a sexual relationship and enjoyment of intercourse under such circumstances seems to me the essence of mature sex freedom and the ultimate in man-woman relatedness, whether in marriage or out, whether associated with procreation or not, and largely regardless of age, except perhaps for the first few years of childhood. But how are we to extend such a conception of sex freedom to unmarried teen-agers in our present society, with many clamoring for it or something resembling it?

I can visualize progress only in terms of successful dialogue between teen-agers and genuinely concerned adults who are flexible enough to welcome constructive change and participate in bringing it about. If active adult participation is lacking, we

should not be surprised that inexperienced, rebellious young
people should come up with such weird answers as sexual anarchy,
promiscuity, outbursts of obscenity, a variety of deviant sex practices, and resort to drug states or magical cultism to cover their
confusion and insecurity.

Some among us try to console ourselves with the delusion that
the present turmoil of change in our sex mores will soon pass.
The hard fact is that it is sure to intensify because of rapidly
mounting population pressures and the equally rapid social and
technological changes that roughly parallel increase in population
density. We must not deceive ourselves about the reality of this.
There is no rational choice but to become involved in a constructive
spirit and to do the best we can to provide friendliness and order
in what develops. It seems to me that we can do no less than to
support the current demand of many young people for earlier
marriage and contribute all that we can to make it successful.
I have observed that very early marriages tend to work out much
better when they have warm adult support. Responsible use of
contraceptives is extremely desirable to guard against starting a
family before the stability of the relationship has been established.
The alternative to early marriage is for young people to live
together unmarried, and in our present society that is likely to
involve damaging stresses that had best be avoided.

I can not presume to estimate precisely what developments lie
ahead in the sex behavior of young people. I have confidence that
if we place our trust in patient, earnest dialogue and progressive
sex education at all levels, combat all forms of exploitation of sex,
pursue a humanistically-oriented effort to improve the quality of
sexual relationships, and make full use of our ability to control
procreation, we shall arrive at the best answers. Unavoidably,
this must be the work of many generations, and no static plateau
will ever be reached, although much leveling off will be achieved
after a time. This is the general approach that makes use of man's
greatest strengths for adjustment and survival—his capability
for effective communication and social cooperation, coupled with
his ability to resist stagnation and adapt to change. With employment of these qualities and the wise utilization of our growing
ability to control procreation, it seems reasonable to believe that
we shall cope successfully (if somewhat slowly and painfully)
with the coming changes in how we are to manage the expression
of human sexuality. Our most advanced actual experience in the

application of this philosophy on a national scale is well under way in Sweden, and the results are more than promising. An illuminating and impressive report on their experience has recently been made by the Swedish Royal Commission on Sex Education, under the direction of Dr. Hans L. Zetterberg.[8]

Whatever the finer details regarding the new sex freedom to which birth control will contribute so much, it seems rather certain that we shall be progressively discarding the fears and guilts that have traditionally hampered our sex lives. We shall gain vastly enhanced enjoyment of sex and make of it a far more constructive force in the human life experience. Genuine democracy and mutuality in the relations of the sexes (now all too rare) can be expected. We shall come to perceive and abhor the exploitative uses of sex now so abundant in our culture. Finally, we shall gain a true picture of the genuinely basic differences between the sexes and will use this knowledge constructively (as opposed to our present indulgence of snide sex hostility based upon ill-founded assumptions or neurotic antagonism). In short, we shall learn to approach sex with immensely increased respect, as a truly cherished aspect of life to be understood, enjoyed, protected, and appreciated as a social force. This revolutionary achievement is possible only upon the solid foundation of reliable control of human fertility, which we shall soon attain.

CHAPTER NOTES

1. See Walter R. Stokes, "Fear of Pregnancy," *Sexology* 28:508, 1962.
2. See Walter R. Stokes, "Our Changing Sex Ethics," *Marriage and Family Living* 24:269, 1962; and Walter R. Stokes, "Sex in the World of Tomorrow," *Sexology* 32:748, 1966.
3. See C. S. Ford and F. Beach, *Patterns of Sexual Behavior* (New York: Harper and Bros., 1954).
4. See Nathan W. Ackerman, *The Psychodynamics of Family Life* (New York: Basic Books, Inc., 1958); Harry F. Harlow, "The Heterosexual Affection System in Monkeys," *American Psychologist* 17:1, 1962; Alfred C. Kinsey et al., *Sexual Behavior in the Human Male* (Philadelphia: W. B. Saunders Co., 1948); Alfred C. Kinsey, et al., *Sexual Behavior in the Human Female* (Philadelphia: W. B. Saunders Co., 1953); W. Masters and V. Johnson, *Human Sexual Response* (Boston: Little, Brown and Co., Inc., 1966); J. Money, J. G. Hampson, and J. L. Hampson, "Hermaphroditism: Recommendations Concerning Assignment of Sex, Change of Sex and Psychological Management," *Bulletin of Johns Hopkins Hospital* 97:284, 1955; J Money, *Sex Errors of the Body: Dilemmas, Education, Counseling* (Baltimore: Johns Hopkins Press, 1968); John Cuber and

Peggy Harroff, *Sex and the Significant Americans: A Study of Sexual Behavior Among the Affluent* (New York: Appleton-Century, 1965); Winston Ehrmann, *Premarital Dating Behavior* (New York: Henry Holt and Co., 1959); Lester Kirkendall, *Premarital Intercourse and Interpersonal Relationships* (Stanford, Calif.: Stanford University Press, 1961); Clark Vincent, *Unwed Mothers* (Glencoe, Ill.: The Free Press, 1961); Ira Reiss, *Premarital Sexual Standards in America* (Glencoe, Ill.: The Free Press, 1960); Ira Reiss, "Universality of the Family: a Conceptual Analysis," *Journal of Marriage and the Family* 27:443, 1965; and Ira Reiss, *Social Context of Premarital Sexual Permissiveness* (Chicago: Holt, Rinehart and Winston, 1967).

5. See C. S. Ford and F. Beach, *Patterns of Sexual Behavior* (New York: Harper and Bros., 1954); J. P. Scott, "Critical Periods in Behavioral Development," *Science* 138:949, 1962; Harry F. Harlow and R. R. Zimmerman, "Affectional Responses in the Infant Monkey," *Science* 130:421, 1959; Harry F. Harlow, "The Heterosexual Affection System in Monkeys," *American Psychologist* 17:1, 1962; John B. Calhoun, "Population Density and Social Pathology," *Scientific American* 206:32, 1962; and John C. Calhoun, "Space and the Strategy of Life," in A. H. Esser, ed., *The Use of Space by Animals and Men* (Bloomington, Ind.: University of Indiana Press, 1969).

6. See Walter R. Stokes, *Married Love in Today's World* (New York: Citadel Press, 1962) and Walter R. Stokes, "Sex in the World of Tomorrow," *Sexology* 32:748, 1966.

7. Ira Reiss, "Universality of the Family: a Conceptual Analysis," *Journal of Marriage and the Family* 27:443, 1965.

8. See Hans L. Zetterberg, *Sweden: the Contraceptive Society* (Totowa, N.J.: Bedminster Press, 1969).

Chapter 18

PREMARITAL SEX FROM AN EXISTENTIAL PERSPECTIVE

By S. Jeffrey Garfield, Ph.D.,
Sander I. Marcus, Ph.D., and
Elizabeth Garfield

Our culture exerts tremendous pressures on teen-agers and young adults. Social forces put the young person in a position where there are no social sanctions for having a sexual relationship with a person of the opposite sex, regardless of the significance of the relationship. Such forces operate in terms of religious rules, standards and expectations from the educational community, influences of popular media, and parental standards and expectations, which are synthesized from all of these.

Although in this century religion as a social force has lost much of its impact, in many cultures and subcultures religion does still exert a strong influence, primarily on people who have deep needs for approval from the community, people who fear making internal evaluations of their own behavior, or people who rely on rules to maintain impulse control. The religious viewpoint, by and large, claims that the meaning and direction of people's lives is derived from adherence to the tenets of the religion, and most religions then evaluate the individual and judge his morality, worth, and integrity by his performance according to their particular standards. Thus the evaluative processes and life-style do not develop from within the individual but are dictated to him by the religious authority, and the meaning of his life ultimately is

not defined by the individual himself. The significance of his life
becomes a matter of "being good" or "doing the right thing." In
this context there is little room for accepting one's sexuality,
which is often defined a priori as sinful by religions, or indeed,
for defining one's place in the cosmic scheme of things.

The educational system in our society makes huge demands on
the time, energy, direction, and choices of young people. Success,
reward, praise, opportunity—all are made to hinge on academic
performance. To perform well academically, the student more
often than not must subjugate his or her intelligence, curiosity,
and initiative in an effort to get the "right" answer on a multiple-
choice exam, a teaching approach that reduces life to a series of
correct answers. Except in the "real" sciences, such avoidance
of controversy or innovation has long characterized the academic
establishment. Learning institutions that could and should be a
source of understanding and opportunity for dialogue on a crucial
life issue such as sex thus become places where even the recognition of sexuality is denied. The most a student will typically
receive are sterile guidelines in the form of do's and don'ts, and
what could be an important center for meaningful dialogue in
sexuality is absent from young people's lives.

Popular media and mass communication methods have become
a powerful force for influencing people. Sex is merchandised over
television in the form of products obviously designed to make any
person more alluring to the opposite sex. Americans are told that
the attraction between a man and a woman is based on various
aphrodisiacs disguised as hair sprays, deodorants, mouthwashes,
or after-shave lotions. Cars are sold to the American male,
washing machines and household appliances to the American
female, clothes and cosmetics to American teen-agers of either
sex by promising instant sexual gratification to the user of the
product. Sex and violence sell television programs. Sex scenes are
explicit in contemporary movies, and sex scenes are *live* in contemporary theater. Sex has become a material commodity in the
marketplace, and is used as bait to lure the potential customer.
In the process of commercializing sex, all sense of intimacy is lost,
and the entire sexual experience is diminished and dehumanized.
There is no room for intimacy on television or in the movies.

There is a very real problem for the teen-ager with an emerging
sense of sexuality. Religions try to suppress sexuality. The schools
try to deny sexuality. Adherence to peer group mores ritualize the

style of sexuality. Laws prohibit various sexual proclivities. At the same time, popular books, magazines, movies, and music bombard the public with sexual stimulants. It is in the midst of this variety that the adolescent is attempting to deal with his sexuality and to formulate a sexual identity.

At the very ages during which sexual relationships are considered taboo, the individual has perhaps the greatest need for, and interest in, sexual outlet. A certain period of sexual experimentation, exploring, and experiencing is a valuable prerequisite for making a mature decision as to a marriage partner, and yet such a learning experience is discouraged by society at large. Only the socially sanctioned act is generally considered to be an appropriate mode of behavior, and many people continue to accept societal guidelines as unequivocal truth. They accede to a variety of external social controls because without structure, guidelines, or "right answers" to rely on, the individual must accept the responsibility for making decisions on admittedly complex issues to which there are no easy answers. The main issue is not how to change cultural or societal mores, however, but how a mature human being can make reasonable choices for a sexually satisfying life in such a society.

Behavior itself means nothing; many people can perform an identical act for entirely different reasons. The sexual act can represent different kinds of meaning and different kinds of gratification to different people. For example, to interpret all "oral" sex as representing a certain kind of sickness (or health, depending upon one's point of view) results in an artificial meaning for an act of behavior that can have various meanings, depending upon the personality and dynamics of the individual. To assess the meaning of any kind of sexual behavior, one must understand the dynamics of the individual; only then does the particular sexual behavior of that individual become clinically meaningful. Sexual behavior may be used variously for "healthy" or "pathological" reasons. The health or pathology must be judged, not by the nature of the sexual behavior itself, but by a clinical assessment of the underlying dynamics.

A typical hysterical neurotic individual is driven by sexual impulses, but they are inextricably bound up with issues of childhood sexuality, as described most clearly by Freud. The classical hysterical neurotic has not as yet made an adequate sexual differentiation in a mature sense, since he or she has not accomplished the transference relationship and identification with the parent of the same sex. The struggle for approval is still a major issue, as is the impulsive sexuality toward the parents, together with fears of what would happen if that sexuality were ever realized. The sexual relationships of the neurotic, as an expression of this kind of ambivalence, may thus reflect the dynamics by being impulsive and anxiety-ridden but unsatisfying. A hysterical neurotic female will frequently have a sexual life that is divorced from her emotional life. She may have a great frequency of sexual relationships but reach orgasm only rarely if at all.

A person in the midst of a severe adolescent reaction may have a sexual pattern similar to the neurotic, but the focus and meaning of the sexuality are considerably different. For the adolescent reaction, sexual relationships represent an expression of rebellion against authority and in some sense are an attempt at independence, albeit an immature one. The reacting adolescent is trapped in a vicious cycle by having an extremely high set of standards for himself coupled with an extremely low opinion of himself. In this dilemma, he projects his lack of self-acceptance onto the world and then rebels against the "imperfect" world that apparently threatens his independence. Whatever the world demands of him, the reacting adolescent will reject and do the opposite, thereby "proving" his independence. Obviously, decisions made on this basis are not independent at all, but nevertheless, the focus is around the issue of independence. In addition, the adolescent is afraid of dealing with issues such as intimacy or commitment, since these represent threats to his fragile sense of independence. Thus, his sexual relationships, like those of the hysterical neurotic, may be characterized by a lack of emotional involvement and a real avoidance of intimacy. Again, whatever the specific behavior, it is the underlying dynamics that provide a meaning for the sexual act.

The meaning of the sexual act within the framework of the individual's personality far transcends the question of the apparent social propriety of the sexual act itself. This does not mean that a sexual need is inappropriate any time it is used for personal gratification. It does mean that if the sexual relationships an individual experiences are used *solely* for the purpose of impulse gratification, without regard to the nature of the relationship with the sexual partner, one can define this as inappropriate. What, then, is appropriate?

The "health" of a relationship can be described in terms of its emphasis on the emotional relationship and involvement between the partners, the intimate sharing quality of the sexual experience as an expression of the intimate sharing quality of the relationship, spontaneity within the sexual experience as an expression of the spontaneity within a healthy relationship, and the transcendent quality in which two people become one while both retain their individuality. This discussion is not intended as a how-to-do-it recipe, but rather as a description of an appropriate, dynamic, mutually satisfying relationship.

In a meaningful relationship, the sexual experience is an expression of the emotional relationship itself. The goal of the sexual experience does, of course, retain its impulse gratification aspect, but this is intermeshed with, and in many ways subservient to, a meaningful relationship between two people. A sexual relationship cannot be meaningful when the partners view it solely for the purpose of their own impulse gratification, without experiencing it as a relationship. Without the experience of relating to, and being involved with, another human being, without an allover sense of being together, such a sexual encounter becomes no more than a glorified form of masturbation. It is the significance of the sexual experience within the context of a relationship that makes that experience meaningful, not the apparent social appropriateness of the specific sexual act.

One of the hallmarks of a meaningful relationship with another human being is an intimate emotional sharing, which may or may not express itself physically within a sexual act. This is the concept of intimacy that Erikson deals with in *Childhood and Society* (1950). A perfectly timed mutual climax may be experienced as no more than an exchange of goods or a trade agreement, rather than as an intimate experience openly shared by two people who are deeply involved with each other. Conversely, a sexual experience in which one partner "takes" another in some form of lustful abandon may be a deeply moving and intimately felt emotional experience that is shared by both, rather than a rape. Again, it is not a question of what kind of sexual activity, but of how intimately the experience is shared within the context of a relationship.

When this kind of intimacy and sharing occurs, a genuine transcendent quality may emerge in which two people, while retaining their own individuality, become one and experience a true union. Each person extends past the boundaries of his or her own skin and experiences togetherness that becomes so intimate that the partners may feel that they experience each other as being part of themselves.

The description thus far does not mean that a balance is always maintained, for in a truly meaningful and open relationship, there is a quality of spontaneity that leaves any reasonable possibility open to experience. To structure emotional sharing or even limit physical activity destroys the spontaneity of the relationship and thereby lessens the sense of humanness.

Accepting the fact that in any real relationship there are many gradations, sexual experience may be generalized into two types, "trivial" and "emotional." The first is relatively uninvolving. The individual by virtue of his or her own choice makes no commitment to extend the initial encounter; he or she deliberately decides to keep it on a physical basis. The latter type involves a decision to enter into the partner's life and open one's self emotionally to the partner, which involves time, effort, and considerable risk.

One may alternate between these two kinds of experience. Indeed, one may vacillate between trivial and emotional sexuality within a relationship with the same person. In a prolonged situation where there is little possibility of emotional involvement, a casual sexual encounter may well be reasonable. The propriety of the choice depends upon whether or not the experience is in fact a choice. Thus, appropriate sexuality depends not on either the specific sexual activity or the casualness of the encounter, but rather upon whether the experience represents a reasonable choice of involvement, partner, activity, and goal, and whether the choice grows out of the individual's sense of maturity and knowledge of self.

What, then, is to be said of premarital sex? Can we categorize premarital sex as unhealthy or "bad" while evaluating marital sex as healthy or "good" by definition? Obviously not, since one may have a rigid, stereotyped, and unintimate married sexual life, or an open, fulfilling, and loving premarital relationship. The issue is not whether sex occurs before or after marriage, but rather what the significance of the relationship is in terms of appropriateness, maturity, choice, responsibility, intimacy, and similar factors.

The choice for intimacy carries with it the freedom and responsibility for making such a choice. The person who freely makes a commitment to another human being also carries the ultimate responsibility for his or her own part in the relationship, and the personal risks involved are considerable, whether or not the sexual behavior is socially sanctioned. A relationship has meaning when it evolves as a function of freedom, choice, responsibility, and a Nietzschean sense of will—not when the depth and purpose of the relationship are defined by an outside societal agent.

Contemporary literature, research, discussion, and concern seek a consensus on human sexuality when, in fact, it is the responsibility of the individual to attribute such meaning and accept responsibility for his behavior in the world. A consensus of morality by which everybody can be evaluated is irrelevant to the task of promoting personal growth so that choices for activity develop from a sense of freedom, maturity, responsibility, and appropriateness. As a culture we have been addressing ourselves to inappropriate questions.

Chapter 19

SEX AND AMERICAN ATTITUDES

By Robert A. Harper, Ph.D.

Harry Stack Sullivan used to say that all people are more alike than they are different. That applies to sex: people are more alike in being human than they are different in being male or female. In their sexuality or sexiness—that is, behavior stemming mainly from their genitality—similarities are certainly more significant and notable among males and females than dissimilarities. It is interesting to observe, however, that our culture has only recently begun to recognize the basic sexuality of women. Women's (as yet incomplete) liberation to become first-class citizens and full-fledged persons has been to a considerable extent related to the gradual awareness on the part of both sexes that women are as embued with sexuality as men. Regardless of sex, then, there is no true humanness devoid of sexuality. The healthy human being has no self apart from the sexual aspects of his being; to be freely and fully human is to be freely and fully sexual.

For the individual to discover himself, for him to have the fulfillment of his true humanness, he needs opportunity for the unfettered expression of his sexuality. With such a generality, especially if we were to insert a few terms like "wholesome" and "spiritual" here or there, even many present-day puritans are not likely to quarrel. It is only when one gets at all specific about means of freeing the individual from false and constraining sexual attitudes and behavior, in order to permit his constructive sexual functioning, that moral hackles quickly rise.

Official codes, general and theoretical pronouncements, personal beliefs and feelings, and overt sexual behavior are all in widely varying states of incongruence and confusion in our society today. What is alleged to be sexual freedom (whether by swingers or hippies or the co-called sophisticated) often reveals itself to be, not deep and healthy sexuality, but either guilt-ridden rebellion or the obsessive-compulsive scratching of some itch of anxiety. The defiers as well as the defenders of the sexual faith of our fathers are often quite ambivalent in their sexual beliefs, feelings, and actions. Most of us have drunk deeply early in life of our culture's schizoid sexual potion, and we are likely to remain sexually befuddled in one way or another the rest of our lives. Sexual activity and self-discovery are not automatic concomitants.

There is currently little basis for optimism, in my opinion, that the so-called Sexual Revolution will release future generations of Americans for full and fulfilling experience of their sexuality. Whatever they say or fail to say, most American parents today indicate that they basically believe that masturbation, premarital petting, and premarital coitus are morally wrong, especially for *their* children. As far as I can discern, these attitudes of the current crop of parents are not only transmitted to, but uncritically accepted by, most children as fundamentally true. The fact that many of these children nevertheless proceed to masturbate and pet and copulate profusely does not basically alter the anti-sexual attitudes with which they have been instilled.

So many patients with sexual problems say to me that their parents cannot be held responsible for their sexual hang-ups, because sex was never even mentioned in the home. It is difficult for them to come to understand that silence on sex, in sharp contrast to relatively free talk on other topics, is the most effective device for communicating guilt and anxiety and apathy and ambivalent fascination and revulsion.

Whatever else we may wish to credit to Freud, he performed and important reality-facing service in calling reluctant scientific attention to the long-repressed fact that sexuality is an attibute of human beings from infancy onward. As called to my attention in a personal discussion of this topic with two well-known Philadelphia psychiatrists, O. Spurgeon English and Warren Hampe, full orgastic satisfaction and a kind of self-transcendence can be observed in the masturbatory activities, not of adolescents, but of infants in our society. This is surely no puzzle, for the messages of sin and guilt (or, at the very least, not-nice-ness) have not yet reached most infants, but they have scarcely missed a single adolescent in our society.

So many parents, educators, clergymen, and others seem to pride themselves these days on the point that not many of them are still telling children that masturbation leads to acne, growth of hair on the palm, impotence, insanity, and early death by dread disease. But anti-masturbatory soft sells are still with us. They go something like this: "There isn't anything *terribly wrong* about masturbation, if not done to *excess*" ("excess" is not defined, so the poor child is left to imagine that even his fearful and guilty occasional sexual encounter with himself may indeed be over the hill into horrible excess). *"But,"* the typical contemporary message goes, whether verbally or nonverbally communicated, "there are *lots* of *nicer* and more wholesome and more enjoyable things we can do with ourselves, *aren't* there? How about a nice jog around the block, or a nice game of hostility darts, or three-dimensional tic-tac-toe? *There's* a good child."

Thus, more gently than by the Beelzebub-is-in-your-pants methods of the past, the child is blocked from the self-discovering potential of masturbation. Does it sound silly and vulgar to speak of masturbation as a means of self-awareness and self-discovery? Undoubtedly so to many of us, for we have been anti-sexually conditioned as children of our culture. There is surely no inherently realistic reason why nature's outstanding built-in means of joy and satisfaction should not be freely and happily used as a step along the road to self-discovery and self-fulfillment.

It may seem we linger too long on masturbation, which can surely produce only a most elementary form of self-discovery. But the essential point to be understood is that persons blocked in their sexual expression at this rudimentary level cannot, sometimes even with the aid of intensive therapy, move on to more advanced levels of sexuality and self-discovery. The major message that stays with most of us from the anti-masturbatory conditioning of childhood (largely attributable to the Christian aspects of our culture) is that sexual desire is of itself evil. The manifest psychological truth, however, is that a person functioning at any level will find it impossible to get integratively in touch with himself so long as he reacts to a major portion of his being—his most formidable, pleasure-giving drive—as something from which to dissociate his "better self."

Masturbation is nevertheless an incomplete sexual experience. The sexual urge, from the first hours of experiencing maternal warmth and suckling satisfaction, is toward the human union of loving and being loved. It is only when the individual finds himself in loving interaction—in complete, sustained, and frequent sexual union—that he is likely to find himself in the process of self-discovery and self-fulfillment.

James Michener puts it quite well, I think, in one of his lesser-known works, *The Fires of Spring:* "If a man happens to find himself—if he knows what he can be depended upon to do, the limits of his courage, the position from which he will no longer retreat, the degree to which he can surrender his inner life to some woman, the secret reservoirs of his determination, the extent of his dedication, the depth of his feeling for beauty, his honest and unpostured goals then he has found a mansion which he can inhabit with dignity all the days of his life."

Our society sees to it that few indeed find such a mansion in which to dwell. Even without such dedicated love, however, sexual relations can be helpful in the pursuit of self-discovery. Many people, including a majority of writers on the subjects of sex and marriage, seem to jump to the conclusion that because sex *with* full love is a wonderfully deep and meaningful experience, sex *without* love somehow becomes a debased, disturbed, and generally undesirable activity. Because ice cream *with* chocolate sauce is great does not mean that ice cream *without* chocolate sauce is dreadful. Because it is usually more fun to kiss a lover than one's mother does not mean it is an awful experience, in most cases, to kiss one's mother.

The contention that love is necessary (rather than desirable) for the enjoyment of sex is part of the hierarchy of barriers against sex raised by our prudish culture. The first line of defense is that sex is bad under any circumstances and those persons who persistently avoid it are spiritually superior. The second rampart is that sex is okay for reproductive purposes, but not pleasure. The third is that perhaps it is all right to enjoy sex in marriage, but certainly not elsewhere. The fourth bastion is that maybe sex is even forgivable at times outside of marriage, but only when the sexual participants are in love. Each line of defense in the hierarchy is somewhat colored by the preceding positions. The sex-only-with-love adherents usually still carry an underlying conviction that sex is basically a not-nice drive, even though it has been antisepticized with love and declared fine and beautiful under prescribed circumstances.

As I indicated earlier, I am not overly impressed with the sexually liberating effects of what has been called the Sexual Revolution. People seem to mean varying things by the phrase: sometimes increased and more detailed references to sex in print and speech, sometimes overt sexual behavior, and, more rarely, changes in sexual attitudes. While I in no sense belittle the desirability of letting people write and say anything they want to write and say about sex or anything else (and I support any revolution that is directed toward the removal of any type of censorship), I am not sure how far sexual revolution in this country has gone beyond the greater freedom of written and spoken discussion. Even if we were to take such a gross criterion as total number of annual copulations divided by total population, I am impressed more by the absence of evidence of sexual behavioral change than by its presence. Obviously, though, even if we were to agree that members of the present generation copulate two or three times as much as earlier generations, we'd say little or nothing about sexuality in relation to self-discovery. Only by a change in attitudes that leads to the free and open and positive utilization of the individual's sexual potential will we have a sexual revolution with promise of greater self-discovery and self-fulfillment.

To produce an attitudinal sexual revolution we must, I believe, bring out the big guns to demolish certain cherished myths in our social morality. If self-discovery through sexual experience is to be more than sterile talk for idle hours, some really revolutionary programs need to be undertaken. The ideas we discuss below are, of course, to be considered suggestive, not definitive. The best thinking of large numbers of social, biological, and psychological scientists needs to be brought to bear on any actual social programs for effective revolution in sexual attitudes and behavior.

First, intensive sex therapy, as distinguished from sex education, is needed on a widespread basis for people in general and children and youth in particular. Combinations of behavior therapy (perhaps along the intensive lines reported by Masters and Johnson) and intensive group therapy probably hold the greatest promise of reaching large numbers of young people with effective attitudinal changes. The early work in sex therapy has to be done by and with experienced therapists to get their sex attitudes in better shape to deal effectively with the reconditioning of other people's sexual attitudes. Therapists are, of course, also products of this anti-sexual society, but if they have faced and worked through their interpersonal problems and have themselves been rather thoroughly reconditioned sexually, they are most likely to be in an attitudinal condition to provide freedom, safety, encoragement, and knowledge for young people to engage in the difficult process of working through their attitudinal distortions.

There has been a tendency among marriage and family educators and counselors to assume that we can somehow do a sort of light retouching job on young people by a course or two on sex in the schools. Even ineffective and mores-undisturbing sex courses have met with more resistance and apathy than acceptance and enthusiasm in most communities. I think we need blockbuster intensive therapeutic efforts, financed by the federal government and run independently of the schools. By the time many children reach school age, anxiety has usurped the place of emotional security, deep-seated guilt and hostility have displaced love, and sex attitudes have become tenacious, perverted dynamisms that cannot be altered by a casual, superficial sex education that is sandwiched once a week or less between gym and homeroom, taught by a birdsy-and-beesy adherent of the basically puritanical mores, and nervously watered down to complete emotional and social unreality by administrators who fear the next phone call will bring their occupational demise.

Intensive behavioral reconditioning and group therapy for large sections of our children and youth to overcome the contamination and crippling of their sexual beings by our culture may sound very expensive and impractical. The expense would be considerable, but not as overwhelming as first glance would suggest. And the results, I predict, would be very practical indeed in contrast with the diffused inadequacy of present sex education efforts. Quite practical, radical, and healthy emotional and social changes would begin very soon to emerge from such an intensive therapeutic program.

Even before the benefits of such massive remedial work can be experienced, major social revisions are needed to try to prevent the sexual corruption and pollution of unborn generations. As I have already stated, the planning and implementing of such social reforms call for the cooperative efforts of our best behavioral and social scientists. One obvious and immediate step, however, would be to make contraceptive and prophylactic information and equipment freely and completely available to persons who reach the age of possible fertility. Fear of pregnancy and venereal disease still has strong puritanical force in preventing many young people from achieving constructive sex attitudes and actions. I have been reliably informed, by the way, that pharmaceutical research could be effectively hastened by our government to produce much more adequate and probably safer contraceptive drugs than those now available.

Self-discovering and self-fulfilling sex would be further enhanced by a simple policy of readily obtainable abortion by request at any licensed hospital. A free and open approach to abortion seems much less fantastic social policy than it did even a few years ago. The recent efforts in New York and elsewhere to abolish all laws against abortion represent a much more promising approach than the earlier attempts to liberalize the definition of therapeutic abortion. Whether you call it therapeutic or not, abortion is desirable whenever a mother is unprepared to deal realistically and willingly with the problems of childbearing and child-rearing. It seems to me quite insane to contend that it is anything but undesirable for the parents, the children, and the society further to inflate the already pathologically swollen population by withholding abortions.

Such an approach to abortion as herein suggested would, defenders of the old morals say, bring about loss of respect for human life. The life removed by a simple D & C type operation sometime before the end of the third month of the pregnancy (as would almost invariably be the case, if the mother was not going through the moral struggle of having, and the frantic search of finding, an illegal abortion) is not human, anyhow. As a matter of fact, freely obtained abortion would probably bring greater respect for human life and every human representative of that life. Entrance into human life would become less the product of unhappy chance and increasingly the product of man's well-worked-out plans, his most realistic judgment.

Another aid to the prevention of the kind of sexual contamination of the individual that blocks self-discovery would be for groups of our least mores-bound parents to get together actively to encourage, help, and foster sexual play in their preadolescent children. It is inimical to personality growth to keep people in an inhibitory sexual jailhouse for the first eighteen years or so of life and then bravely and tearfully hand them contraceptives for self-discovery from that point onward. To prevent sexual hang-ups in interactional as well as masturbatory sex, we have to start when children are barely toddlers. Vigorous and joyful sex play in the nursery school is obviously shocking and abhorrent only to those of us who still think sex is a basically undesirable activity.

To help bring about a sex revolution designed for self-discovery and self-actualization, we need a great expansion of scientific research into sex. A rational sex ethic would come to be based increasingly on the results of such research into the psychological, biological, and sociological aspects of human sexual behavior and would decreasingly concern itself with universal moral edicts, mystical observations, or *a priori* enunciations from authority figures. What Moses, for example, said about adultery or what Freud said about kinds of female orgasms would be desirably taken as hypotheses for investigation and not creeds to be unquestionably followed.

The foregoing comment may seem so elementary it need not be uttered. And yet most of us have had our consciences on sexual matters solidly molded early in our uncritically childhood states by parents and others who have taken as inexorable truth the limited teachings on sex attributed to such doubtfully qualified behavioral scientists as Saul of Tarsus and Jesus of Nazareth.

A revolutionized system of sexual values would exclude prejudice against individuals on any basis such as age, gender, type of sexual preference, ethnic group, religion, or socio-economic status. Gender bias is still widespread in various manifestations of the double standard. A rational sex code would also remove such discriminations directed against the sex-love activities of children and adolescents. Limitations, if any, on anybody's sex activities would need to be demonstrably related to particular or general health and well-being. People would be prevented from needlessly, forcefully, or unfairly harming others, and each individual would likewise desirably be discouraged from any activity that would harm himself. Other sorts of limitation are unrealistic and in themselves frustrating to needed and desirable varietism in the pursuit of self-discovery and self-fulfillment.

Some students of the behavioral and social sciences who readily admit that many of the current sex attitudes and sex practices of our society are intrinsically ridiculous defend these attitudes and practices on the basis that they are closely tied to the marriage and family institutions, which, they contend, should not be seriously tampered with or shaken. But a revolution designed to create opportunities for the individual increasingly to discover and fulfill his various capacities, especially his capacity to love, cannot leave undisturbed the antiquated and repressive structures and functions of the marriage and family institutions. They must indeed be tampered with and shaped until their human-degrading procedures are radically altered. A great deal of imaginative planning and creative social experimentation is needed to find more person-enhancing systems of bringing up children as well as sharply reducing the number of children reproduced.

Although population control may seem outside the scope of this paper, it is really central to it. No human-enhancing sexual revolution, no change in human attitudes and actions directed toward self-discovery and self-fulfillment, can ignore the imminent devastation of all truly positive human values by the population explosion. Population increments not only need to be slowed down, but active and, for a time, drastic population *decrements* need to be achieved. What only a relatively few students of society seem to have squarely faced is that radical changes in the birth rates are manifestly hopeless by any voluntary means alone. While educational programs in population reduction need to be continued (and expanded beyond family planning as the solitary educational plank), people quite clearly cannot be persuaded voluntarily to curtail reproduction sharply enough to prevent human chaos.

Dr. Judith Blake, chairman of the Department of Demography at the University of California at Berkeley, pointed out in the May 2, 1969, issue of *Science* some needed tradition-defying ways of educating toward population reduction. She writes:

> If we wish to limit our growth, such a desire implies basic changes in the social organization of reproduction that will make non-marriage, childlessness, and small (two-child) families far more prevalent than they are now. A new policy to achieve such ends can take advantage of the antinatalist tendencies that our present institutions have suppressed. This will involve the lifting of penalties for antinatalist behavior rather than the "creation" of new ways of life. This behavior already exists among us as part of our covert and deviant culture, on the one hand, and our elite and artistic culture, on the other. Such antinatalist tendencies have also found expression in feminism, which has been stifled in the United States by means of systematic legal, educational, and social pres-

sures concerned with women's "obligations" to create and care for children. A fertility-control policy that does not take into account the need to alter the present structure of reproduction in these and other ways merely trivializes the problem of population control and misleads those who have the power to guide our country toward completing the vital revolution.[1]

The implementation of such suggestions as those of Dr. Blake's would be most desirable, but insufficient alone to stem the population tide. The only solution I can see, and my democratic impulses were shocked for a long time by encountering the idea, is to take away the *right* to reproduce. The *privilege* to reproduce could then be granted, and the rules governing such privilege-granting could be worked out in whatever wholly democratic ways people would want. But the original removal of the *right* to reproduce would have to be done whether or not it was with the individual's approval and consent.

Such a proposal is neither so radical nor so impractical as it seems at first. Even now, we as a society *try* to take away the individual's right to reproduce *unless* he or she goes through certain ritualistic and legalistic procedures we designate as "getting married." My recommendation is simply, in one full and nondiscriminatory sweep, to take this right away from all of us.

But is any practical method of curtailing reproduction available? Not immediately. But informed biological and pharmaceutical opinion indicates that several years of research can probably produce temporary sterilants that could be added to water supplies and staple foods effectively to remove reproductive rights. I have also been assured by scientists, who should know, that research can probably fairly quickly produce time-capsule contraceptives that could be administered to all females of reproductive age—to be temporarily withdrawn for those who are from time to time designated as reproductively privileged.

Obviously such plans would make unnecessary complicated education in, and dispensation of, contraceptives like those mentioned earlier. The connection between sex and reproduction in the future would then exist only under rare and special circumstances approved both by the participating individuals and by, say, a panel of sociological, psychological, and biological experts. Birth would be a really rationally planned procedure directed toward goals that would gradually decrease the quantity, but vastly improve the quality of mankind.

Is all this wild and silly utopianism? It need not be. I am reminded of the story told of Lloyd George as he joined Woodrow Wilson and the other national representatives at the peace conference that followed World War I. Lloyd George asked his fellow conference planners whether or not they were seriously interested in undertaking the difficult and radical planning necessary to bring about lasting international peace. His question was greeted with silence, and he said: "Gentlemen, I understand." So we got the Treaty of Versailles, Hitler, World War II, the Cold War, and lots of localized hot wars.

Mankind still helplessly and hopelessly looks for peace while continuing to develop ever more cataclysmic forms of warfare. Meantime, though, a formidable rival in impending devastation has emerged in the form of the exploding population crisis. Will our national and international leaders demonstrate the same imbecilic futility in forestalling this new type of devastation as they have in dealing with war? Very probably. But even if my pessimism is somehow happily unjustified, the topic of this paper demanded some effort at facing the population crisis. To speak of self-discovery and self-fulfillment via individual sex expression at this point in history without at least making some reference to such impending devastation is to speak vapid nonsense.

It is no way suggested that my simplistic discussion of population control leads to solution of this complex crisis. But for such fundamental human goals as world peace, optimal population planning, and creation of a social environment that would enhance self-actualization for great numbers of individuals (of which the kind of attitudinal sexual revolution herein discussed would be one important part), we must all get down to the hard work of conceiving and implementing radical social change. It is no longer enough for social and behavioral scientists in meetings, journals, and books to pass back and forth among themselves professional trade stamps of empty platitudes.

CHAPTER NOTES

1. Judith Blake, "Population Policy for Americans: Is the Government Being Misled?" *Science* 164 (May 2, 1969) : 529.

Chapter 20

SEXUALITY—A CREATIVE FORCE?

By Mary S. Calderone, M.D., M.P.H.

At the outset this author must emphasize that she writes, not from a background in the behavioral sciences, but as a physician specializing in the point of view of public health and preventive medicine. This particular background teaches the art of dealing with the health problems of people as a mass rather than as individuals. Thus it approaches any dis-ease in the general society from two points of view: therapeutic and preventive. The *therapeutic* aspect applies to that portion of the population already ill, but concurrent *preventive* action should always be applied to the incoming generation of susceptibles to prevent their becoming infected with the same dis-ease. One might therefore pustulate that the adult society shows many symptoms of dis-ease regarding sex and sexuality, and thus requires intensive therapy, and that the incoming generations of susceptibles, the children from birth upward, should be accorded an education for knowledge and attitudes that would immunize them against the sexual dis-ease observable in their elders.

This book, many symposia, and similar efforts among a wide range of professional groups—in the behavioral and medical sciences, and among educators and the clergy—exemplify something

The paper on which this chapter is based was presented at a meeting jointly sponsored by the American Psychiatric Association, the American Association of Marriage Counselors, and the Sex Information and Education Council of the U.S. (SIECUS), New York, March 29, 1969.

that is happening in our society today: an intensive search for a full comprehension of man as a sexual being. Although this search takes account of the erotic, it does not focus on it specifically. There are many difficulties placed in the way of the searchers by those who do persist in focusing primarily on the erotic, whether at the positive or negative pole. We see at the extreme left those who are obsessed with erotic exploitation, but at the extreme right we see those who are equally obsessed with eroticism, but as something to be repressed or grimly regulated. This often violent polarization between erotic-exploitives and erotic-repressives makes it increasingly difficult for those who, satisfied neither with rejection of the extremes nor with attempts at compromise, are actively engaged in the search for a positive approach to the totality that we can call *human sexuality*.

One such group is SIECUS, the Sex Information and Education Council of the U.S., formed in 1964 and shortly thereafter listed in the American Medical Association's Directory of Voluntary Health Organizations. Its stated purpose is as follows:

> To establish man's sexuality as a health entity: to identify the special characteristics that distinguish it from, yet relate it to, human reproduction; to dignify it by openness of approach, study, and scientific research designed to lead towards its understanding and its freedom from exploitation; to give leadership to professionals and to society, to the end that human beings may be aided towards responsible use of the sexual faculty and towards assimilation of sex into their individual life patterns as a creative and re-creative force.[1]

The initial phrase "To establish man's sexuality as a health entity," indicates the conviction of the council's founders and of its board members that the modern definition of health as "a state of complete physical, mental, and social well-being" requires that the sexual aspects of man's life should receive the same degree of attention from professionals as other aspects of his health.

The SIECUS board, by this writing numbering over one hundred present or past members, has consistently included leadership from the following disciplines: psychiatry; obstetrics; pediatrics; sociology; psychology; education, from elementary through graduate school; social work; the law; the three major faiths; family life education; marriage counseling; health education; the communications media; and business. As regards differences of attitudes and beliefs about their common area of interest, one might say that the board represents a wide range from right to left, but not the extremes of either.

SIECUS operates at the national level only, as an educational and informational agency, with no branches or affiliates. It takes no positions but rather operates in a spirit of challenge, inquiry, openness, rationality. It has prepared no materials nor curricula; in fact, contrary to the many false statements that have been made about it, SIECUS is not primarily interested in schools but in those who might deal specifically with the individual during all phases of his life—primarily the parent, the educator, the physician, the clergyman, the therapist. In actuality, its primary mission is to develop a valid and viable ideology about human sexuality.

The basic concept of human sexuality as connoting the totality of a person as male or female—in being, attitudes, thoughts, actions, relationships—is serving as an "open sesame" into areas formerly forbidden even for professionals to consider openly. This is fortunate, in view of the concurrent but independent emergence in the society of a number of nonstereotyped forms of sexual behaviors and relationships, quite beyond and distinct from sex or reproductive acts or orgasmic capacity. We see these developments in such disparate groups as the young middle-class single adults—whether the alienated or those in the colleges, in the business world, or in the religious orders. In other words, among many individuals new ways of being-to-each-other as male or female are evolving that may often have little or nothing to do with the sex act that so preoccupies the erotic-exploitives and erotic-repressives.

Actually the polarization of these two extremist sex-obsessed groups appears to be serving to clear the field for real evolution of what may prove to be valid and viable in new sexual patterns, and we see thoughtful, searching individuals of diverse ages and backgrounds, actively engaged in confronting themselves and others as sexual persons, trying to probe into and comprehend the many facets of human behavior that are sex-related, the many nuances of sex-related attitudes and feelings, the distinction between the closed-end boxes of stereotyping and compulsiveness and the open-endedness of self-determined and self-controlled sexual feeling and expression. In short, many people are edging nearer to comprehension of the fuller meanings of being man or woman, and of the many kinds of significances, some never permitted nor perhaps even conceived of in our society, of the man-woman relationship that might include, but also be aside from, the purely erotic.

But many limitations still block the way to openness of approach and understanding of sexuality. One in particular relates to concepts of masculinity, for which traditional and confining patterns are now only beginning to be broken. This is in contrast to the female, whose emergence I personally experienced fifty years ago as a teen-ager. If we are to enter into consideration of sexuality as a creative force, which I believe it is, I think it may, at least for a time, have to be for the two sexes differently inasmuch as each of the two sexes, as a collectivity, is at a different stage of sexual evolution: the male collectivity is predominantly still erotic-obsessive (who purveys and buys erotica?), but the female collectivity, while moving (or having moved) away from the erotic-repressive camp, refuses to go the whole way into erotic obsession. The male collectivity is thus being liberated to move toward a cleared middle ground in which eroticism and sexual identity, sex roles and relationships, might fall into true and creative interaction and balance.

Descartes said, "I think, therefore I am." I have often thought that a truer, more human way of putting it would be, "I feel, therefore I am." The meaning refines itself further if it is stated, "I feel (as a woman, as a man), therefore I am."

For every person, feeling *as* a male or *as* a female or *because* he is male or female, must have different meanings, as it must at different times in the same person's life. These differences lead to many unanswered questions: what degree exists of interplay between erotic expression and gender identity? If his gender identity can be looked upon as a *constant* in the adult life of an individual, and his erotic expression as an explosive experience of *variable* periodicity and intensity, then when or how do either, both, or neither bear on the creativity of that individual?

Erotic tension per se impels the individual toward orgasmic release. Does it per se also impel the individual into creativity? What is the cause of erotic tension? Often attributed in males to "pressure" of spermatic or seminal production this, like many other sexual assumptions, must be mythologically-based for there is no analogous physiological process in the female to explain why she, too, can and does feel she will "explode" without orgasmic release. What are the factors in the mechanism of this build-up—

psychic, physiological, humoral, neural, or a mixture? The genitally localized sexual tension is perceived at what level and where in the central nervous system? What are the pathways that trigger its release? At what neurological levels is incorporation of erotic activity into the personality structure achieved—autonomic, spinal cord, brain stem, cortex? If association pathways involving eroticism move into association with gender and personality identity at ever higher and higher brain levels, does this tend to intensify or to diminish erotic drive?

Or, perhaps, is the trigger mechanism that releases the genital build-up at a relatively low neurological level, but so dependent for its operation on a complex series of neuropsychic connections that it must horseshoe up through association pathways to a given brain level and then back down? Why, for instance, do anxiety or anger increase genital tension at some times and diminish it at others? All of us experience moments of peak creativity; do we have *individualized* patterns that relate such moments to the normally occurring peaks and valleys of erotic tension, or could *standardized* patterns be identified?

I do not know if psycho-neuro-physiologists have the answers to these and many related questions, so I have to admit that it is only my own personal hunch that leads me to postulate that our truest creativity arises out of our profoundest moments or periods of total sexual identification, of which the erotic may or may not be a part: in other words, these may be moments that coincide with intense erotic experience, but, quite conversely, they may also coincide with moments of intense erotic deprivation or denial. Possibly, then, the sexual constant for creativity is not the erotic, but is rather one's sense of a fully achieved gender role within which the erotic certainly functions as a variable that colors, illuminates, highlights, or changes the focus, if not the nature, of the constant.

This takes me back to, "I feel as man or as woman, therefore I am." The probability is that the reaction between the variable of *eroticism* and the base line constant of *gender role* changes with age, as does the creativity that is the resultant of the variable acting on the constant. The adolescent is primarily saying, "I feel erotically, therefore I am." As the individual matures (in the true as well as chronological sense), as his experiencing of self and of others deepens and his sense of gender identity and role strengthens, his eroticism might appear to diminish, whether absolutely or relatively; but if the individual is free, the total in terms of creativity should, I believe, increase.

Thus, if the individual at any age places dependence of creativity on the variable of eroticism, this is treacherous simply because it *is* a variable. But if eroticism, for all of its variability, remains a function of strong gender identity, then the base for creativity can remain stable and assured—and creative production enriched, not weakened, by the range of variability of genitality during the aging process.

In other words, to place total dependence for love, creativity, or any other self-determined goals primarily on eroticism predestines questionable achievement of these goals. About love, Wardell Pomeroy has said it best: "Penises and vaginas can't love each other; only people can do that."[2] Neither can penises and vaginas, in no matter how many orgasms, write poems, build bridges, explore space, make marriages, or accomplish what needs to be accomplished on behalf of human sexuality. Only *people* can make —or fail to make—orgasm into part of creative and lovely wholes of their lives.

So if education for sexuality, in fact *all* education, concentrates on the *person* as male or female to enable this person to emerge in adult life, fully conscient of himself or herself *as* male or female, then genitality must fall into place, neither held out as an ever-luring flame nor trailed along as a guilty hangover. Eroticism must be integrated into the ego structure in a manner appropriate to each stage of ego development, thus eventually to be incorporated into full sexual relationships in ways that enhance the creativity of these relationships and of the individuals concerned in all of their other relationships.

What should be emphasized at this point is how little we really do know about sexuality and its many manifestations in the human being. The researches of Kinsey and of his colleagues told us what men and women remembered that they did sexually under the conditions of the society of the 1940s. Obviously, these conditions have changed radically, and yet one knows of no intensive research being carried on that would provide the sorely needed objective findings on which to base conclusions as to what children and young people need for prevention of those very sexual dis-eases that men and women have been clearly shown to be suffering from today.

The work of Masters and Johnson has provided, for the first time, thoroughly accurate and objective knowledge of the physiology of human sexual response and effective beginnings of therapeutic methods for primary psycho-genital inadequacies. What is now desperately needed is intensive research on the delicate but powerful interrelationships between sexual feelings, attitudes, and action. Thus, any discussion of sexuality as a creative force must still necessarily end with a question mark. Is it indeed a creative force? Even this question must be dissected to discover what about sexuality might or might not lead to creativity —the erotic *act*, the psycho-erotic *relationship*, the drive toward these, or what?

Finally, what is meant by creative? Perhaps for the purpose of this discussion, which in reality is simply a series of questions that need to be answered before larger questions can be posed, I might define creativity simply as the result of the evolution of the person to the point at which fulfillment of his highest potential becomes as easy for him as breathing. In fact, then full creativity, like fulfilled sexuality, becomes literally the breath of life itself.

CHAPTER NOTES
1. From the SIECUS Charter.
2. W. B. Pomeroy, *Boys and Sex* (New York: Delacorte Press, 1968), p. 92.

Appendix

GROWTH CENTERS

WEST

BERKELEY CENTER FOR HUMAN
INTERACTION
1820 Scenic
Berkeley, Calif. 94709
(415) 845-4765
Trevor Hoy

BERKELEY INSTITUTE FOR TRAINING
IN GROUP THERAPY & PSYCHODRAMA
1868 San Juan Avenue
Berkeley, Calif. 94707

BERKELEY MOVERS
4919 Clarke Street
Oakland, Calif. 94609

BINDRIM, PAUL & ASSOCIATES
2000 Cantata Drive
Los Angeles, Calif. 90028

BLUE MOUNTAIN CENTER OF
MEDITATION
1960 San Antonio
Berkeley, Calif. 94707
Eknath Eswaran

BRIDGE MOUNTAIN FOUNDATION
2011 Alba Road
Ben Lomand, Calif. 95005
(408) 336-5787

CASAELYA
2266 Union Street
San Francisco, Calif. 94123
(415) 771-6611

THE CENTER
Box 3014
Stanford, Calif. 94305
(415) 327-7686
David Mastrandrea

THE CENTER FOR CREATIVITY
AND GROWTH
599 College Avenue
Palo Alto, Calif. 94306
(415) 321-4200
Frieda Porat

CENTER FOR HUMAN COMMUNICATION

120 Oak Meadow Drive
Los Gatos, Calif. 95030
(408) 354-6466

CENTER FOR INTERPERSONAL
DEVELOPMENT
3127 Eastern Avenue
Sacramento, Calif. 95821
(916) 454-6188
Margaret McKoane

CENTER FOR STUDIES OF THE PERSON
1125 Torrey Pines Road
La Jolla, Calif. 92037
(714) 459-3861
Carl Rogers

COUNSELING ASSOCIATES OF
SAN MATEO
30 South El Camino Real
San Mateo, Calif. 94401
and
6275 Shadygrove Court
San Jose, Calif. 95129

DIALOGUE HOUSE ASSOCIATES
Box 877
San Jacinto, Calif. 92383
(714) 654-2625

EDMUCKO
P.O. Box 216
Ben Lomond, Calif. 95005
(408) 336-8256
Ed Dalton

ELYSIUM INSTITUTE
5436 Fernwood Avenue
Los Angeles, Calif. 90027
(213) 465-7121
Ed Lange, Aileen Goodson

EMOTIONAL STUDIES INSTITUTE
775 Camino del Sur C-2
Goleta, Calif. 93017
(805) 968-2694
Patrick T. Allison

ESALEN INSTITUTE
Big Sur, Calif. 93920
(408) 667-2335

Richard Price, Ken Price
and
1776 Union Street
San Francisco, Calif. 94123
(415) 431-8771
David Baar, Michael Murphy
and
Stanford University
Stanford, Calif. 94305

EUREKA CENTER FOR COMMUNICATION
AND ENCOUNTER
4300 Crest View Drive
Eureka, Calif. 95501

EXPLORATIONS INSTITUTE
Box 1254
Berkeley, Calif. 94701
(415) 548-1004
James Elliott

FOUNDATION FOR HUMAN
ACHIEVEMENT
291 Geary Street
San Francisco, Calif. 94102

GESTALT THERAPY INSTITUTE
OF LOS ANGELES
337 South Beverly Drive
Suite 206
Beverly Hills, Calif. 90212

GESTALT THERAPY INSTITUTE
OF SAN DIEGO
7255 Girard Avenue, Suite 27
La Jolla, Calif. 92037
(714) 459-2693
Thomas A. Munson

GESTALT THERAPY INSTITUTE
OF SOUTHERN CALIFORNIA
1029 Second Street
Santa Monica, Calif. 90403
Robert Resnick

GUILD FOR PSYCHOLOGICAL STUDIES
2230 Divisadero Street
San Francisco, Calif. 94115
Sadie M. Gregory

HIGH POINT FOUNDATION
1001 East Rosecrans Avenue
Compton, Calif. 90221

HUMAN DYNAMICS WORKSHOP
Box 342
Boulder Creek, Calif. 95006
(408) 338-3926
Jill Wechsler

HUMAN EXPLORATIONS PROGRAM
P.O. Box 1145
Kanehoe, Hawaii 96744

HUMAN POTENTIAL INSTITUTE
2550 Via Tejon
Palos Verdes Estates, Calif. 90274
(213) 376-8533
William F. Hull, Erick H. Marcus,
Henry L. Levy, Anita Mooney

HUMAN RESOURCES INSTITUTE
7946 Ivanhoe Avenue
La Jolla, Calif. 92037
(714) 459-3664
and
1745 South Imperial Avenue
El Centro, Calif. 92243
(714) 354-3501
Philip Kavanaugh, John Emery,
John Aycock

HUMANIST INSTITUTE
1430 Masonic Street
San Francisco, Calif. 94117
(415) 626-0544
Tolbert McCarroll

INSTITUTE OF ABILITY
P.O. Box 798
Lucerne Valley, Calif. 92356

INSTITUTE OF HUMAN ABILITIES
80 Hamilton Place
Oakland, Calif. 94612

INSTITUTE OF INTEGRATIVE
PSYCHOLOGY
School of Social Sciences
University of California
Irvine, Calif. 92664
(714) 833-6336
Joseph T. Hart
c/o Mrs. Ruthie Lewis

INSTITUTE OF BEHAVIORAL DYNAMICS
9000 Sunset Boulevard
Los Angeles, Calif. 90069

INSTITUTE FOR CREATIVE AND
ARTISTIC DEVELOPMENT
5935 Manchester Drive
Oakland, Calif. 94618
(415) 653-9133
Eugene B. Sagan

INSTITUTE FOR GROUP AND
FAMILY STUDIES

347 Alma
Palo Alto, Calif. 94301
(415) 327-5431

INSTITUTE FOR GROWTH
3627 Sacramento Street
San Francisco, Calif. 94118
(415) 563-7988
Joseph Busey, Peter Rogers,
David Wilson

INSTITUTE FOR MULTIPLE
PSYCHOTHERAPY
3701 Sacramento Street
San Francisco, Calif. 94118
(415) 752-3564
Richard Miller,
Lawrence Bloomberg

INTERNATIONAL COOPERATION
COUNCIL
17819 Roscoe Boulevard
Northridge, California 93124

KAIROS
The Ranch
Box 350
Rancho Santa Fe, Calif. 92067
(714) 756-1123
Robert J. Driver
and
Town House
624 Upas Street
San Diego, Calif. 92103
(714) 295-1569
Peter Beemer

KEMERY INSTITUTE
304 Parkway
Chula Vista, Calif. 92010
(714) 427-6225
W. E. Kemery

LAFAYETTE CENTER FOR
COUNSELING AND EDUCATION
Brook Dewing Medical Building
914 Dewing Street
Lafayette, California 94549
(415) 284-5959
Kenneth E. Johnson,
Frank E. Humberger

NATIONAL CENTER FOR THE
EXPLORATION OF HUMAN POTENTIAL
8080 El Paseo Grande
La Jolla, Calif. 92037
(714) 459-4469
Herbert A. Otto, Al Lewis

NEW CONSCIOUSNESS PROGRAM
Old Student Union; Room 142
University of California
Santa Barbara, California 93101

PACIFIC TRAINING ASSOCIATES
3516 Sacramento Street
San Francisco, Calif. 94118
(415) 346-0770
Price Cobb, William Grier

PALO ALTO VENTURE
P.O. Box 11802
Palo Alto, Calif. 94306
Charlene Harman

PERSONAL EXPLORATION GROUPS
2400 Bancroft Way
Stiles Hall
Berkeley, Calif. 94704

SAN FRANCISCO GESTALT
THERAPY INSTITUTE
1719 Union Street
San Francisco, Calif. 94123
(415) 776-4500

SAN FRANCISCO VENTURE
584 Page Street
San Francisco, Calif. 94117

SCHIFFMAN, MURIEL, ·
COMMUNICATION & SELF THERAPY
WORKSHOPS
340 Santa Monica Avenue
Menlo Park, Calif. 94025

S.E.L.F. INSTITUTE
40 Hawthorne Avenue
Los Altos, California 94022
John J. Latini

SELF-OTHER SYSTEMS INSTITUTE
Maple Street
Redwood City, Calif. 94063
(415) 364-1787
Mr. & Mrs. August Winsten

SOCIETY FOR COMPARATIVE
PHILOSOPHY, INC.
Box 857
Sausalito, Calif. 94965
(415) 322-5286
Alan Watts

SWEET'S MILL
Auberry, California 93602

TAHOE INSTITUTE
Box DD

South Lake Tahoe, Calif. 95705
Jerry Nims

THOMAS JEFFERSON RESEARCH
CENTER
1143 North Lake Avenue
Pasadena, Calif. 91104

TOPANGA CENTER FOR
HUMAN DEVELOPMENT
2247 Topanga Canyon Road
Topanga, Calif. 90290
Thomas C. Greening

VIEWPOINTS INSTITUTE
833 North Kings Road
Los Angeles, Calif. 90069

WELL-SPRINGS
2003 Alba Road
Ben Lomond, Calif. 95005
Kay Ottmans Pawley

WESTERN CENTER CONSULTANTS
9400 Culver Boulevard
Suite 206
Culver City, Calif. 90230
(213) 836-5452
Robert N. Stapleton

ANALYSIS INSTITUTE
1394 Westwood Boulevard
Los Angeles, Calif. 90024

NORTHWEST

NORTHWEST FAMILY THERAPY
INSTITUTE
Box 94278
Tacoma, Wash. 98494
Karl Humiston

SEMINARS IN GROUP PROCESS
8475 S.W. Bohmann Parkway
Portland, Oreg. 97223
(503) 244-8806
Robert C. Warren

SENOI INSTITUTE, INC.
Route 2, Box 259
Eugene, Oreg. 97401
(503) 747-4311
Robert C. Warren

STAR WEATHER RANCH INSTITUTE
Box 923
Hailey, Ida. 08333
Josephine Price

VIDA
Ventures in Developing Awareness

1934 East Charleston
Las Vegas, Nev. 89104
(702) 384-4844
Irving S. Katz

CENTRAL STATES

ALVERNA RETREAT HOUSE
8140 Spring Mill Road
Indianapolis, Ind. 46260
(317) 255-1340
Father Maury Smith

AMARE: THE INSTITUTE OF HUMAN
RELATEDNESS
Box 108
Bowling Green, Ohio 43402
Melvin L. Foulds

ANTIOCH GROUP FOR HUMAN
RELATIONS
Antioch College
Yellow Springs, Ohio 45387

ARIZONA TRAINING LABORATORIES FOR
APPLIED BEHAVIORAL SCIENCE
Box 26660
Tempe, Ariz. 85281
Warren Kingsbury

CAMBRIDGE HOUSE
1900 North Cambridge Avenue
Milwaukee, Wis. 53202
(414) 272-4327
Sandra Badtke

CENTER FOR CREATIVE INTERCHANGE
602 Center Street
Des Moines, Iowa 50309
(515) 243-5692
Charles L. Palmgren

COMMUNICATION CENTER NO. 1
1001 Union Boulevard
St. Louis, Mo. 63113
(314) 863-7267
Mel Spehn

CREATIVE RISK-TAKING LABORATORIES
Training Consultants International
Suite 132, 7710 Computer Avenue
Minneapolis, Minn. 55435
David Jones, Richard Byrd

DOMUS
2722 Park Avenue
Minneapolis, Minn. 55407
(612) 332-5333
Wendell Brustman

ESPIRITU
1214 Miramar
Houston, Tex. 77006
(713) 528-3301
Leland Johnson

EVERGREEN INSTITUTE
3831 West Wagon Trail Drive
Littleton, Colo. 80120
(303) 798-6351, 225-0554
Carl Hollander

FOREST GROWTH CENTER
555 Wilson Lane
Des Plaines, Ill. 60016

GESTALT INSTITUTE OF CLEVELAND
12921 Euclid Avenue
Cleveland, Ohio 44112
(216) 421-0469
Edwin C. Nevis

GREENERFIELDS UNLIMITED
1740 Waukegan Road
Glenview, Ill. 60025

HARA, INC.
7322 Blairview
Dallas, Tex. 75230
(214) 361-7444
Ben Goodwin

HUMAN POTENTIAL
Unity Village, Mo. 64063
Warren Kreml

HUMAN RESOURCE DEVELOPERS
520 North Michigan, #520
Chicago, Ill. 60611
Dean C. Dauw

INSCAPE
2845 Comfort
Birmingham, Mich. 48010

INSTITUTE OF GENERAL SEMANTICS
University of Denver
Denver, Colo. 80210
(303) 753 2387
Elwood Murray, Mark Liebig

KEYSTONE EXPERIENCE
West Georgia College
Psychology Department
Carrollton, Ga. 30117

KOPAVI
Box 16
Wayzata, Minn. 55391
Alan N. Hale

THE LAOS HOUSE: SOUTHWEST
CENTER FOR HUMAN POTENTIAL
700 West 19th
Austin, Tex. 78701
(512) 477-4471
Robert R. Bryant

MIDWEST PERSONAL GROWTH CENTER
200 South Hanley Road
Clayton, Mo. 63105
(314) 863-8476
Donald Sundland

OASIS: MIDWEST CENTER FOR
HUMAN POTENTIAL
20 East Harrison
Chicago, Ill. 60605
(314) 922-8294
Robert B. Shapiro

OMEGA CENTER
Unity Village, Mo. 64063

ONTOS, INC.
40 South Clay
Hindsdale, Ill. 60521
(312) 325-6384
John D. Burton

OUTREACH
University of Michigan
Psychology Department
Ann Arbor, Mich. 48104
Ken Winter

PEOPLE
4340 Campbell
Kansas City, Mo. 64110
(816) 561-6847
Kathy Dickman

ROCKY MOUNTAIN BEHAVIORAL
INSTITUTE
12086 West Green Mountain Drive
Denver, Colo. 80228
O.A. Ham
Hinsdale, Ill. 60521

SEMINARS FOR GROUP STUDIES
Center for Continuing Education
University of Chicago
1307 East 60th Street
Chicago, Ill. 60637
(312) 288-2500

SHADYBROOK HOUSE
Rural Route 1
Mentor, Ohio 44060
(216) 255-3406
Donald R. Boyce

S.I.P.O.D.
2606 East Grove
Houston, Tex. 77027

SOUTHWEST MOTIVATION
CENTER, INC.
Cambridge Tower
1801 Lavaca
Austin, Tex. 78701

UNIVERSITY ASSOCIATES
Box 615
Iowa City, Iowa 52240
(319) 351-7322
and
Box 24402
Indianapolis, Ind. 46224
(317) 637-7140

UOMES
110 Anderson Hall
University of Minnesota
Minneapolis, Minn. 55455

YOGI ACADEMY FOUNDATION
3209 Burton Avenue, SE
Albuquerque, N. Mex. 87107

EAST

ADANTA
3379 Peachtree Road, NE
Suite 250
Atlanta, Ga. 30326

ANTHOS
24 East 22nd Street
New York, N.Y. 10010
(212) 673-9067
Bob Kriegel

ASSOCIATES FOR HUMAN RESOURCES
387 Sudbury Road
Concord, Mass. 01742
(617) 369-7810
John B. Marin

ATHENA CENTER FOR CREATIVE
LIVING
2308 Smith Avenue
Aliquippa, Pa. 15001
Leslie H. Salov

ATLANTA WORKSHOP FOR
LIVING-LEARNING
3167 Rilman Road, N.W.
Atlanta, Ga. 30327
(404) 233-4414
Sarah S. Hollums

AUREON INSTITUTE
71 Park Avenue
New York, N.Y. 10016
(212) 532-4171
Harold Streitfeld

AWOSTING RETREAT
315 West 57th Street
New York, N.Y. 10019

BOSTON TEA PARTY
55 Berkeley Street
Boston, Mass. 02116
(617) 338-7026
Ray Riepen

BUCKS COUNTY SEMINAR HOUSE
Erwimna, Pa. 18920
(215) 294-9243
Grenville Moat

THE CENTER
Box 157
Syria. Va. 22743
(707) 923-4436

THE CENTER OF MAN
Micanopy, Fla. 32667
(904) 466-3459, 466-3351
Sidney Jourard, Theodore Landsman,
Vincent F. O'Connell

CENTER FOR HUMAN DEVELOPMENT
217 North Craig Street
Pittsburgh, Pa. 15213
(412) 687-1400
Robert Sone, Leslie Cohen

CENTER FOR THE WHOLE PERSON
1633 Race Street
Philadelphia, Pa. 19103
(215) 563-4560
William Swartley

COMMUNITY CONSULTATION SERVICES
285 Central Park West
New York, N.Y. 10024
(212) 873-3668
Carmi Harari

CUMBRES
Box C
Dublin, N.H. 03444
(603) 563-7591

DIALOGUE HOUSE ASSOCIATES
45 West 10th Street
New York, N.Y. 10011
(212) 228-9180
Ira Progoff

ENCOUNTERS: WORKSHOPS IN
PERSONAL AND PROFESSIONAL GROWTH
5225 Connecticut Avenue, NW
Suite 209
Washington, D.C. 20015
(202) 530-4485; 363-3033
Lawrence Tirnauer

THE FAMILY RELATIONS INSTITUTE
3509 Farm Hill Drive
Annandale, Va. 22044
Lori Eisenberg

FOUNDATION FOR GIFTED AND
CREATIVE CHILDREN
395 Diamond Hill Road
Warwick, R.I. 02866
John Friedel

GROUPS FOR MEANINGFUL
COMMUNICATION
645 West End Avenue
New York, N.Y. 10025
(212) 724-8788
Joseph Wysong

G.R.O.W.
312 West 82nd Street
New York, N.Y. 10024
(212) 874-1955

THE HAN INSTITUTE
c/o Denis O'Donovan
Executive Suite N
Weir Plaza Building
855 South Federal Highway
Boca Raton, Fla. 33432
Glory B. King

HELIOTROPE
Box 9041
Fort Lauderdale, Fla. 33312
(305) 584-2305
Gary D. Seiler

HUMAN DIMENSIONS INSTITUTE
4380 Main Street
Buffalo, N.Y. 14226
(716) 839-3600
Jeanne Rindge

HUMAN RELATIONS CENTER
Boston University
270 Bay State Road
Boston, Mass. 02215

HUMAN RESOURCES DEVELOPMENT
Hidden Springs
South Acworth, N.H. 03607

HUMAN RESOURCES INSTITUTE
Box 3296
Baltimore, Md. 21228

HUMANIST SOCIETY OF GREATER
NEW YORK
2109 Broadway at 73rd Street
New York, N.Y. 10023
(212) 799-0191
Joseph Ben-David

INSTAD—INSTITUTE FOR TRAINING
AND DEVELOPMENT
625 Stanwix Street, Suite 2306
Pittsburgh, Pa. 15222

INSTITUTE OF APPLIED
PSYCHOTHERAPY
251 West 92nd Street
New York, N.Y. 10025
(212) 877-3293
Ronald Jarvis

INSTITUTE FOR EXPERIMENTAL
EDUCATION
Box 446
Lexington, Mass. 02173
(617) 862-0869
Robert Horn, Buryl Payne

INSTITUTE FOR LIVING
300 South 19th Street
Philadelphia, Pa. 19103
(215) 546-7344
Kurt Konietzsko

INSTITUTE FOR RATIONAL LIVING
45 East 65th Street
New York, N.Y. 10021
(212) 535-0822
Albert Ellis

INSTITUTE FOR RESEARCH INTO
PERSONAL FREEDOM
327 Sixth Avenue
New York, N.Y. 10014

INTERFACE, INC.
Park Plaza #534
1629 Columbia Road, NW
Washington, D.C. 20009

ITHACA SEED COMPANY
Box 651
Ithaca, N.Y. 14850

KIRKRIDGE
Bangor, Pa. 18013

LABORATORY FOR APPLIED
BEHAVIORAL SCIENCE
Newark State College
Union, N.J. 07083
(201) 289-4345

LIFWYN FOUNDATION
52 South Morningside Drive
Westport, Conn. 06880

MAITREYAN FOUNDATION
220 SW 2nd Street
Boca Raton, Fla. 33432

MID-ATLANTIC INSTITUTE OF
CHRISTIAN EDUCATION
Suite 325
1500 Massachusetts Ave., NW
Washington, D.C. 20005

N.T.L. INSTITUTE FOR APPLIED
BEHAVIORAL SCIENCE
1201 Sixteenth Street, N.W.
Washington, D.C. 20036
(202) 223-9400

NEW ENGLAND CENTER FOR PERSONAL
AND ORGANIZATIONAL DEVELOPMENT
Box 575
Amherst, Mass. 01002
(413) 253-9686
John T. Canfield, Don Carew

NEW YORK INSTITUTE FOR THE
ACHIEVEMENT OF HUMAN POTENTIAL
36 East 36th Street
New York, N.Y. 10016
Harry Valentine III

NUMBER NINE
266 State Street
New Haven, Conn. 06511
(203) 787-2127
Dennis T. Jaffe

OMEGA INSTITUTE
Box 263
Merrifield, Va. 22116
Lila M. Mallette

ORIZON INSTITUTE
2710 - 36th Street, NW
Washington, D.C. 20007
(301) 233-5689
Barbara Mullens

PENDLE HILL
Wallingford, Pa. 19086
(215) 566-4507
Robert Blood

PERSONAL GROWTH LABORATORIES
112 Hunter Lane
North Wales, Pa. 19454
(215) 368-0767
Joseph D. Kovatch

THE PIEDMONT PROGRAM
Box 6129
Winston-Salem, N.C. 27109
(919) 723-6406
John Woodmansee

PLAINFIELD CONSULTATION CENTER
831 Madison Avenue
Plainfield, N.J. 07060
(201) 757-4921
Lawrence Kesner

PRINCETON ASSOCIATES FOR
HUMAN RESOURCES
341 Nassau Street
Princeton, N.J. 08540
(609) 921-2727
Leonard Blank

QUEST
3000 Connecticut Avenue, NW
Washington, D.C. 20008

RELATIONSHIP DEVELOPMENT CENTER
P.O. Box 23; Gedney Station
White Plains, N.Y. 10605
(914) 428-8367
Julius Rosen

SENSITIVITY TRAINING FOR
EDUCATIONAL PERSONNEL
Herbert H. Lehman College
Bedford Park Boulevard West
Bronx, N.Y. 10468

SENTIO
247 West 72nd Street
New York, N.Y. 10023

SKY FARM INSTITUTE
Maple Corner
Calais, Vt. 05648

SPRUCE INSTITUTE
1828 Spruce Street
Philadelphia, Pa. 19103
Robert B. Martin

TARRYTOWN HOUSE
Box 222
Tarrytown, N.Y. 10592
(914) 591-8200, 634-5588
Robert L. Schwartz

TAO HOUSE
522 Eastbrook Road
Ridgewood, N.J. 07450
(201) 447-2098
Martha Hard Borod

TRAINING FOR LIVING INSTITUTE
80 Fifth Avenue
New York, N.Y. 10011
(212) 242-5410
Sr. Elizabeth Croake

WAINWRIGHT HOUSE
Milton Point
Rye, N.Y. 10580
(914) 967-6080
Weyman C. Huckabee

W.I.L.L. (WORKSHOP INSTITUTE
FOR LIVING-LEARNING)
333 Central Park West
New York, N.Y. 10025

FOREIGN COUNTRIES

CANADA

CLAREMONT EXPERIMENT
P.O. Box 123
Weston, Ont.

COLD MOUNTAIN INSTITUTE
P.O. Box 2884
Vancouver, B.C.
and
P.O. Box 4362
Edmonton 60, Alta.

DYNACOM
2955 Fendall
Montreal 250, Que.

THE GESTALT TRAINING INSTITUTE
OF CANADA
Lake Cowichan, Box 39
Vancouver, B.C.

HUMAN DEVELOPMENT ASSOCIATION
P.O. Box 811, Station B
Montreal, Que.

SHALAL
750 West Broadway
Vancouver, B.C.

STRATHMERE
North Gower, Ont.

SYNERGIA
P.O. Box 1685, Station B
Montreal 2, Que.

TORONTO GROWTH CENTRE
Box 11
Downsview, Ont.
Paul Blythe

FOREIGN

AUSTRALIAN INSTITUTE OF
HUMAN RELATIONS
12 Webb Street
Altona, Australia

CENTER HOUSE
10 -A Airlie Gardens
Kensington, London W8, England

CENTRE FOR APPLIED SOCIAL
RESEARCH
The Tavistock Institute
Belzise Lane
London NW 3, England

M. FERDINAND CUVELIER
179 Passtraat
Geel, Belgium

DIIPF
Box 900280, Schloss Strasse 29
6 Frankfurt 90, Germany

ESALEN-IN-CHILE
c/o Claudio Naranjo
1413 Allston Way
Berkeley, California 94702

HUMAN INTERACTION SEMINARS
Box 4984
G.P.O. Sydney 2001 NSW
Australia

JOHN C. LILLY
c/o Oscar Ichazo
Casilla 614
Arika, Chile

QUAESITOR
Vernon Road
Sutton, Surrey, England

TARANGO-CENTRO DE DESARROLLO
HUMANO
Norte 59 #896
Industrial Vallejo
Mexico 16, D.F.
567-29-66
Mr. A. Leites

YOLOTI
Sierra Vertientes 365
Mexico D.F. 10, Mexico

Index